FOXE'S
BOOK OF
MARTYRS

by JOHN FOXE

Whitaker House

Publisher's note:
This text was abridged from John Foxe's original work
by William Grinton Berry (1873–1926), who endeavored
to disentangle Foxe's lengthy national and religious
historical discourses from the powerfully moving
biographies in order to highlight the personal accounts.
Berry minimized the repetitious judicial examinations
that were common to many of the depicted martyrs
while conserving Foxe's literary craftsmanship
and simplicity of style as expressed in these
vivid narratives of faith of courage.

FOXE'S BOOK OF MARTYRS

ISBN-13: 978-0-88368-095-7
ISBN-10: 0-88368-095-5
Printed in the United States of America
© 1981 by Whitaker House

Whitaker House
1030 Hunt Valley Circle
New Kensington, PA 15068
www.whitakerhouse.com

18 19 20 21 22 23 **UI** 15 14 13 12 11 10

CONTENTS

About the Author

ABOUT THE AUTHOR

John Foxe was born at Boston, Lincolnshire, England in 1516. As a devout and scholarly boy, he was sent to Brasenose College, Oxford and then on to Magdalen College where he held a fellowship for seven years.

During this time of study, Foxe gained a reputation for his scholarly wisdom and piety and could have led a quiet and successful life. But becoming aware of certain spiritual truths, Foxe embraced Protestantism. As a result, in 1545, he had to resign his fellowship at the University and become a tutor for the Lucy family of Warwickshire. Shortly after, he married Agnes Randall of Conventry, a woman who shared his views on life in Jesus Christ.

During the next five years, John Foxe worked for the Reformation, writing tracts and beginning his famous history of the persecutions and martyrdoms in England from John Wycliffe through the early 1500's.

When Queen Mary, a staunch Roman Catholic, took the throne in 1553, Foxe and his family fled England in danger of their lives. They journeyed to the Continent where he continued work on his manuscript and became acquainted with John Knox.

Foxe earned a meager income while outside of England, but his chief labor was always his manuscript. With new material from home, he extended his chronicle through to Thomas Cranmer's death in 1556. Soon after, Protestant Elizabeth gained the throne of England, and Foxe returned to London with his family.

The manuscript was finally printed in 1563 as *The Acts*

and Monuments of These Latter and Perilous Days. It quickly became popular as *The Book of Martyrs.* Even though in print, Foxe did not let up on his monumental work. He labored for seven more years, paying careful attention to the details and accuracy of the book. In 1570 he produced his second edition which was greatly improved and has held up under any attempts to disprove his accounts made by future generations. The work took a great toll on Foxe's personal health from which he never recovered, but it was his life's crowning achievement. Foxe died in 1587 at the age of seventy-one.

Some have described John Foxe as a man of integrity and warmth who was often sought out as a spiritual counselor. His boldness in Christ gave him the courage to speak the truth before the great and the small. He won the friendship of Sir Francis Drake who read his book aloud on the western seas as he journeyed to the New World.

In his honest and compassionate accounts of man's search for spiritual truth, and the persecution and death that accompanied that search, John Foxe etched a detailed picture of the English Reformation that would have otherwise remained unknown. But more importantly, he has left the Christian faith of all ages a legacy of inspiration and courage.

Chapter One

THE EARLY CHRISTIANS

CHRIST our Saviour, in the Gospel of St Matthew, hearing the confession of Simon Peter, who, first of all other, openly acknowledged Him to be the Son of God, and perceiving the secret hand of His Father therein, called him (alluding to his name) a rock, upon which rock He would build His Church so strong, that the gates of hell should not prevail against it. In which words three things are to be noted : First, that Christ will have a Church in this world. Secondly, that the same Church should mightily be impugned, not only by the world, but also by the uttermost strength and powers of all hell. And, thirdly, that the same Church, notwithstanding the uttermost of the devil and all his malice, should continue.

Which prophecy of Christ we see wonderfully to be verified, insomuch that the whole course of the Church to this day may seem nothing else but a verifying of the said prophecy. First, that Christ hath set up a Church, needeth no declaration. Secondly, what force of princes, kings, monarchs, governors, and rulers of this world, with their subjects, publicly and privately, with all their strength and cunning, have bent themselves against this Church! And, thirdly, how the said Church, all this notwithstanding, hath yet endured and holden its own! What storms and tempests it hath overpast, wondrous it is to behold: for the more evident declaration whereof, I have addressed this present history, to the end, first, that the wonderful works of God in His Church might appear to His glory; also that, the continuance and proceedings of the Church, from time to time, being set forth, more knowledge and experience may redound thereby, to the profit of the reader and edification of Christian faith.

At the first preaching of Christ, and coming of the Gospel, who should rather have known and received him than the Pharisees and Scribes of that people which had His law? and yet who persecuted and rejected Him more than they themselves? What followed? They, in refusing Christ to be their King, and choosing rather to be subject unto Cæsar, were by the said Cæsar at length destroyed.

The like example of God's wrathful punishment is to be noted no less in the Romans themselves. For when Tiberius Cæsar, having learnt by letters from Pontius Pilate of the doings of Christ, of His miracles, resurrection, and ascension into heaven, and how He was received as God of many, himself moved with belief of the same, did confer thereon with the whole senate of Rome, and proposed to have Christ adored as God; they, not agreeing thereunto, refused Him, because that, contrary to the law of the Romans, He was consecrated (said they) for God before the senate of Rome had so decreed and approved Him. Thus the vain senate (being contented with the emperor to reign over

2

them, and not contented with the meek King of glory, the Son of God, to be their King) were scourged and entrapped for their unjust refusing, by the same way which they themselves did prefer. For as they preferred the emperor, and rejected Christ, so the just permission of God did stir up their own emperors against them in such sort, that the senators themselves were almost all destroyed, and the whole city most horribly afflicted for the space almost of three hundred years.

For first, the same Tiberius, who, for a great part of his reign, was a moderate and a tolerable prince, afterward was to them a sharp and heavy tyrant, who neither favoured his own mother, nor spared his nephews nor the princes of the city, such as were his own counsellors, of whom, being of the number of twenty, he left not past two or three alive. Suetonius reporteth him to be so stern of nature, and tyrannical, that in one day he recordeth twenty persons to be drawn to the place of execution. In whose reign through the just punishment of God, Pilate, under whom Christ was crucified, was apprehended and sent to Rome, deposed, then banished to the town of Vienne in Dauphiny, and at length did slay himself. Agrippa the elder, also, by him was cast into prison, albeit afterward he was restored.

After the death of Tiberius, succeeded Caligula, Claudius Nero and Domitius Nero; which three were likewise scourges to the Senate and people of Rome. The first commanded himself to be worshipped as god, and temples to be erected in his name, and used to sit in the temple among the gods, requiring his images to be set up in all temples, and also in the temple of Jerusalem; which caused great disturbance among the Jews, and then began the abomination of desolation spoken of in the Gospel to be set up in the holy place. His cruelty of disposition, or else displeasure towards the Romans, was such that he wished that all the people of Rome had but one neck, that he, at his pleasure, might destroy such a multitude. By this said Caligula, Herod Antipas, the murderer of John Baptist and condemner of Christ, was condemned to perpetual banishment, where he died miserably. Caiaphas also, who wickedly sat upon Christ, was the same time removed from the high priest's room, and Jonathan set in his place.

The raging fierceness of this Caligula had not thus ceased, had not he been cut off by the hands of a tribune and other gentlemen, who slew him in the fourth year of his reign. After whose death were found in his closet two small books, one called the *Sword*, the other the *Dagger*: in which books were contained the names of those senators and noblemen of Rome, whom he had purposed to put to death. Besides this *Sword* and *Dagger*, there was found also a coffer, wherein divers kinds of poisons were kept in glasses and vessels, for the purpose of destroying a wonderful number of people; which poisons, afterward being thrown into the sea, destroyed a great number of fish.

But that which this Caligula had only conceived, the same did the other two, which came after, bring to pass; namely, Claudius Nero, who reigned thirteen years with no little cruelty; but especially the third of these Neros, called Domitius Nero, who, succeeding after Claudius, reigned fourteen

4

years with such fury and tyranny that he slew the most part of the senators and destroyed the whole order of knighthood in Rome. So prodigious a monster of nature was he (more like a beast, yea rather a devil than a man), that he seemed to be born to the destruction of men. Such was his wretched cruelty, that he caused to be put to death his mother, his brother-in-law, his sister, his wife and his instructors, Seneca and Lucan. Moreover, he commanded Rome to be set on fire in twelve places, and so continued it six days and seven nights in burning, while that he, to see the example how Troy burned, sang the verses of Homer. And to avoid the infamy thereof, he laid the fault upon the Christian men, and caused them to be persecuted.

And so continued this miserable emperor till at last the senate, proclaiming him a public enemy unto mankind, condemned him to be drawn through the city, and to be whipped to death; for the fear whereof, he, flying the hands of his enemies, in the night fled to a manor of his servant's in the country, where he was forced to slay himself, complaining that he had then neither friend nor enemy left, that would do so much for him.

The Jews, in the year threescore and ten, about forty years after the passion of Christ, were destroyed by Titus, and Vespasian his father, (who succeeded after Nero in the empire) to the number of eleven hundred thousand, besides those which Vespasian slew in subduing the country of Galilee. They were sold and sent into Egypt and other provinces to vile slavery, to the number of seventeen thousand; two thousand were brought with Titus in his triumph; of whom, part he gave to be devoured of the wild beasts, part otherwise most cruelly were slain.

As I have set forth the justice of God upon these Roman persecutors, so now we declare their persecutions raised up against the people and servants of Christ, within the space of three hundred years; which persecutions in number commonly are counted to be ten, besides the persecutions first moved by the Jews, in Jerusalem and other places, against the apostles. After the martyrdom of Stephen, suffered next James the holy apostle of Christ, and brother of John. 'When this James,' saith Clement, 'was brought to the tribunal seat, he that brought him and was the cause of his trouble, seeing him to be condemned and that he should suffer death, was in such sort moved therewith in heart and conscience that as he went to the execution he confessed himself also, of his own accord, to be a Christian. And so were they led forth together, where in the way he desired of James to forgive him what he had done. After that James had a little paused with himself upon the matter, turning to him he saith "Peace be to thee, brother;" and kissed him. And both were beheaded together, A.D. 36.'

Thomas preached to the Parthians, Medes and Persians, also to the Carmanians, Hyrcanians, Bactrians and Magians. He suffered in Calamina, a city of India, being slain with a dart. Simon, who was brother to Jude, and to James the younger, who all were the sons of Mary Cleophas and of Alpheus, was Bishop of Jerusalem after James, and was crucified in a city of Egypt in the time of Trajan the emperor. Simon the apostle, called Cananeus and Zelotes, preached in Mauritania, and

6

in the country of Africa, and in Britain: he was likewise crucified.

Mark, the evangelist and first Bishop of Alexandria, preached the Gospel in Egypt, and there, drawn with ropes unto the fire, was burnt and afterwards buried in a place called there 'Bucolus,' under the reign of Trajan the emperor. Bartholomew is said also to have preached to the Indians, and to have translated the Gospel of St Matthew into their tongue. At last in Albinopolis, a city of greater Armenia, after divers persecutions, he was beaten down with staves, then crucified; and after, being excoriate, he was beheaded.

Of Andrew the apostle and brother to Peter, thus writeth Jerome. 'Andrew did preach, in the year fourscore of our Lord Jesus Christ, to the Scythians and Sogdians, to the Sacæ, and in a city which is called Sebastopolis, where the Ethiopians do now inhabit. He was buried in Patræ, a city of Achaia, being crucified by Ægeas, the governor of the Edessenes.' Bernard, and St Cyprian, do make mention of the confession and martyrdom of this blessed apostle; whereof partly out of these, partly out of other credible writers, we have collected after this manner: When Andrew, through his diligent preaching, had brought many to the faith of Christ, Ægeas the governor, knowing this, resorted to Patræ, to the intent he might constrain as many as did believe Christ to be God, by the whole consent of the senate, to do sacrifice unto the idols, and so give divine honours unto them. Andrew, thinking good at the beginning to resist the wicked counsel and the doings of Ægeas, went unto him, saying to this effect unto him: 'that it behoved him who

7

was judge of men, first to know his Judge which dwelleth in heaven, and then to worship Him being known; and so, in worshipping the true God, to revoke his mind from false gods and blind idols.' These words spake Andrew to the proconsul.

But Ægeas, greatly therewith discontented, demanded of him, whether he was the same Andrew that did overthrow the temple of the gods, and persuade men to be of that superstitious sect which the Romans of late had commanded to be abolished and rejected. Andrew did plainly affirm that the princes of the Romans did not understand the truth and that the Son of God, coming from heaven into the world for man's sake, hath taught and declared how those idols, whom they so honoured as gods, were not only not *gods*, but also most cruel *devils*; enemies to mankind, teaching the people nothing else but that wherewith God is offended, and, being offended, turneth away and regardeth them not; and so by the wicked service of the devil, they do fall headlong into all wickedness, and, after their departing, nothing remaineth unto them, but their evil deeds.

But the proconsul charged and commanded Andrew not to teach and preach such things any more; or, if he did, he should be fastened to the cross with all speed.

Andrew, abiding in his former mind very constant, answered thus concerning the punishment which he threatened : 'He would not have preached the honour and glory of the cross, if he had feared the death of the cross.' Whereupon sentence of condemnation was pronounced; that Andrew, teaching and enterprising a new sect, and taking away the religion of their gods, ought to be crucified.

Andrew, going toward the place, and seeing afar off the cross prepared, did change neither countenance nor colour, neither did his blood shrink, neither did he fail in his speech, his body fainted not, neither was his mind molested, nor did his understanding fail him, as it is the manner of men to do, but out of the abundance of his heart his mouth did speak, and fervent charity did appear in his words as kindled sparks; he said, 'O cross, most welcome and long looked for! with a willing mind, joyfully and desirously, I come to thee, being the scholar of Him which did hang on thee: because I have always been thy lover, and have coveted to embrace thee.'

Matthew, otherwise named Levi, first of a publican made an apostle, wrote his Gospel to the Jews in the Hebrew tongue. After he had converted to the faith Æthiopia and all Egypt, Hircanus, their king, sent one to run him through with a spear.

Philip, the holy apostle, after he had much laboured among the barbarous nations in preaching the word of salvation to them, at length suffered, in Hierapolis, a city of Phrygia, being there crucified and stoned to death; where also he was buried, and his daughters also with him.[1]

Of James, the brother of the Lord, thus we read:

James, took in hand to govern the Church with the apostles, being counted of all men, from the time of our Lord, to be a just and perfect man. He drank no wine nor any strong drink, neither did he eat any animal food; the razor never came upon his

---

[1] It should be understood that the accounts of the martyrdoms of apostles are mainly traditional.

head. To him only was it lawful to enter into the holy place, for he was not clothed with woollen, but with linen only; and he used to enter into the temple alone, and there, falling upon his knees, ask remission for the people; so that his knees, by oft kneeling (for worshipping God, and craving forgiveness for the people), lost the sense of feeling, being benumbed and hardened like the knees of a camel. He was, for the excellency of his just life, called 'The Just,' and, 'the safeguard of the people.'

When many therefore of their chief men did believe, there was a tumult made of the Jews, Scribes and Pharisees, saying; There is danger, lest all the people should look for this Jesus, as the Christ. Therefore they gathered themselves together, and said to James, 'We beseech thee restrain the people, for they believe in Jesus, as though he were Christ; we pray thee persuade all them which come unto the feast of the passover to think rightly of Jesus; for we all give heed to thee, and all the people do testify of thee that thou art just, and that thou dost not accept the person of any man. Therefore persuade the people that they be not deceived about Jesus, for all the people and we ourselves are ready to obey thee. Therefore stand upon the pinnacle of the temple, that thou mayest be seen above, and that thy words may be heard of all the people; for all the tribes with many Gentiles are come together for the passover.'

And thus the forenamed Scribes and Pharisees did set James upon the battlements of the temple, and they cried unto him, and said, 'Thou just man, whom we all ought to obey, this people is going astray after Jesus which is crucified.'

And he answered with a loud voice, 'Why do you ask me of Jesus the Son of Man? He sitteth on the right hand of the Most High, and shall come in the clouds of heaven.'

Whereupon many were persuaded and glorified God, upon this witness of James, and said, 'Hosannah to the Son of David.'

Then the Scribes and the Pharisees said among themselves, 'We have done evil, that we have caused such a testimony of Jesus; let us go up, and throw him down, that others, being moved with fear, may deny that faith.' And they cried out, saying, 'Oh, oh, this just man also is seduced.' Therefore they went up to throw down the just man. Yet he was not killed by the fall, but, turning, fell upon his knees, saying, 'O Lord God, Father, I beseech thee to forgive them, for they know not what they do.' And they said among themselves, 'Let us stone the just man, James;' and they took him to smite him with stones. But while they were smiting him with stones, a priest, said to them, 'Leave off, what do ye? The just man prayeth for you.' And one of those who were present, a fuller, took an instrument, wherewith they did use to beat and purge cloth, and smote the just man on his head; and so he finished his testimony. And they buried him in the same place. He was a true witness for Christ to the Jews and the Gentiles.

Now let us comprehend the persecutions raised by the Romans against the Christians in the primitive age of the Church, during the space of three hundred years. Wherein marvellous it is to see and read the numbers incredible of Christian innocents that were tormented and slain. Whose kinds of punishments, although they were divers, yet the manner of constancy in all these martyrs was one. And yet, notwithstanding the sharpness of these so many and sundry torments, and also the like cruelness of the tormentors, such was the number of these constant saints that suffered, or rather such was the power of the Lord in His saints, that, as Jerome saith, 'There is no day in the whole year unto which the number of five thousand martyrs cannot be ascribed, except only the first day of January.'

The first of these ten persecutions was stirred up by Nero about the year of our Lord threescore and four. The tyrannous rage of which emperor was very fierce against the Christians, 'insomuch that (as Eusebius recordeth) a man might then see cities full of men's bodies, the old there lying together with the young, and the dead bodies of women cast out naked, without all reverence of that sex, in the open streets.' Many there were of the Christians in those days, who, seeing the filthy abominations and intolerable cruelty of Nero, thought that he was antichrist.

In this persecution, among many other saints, the blessed apostle Peter was condemned to death, and crucified, as some do write, at Rome; albeit some others, and not without cause, do doubt thereof. Hegesippus saith that Nero sought matter against Peter to put him to death; which, when the people perceived, they entreated Peter with much ado that he would fly the city. Peter, through their importunity at length persuaded, prepared himself to avoid. But, coming to the gate, he saw the Lord Christ come to meet him, to Whom he, worshipping.

said, 'Lord, whither dost Thou go?' To whom He answered and said, 'I am come again to be crucified.' By this, Peter, perceiving his suffering to be understood, returned back into the city. Jerome saith that he was crucified, his head being down and his feet upward, himself so requiring, because he was (he said) unworthy to be crucified after the same form and manner as the Lord was.

Paul, the apostle, who before was called Saul, after his great travail and unspeakable labours in promoting the Gospel of Christ, suffered also in this first persecution under Nero. Abdias, declareth that unto his execution Nero sent two of his esquires, Ferega and Parthemius, to bring him word of his death. They, coming to Paul instructing the people, desired him to pray for them, that they might believe; who told them that shortly after they should believe and be baptised at his sepulchre. This done, the soldiers came and led him out of the city to the place of execution, where he, after his prayers made, gave his neck to the sword.

The first persecution ceased under Vespasian who gave some rest to the poor Christians. After whose reign was moved, not long after, the second persecution, by the emperor Domitian, brother of Titus. He, first beginning mildly and modestly, afterward did so far outrage in pride intolerable, that he commanded himself to be worshipped as god, and that images of gold and silver in his honour should be set up in the capitol.

In this persecution, John, the apostle and evangelist, was exiled by the said Domitian into

Patmos. After the death of Domitian, he being slain and his acts repealed by the senate, John was released, and came to Ephesus in the year fourscore and seventeen; where he continued until the time of Trajan, and there governed the churches in Asia, where also he wrote his Gospel; and so lived till the year after the passion of our Lord, threescore and eight, which was the year of his age about one hundred.

Clement of Alexandria addeth a certain history of the holy apostle, not unworthy to be remembered of such as delight in things honest and profitable The words be these: When John was returned to Ephesus from the isle of Patmos, he was requested to resort to the places bordering near unto him. Whereupon, when he was come to a certain city, and had comforted the brethren, he beheld a young man robust in body, of a beautiful countenance, and of a fervent mind. Looking earnestly at the newly-appointed bishop, John said: ‘I most solemnly commend this man to thee, in presence here of Christ and of the Church.’

When the bishop had received of him this charge, and had promised his faithful diligence therein, again the second time John spake unto him, and charged him as before. This done, John returned to Ephesus. The bishop, receiving the young man committed to his charge, brought him home, kept him, and nourished him, and at length baptized him; and after that, he gradually relaxed his care and oversight of him, trusting that he had given him the best safeguard possible in putting the Lord's seal upon him.

The young man thus having his liberty more, it

14

chanced that certain of his old companions and acquaintances, being idle, dissolute, and hardened in wickedness, did join in company with him, who first invited him to sumptuous and riotous banquets; then enticed him to go forth with them in the night to rob and steal; after that he was allured by them unto greater mischief and wickedness. Wherein, by custom of time, and by little and little, he, becoming more expert, and being of a good wit, and a stout courage, like unto a wild or unbroken horse, leaving the right way and running at large without bridle, was carried headlong to the profundity of all misorder and outrage. And thus, utterly forgetting and rejecting the wholesome doctrine of salvation which he had learned before, he entered so far in the way of perdition, that he cared not how much further he proceeded in the same. And so, associating unto him a band of companions and fellow thieves, he took upon himself to be as head and captain among them, in committing all kind of murder and felony.

It chanced that John was sent for to those quarters again, and came. Meeting the bishop afore specified, he requireth of him the pledge, which, in the presence of Christ and of the congregation then present, he left in his hands to keep. The bishop, something amazed at the words of John, supposing he had meant them of some money committed to his custody, which he had not received (and yet durst not mistrust John, nor contrary his words), could not tell what to answer. Then John, perceiving his perplexity, and uttering his meaning more plainly: 'The young man,' saith he, 'and the soul of our brother committed to your custody, I do require.' Then the bishop, with a loud voice sorrowing and weeping, said, 'He is dead.' To whom John said, 'How, and by what death?' The other said, 'He is dead to God, for he became an evil and abandoned man, and at length a robber. And now he doth frequent the mountain instead of the Church, with a company of villains and thieves, like unto himself.'

Here the apostle rent his garments, and, with a great lamentation, said, 'A fine keeper of his brother's soul I left here! get me a horse, and let me have a guide with me:' which being done, his horse and man procured, he hasted from the Church, and coming to the place, was taken of thieves that lay on the watch. But he, neither flying nor refusing, said, 'I came hither for the purpose: lead me,' said he, 'to your captain.' So he being brought, the captain all armed fiercely began to look upon him; and eftsoons coming to the knowledge of him, was stricken with confusion and shame, and began to fly. But the old man followed him as much as he might, forgetting his age, and crying, 'My son, why dost thou fly from thy father? an armed man from one naked, a young man from an old man? Have pity on me, my son, and fear not, for there is yet hope of salvation. I will make answer for thee unto Christ; I will die for thee, if need be; as Christ hath died for us, I will give my life for thee; believe me, Christ hath sent me.'

He, hearing these things, first, as in a maze, stood still, and therewith his courage was abated. After that he had cast down his weapons, by and by he trembled, yea, and wept bitterly; and, coming to the old man, embraced him, and spake unto him with weeping (as well as he could), being even then baptized afresh with tears, only his right hand being hid and covered.

Then the apostle, after that he had promised that he should obtain remission of our Saviour, prayed, falling down upon his knees, and kissing his murderous right hand (which for shame he durst not show before) as now purged through repentance, and brought him back to the Church. And when he had prayed for him with continual prayer and daily fastings, and had comforted and confirmed his mind with many sentences, he left him restored to the Church again; a great example of sincere penitence and proof of regeneration, and a trophy of the future resurrection.

The causes why the Roman emperors did so persecute the Christians were chiefly these—fear and hatred.

First, fear, for that the emperors and senate, of blind ignorance, not knowing the manner of Christ's kingdom, feared and misdoubted lest the same would subvert their empery; and therefore sought they all means possible, how, by death and all kinds of torments, utterly to extinguish the name and memory of the Christians.

Secondly, hatred, partly for that this world, of its own natural condition, hath ever hated and maliced the people of God, from the first beginning of the world. Partly again, for that the Christians being of a contrary nature and religion, serving only the true living God, despised their false gods, spake against their idolatrous worshippings, and many times stopped the power of Satan working in their idols: and therefore Satan, the prince of this world, stirred up the Roman princes and blind idolaters to bear the more hatred and spite against them. Whatsoever mishappened to the city or provinces of Rome, either famine, pestilence, earthquake, wars, wonders, unseasonableness of weather, or what other evils soever, it was imputed to the Christians.

The tyrants and organs of Satan were not contented with death only, to bereave the life from the body. The kinds of death were divers, and no less horrible than divers. Whatsoever the cruelness of man's invention could devise for the punishment of man's body, was practised against the Christians— stripes and scourgings, drawings, tearings, stonings, plates of iron laid unto them burning hot, deep dungeons, racks, strangling in prisons, the teeth of wild beasts, gridirons, gibbets and gallows, tossing upon the horns of bulls. Moreover, when they were thus killed, their bodies were laid in heaps, and dogs there left to keep them, that no man might come to bury them, neither would any prayer obtain them to be interred.

And yet, notwithstanding all these continual persecutions and horrible punishments, the Church daily increased, deeply rooted in the doctrine of the apostles and of men apostolical, and watered plenteously with the blood of saints.

In the third persecution Pliny the second, a man learned and famous, seeing the lamentable slaughter of Christians, and moved therewith to pity, wrote to Trajan, certifying him that there were many thousands of them daily put to death, of which none did any thing contrary to the Roman laws worthy persecution. ' The whole account they gave of their crime or error (whichever it is to be called) amounted only to this,—viz. that they were accustomed on a stated day to meet before day-light, and to repeat together a set form of prayer to Christ as a God, and to bind themselves by an obligation—not indeed to commit wickedness ; but, on the contrary,—never to commit theft, robbery or adultery, never to falsify their word, never to defraud any man : after which it was their custom to separate, and reassemble to partake in common of a harmless meal.'

In this persecution, suffered the blessed martyr, Ignatius, who is had in famous reverence among very many. This Ignatius was appointed to the bishopric of Antioch next after Peter in succession. Some do say, that he, being sent from Syria to Rome, because he professed Christ, was given to the wild beasts to be devoured. It is also said of him, that when he passed through Asia, being under the most strict custody of his keepers, he strengthened and confirmed the churches through all the cities as he went, both with his exhortations and preaching of the Word of God. Accordingly, having come to Smyrna, he wrote to the church at Rome, exhorting them not to use means for his deliverance from martyrdom, lest they should deprive him of that which he most longed and hoped for. 'Now I begin to be a disciple. I care for nothing, of visible or invisible things, so that I may but win Christ. Let fire and the cross, let the companies of wild beasts, let breaking of bones and tearing of limbs, let the grinding of the whole body, and all the malice of the devil, come upon me; be it so, only may I win Christ Jesus!' And even when he was sentenced to be thrown to the beasts, such was the burning desire that he had to suffer, that he spake, what time he heard the lions roaring, saying, 'I am the wheat of Christ: I am going to be ground with the teeth of wild beasts, that I may be found pure bread.'

After the decease of the quiet and mild prince Antoninus Pius followed his son Marcus Aurelius, about the year of our Lord 161, a man of nature more stern and severe; and, although in study of philosophy and in civil government no less commendable, yet, toward the Christians sharp and fierce; by whom was moved the fourth persecution.

In the time of the same Marcus a great number of them which truly professed Christ suffered most cruel torments and punishments, among whom was Polycarp, the worthy bishop of Smyrna. Of whose end and martyrdom I thought it here not inexpedient to commit to history so much as Eusebius declareth to be taken out of a certain letter or epistle, written by them of his (Polycarp's) own church to all the brethren throughout the world.

Three days before he was apprehended, as he was praying at night, he fell asleep, and saw in a dream the pillow take fire under his head, and presently consumed. Waking thereupon, he forthwith related the vision to those about him, and prophesied that he should be burnt alive for Christ's sake. When the persons who were in search of him were close at hand, he was induced, for the love of the brethren, to retire to another village, to which, notwithstanding, the pursuers soon followed him; and having caught a couple of boys dwelling thereabout, they whipped one of them till he directed them to Polycarp's retreat. The pursuers having arrived late in the day, found him gone to bed in the top room of the house, whence he might have escaped into another house, if he would; but this he refused to do, saying, 'The will of the Lord be done.'

Hearing that they were come, he came down, and spoke to them with a cheerful and pleasant countenance: so that they were wonder-struck, who, having never known the man before, now beheld his venerable age and the gravity and composure of his manner, and wondered why they should be so earnest for the apprehension of so old a man. He immediately ordered a table to be laid for them, and exhorted them to eat heartily, and begged them to allow him one hour to pray without molestation; which being granted, he rose and began to pray, and was so full of the grace of God, that they who were present and heard his prayers were astonished, and many now felt sorry that so venerable and godly a man should be put to death.

When he had finished his prayers, wherein he made mention of all whom he had ever been connected with, small and great, noble and vulgar, and of the whole catholic Church throughout the world, the hour being come for their departure, they set him on an ass and brought him to the city. There met him the irenarch Herod, and his father Nicetes, who taking him up into their chariot, began to exhort him, saying, 'What harm is it to say "Lord Cæsar," and to sacrifice, and save yourself?' At first he was silent: but being pressed to speak, he said, 'I will not do as you advise me.' When they saw that he was not to be persuaded, they gave him rough language, and pushed him hastily down, so that in descending from the chariot he grazed his shin. But he, unmoved as if he had suffered nothing, went on cheerfully, under the conduct of his guards, to the Stadium. There, the noise being so great that few could hear anything, a voice from heaven said to Polycarp as he entered the Stadium, 'Be strong, Polycarp, and play the man.' No one saw him that spake, but many people heard the voice. When he was brought to the tribunal, there was a great tumult as soon as it was generally understood that Polycarp was apprehended. The proconsul asked him, if he were Polycarp. When he assented, the former counselled him to deny Christ, saying, 'Consider thyself, and have pity on thy own great age'; and many other such-like speeches which they are wont to make:—'Swear by the fortune of Cæsar'— 'Repent'—'Say, "Away with the atheists."'

Then Polycarp, with a grave aspect, beholding all the multitude in the Stadium, and waving his hand to them, gave a deep sigh, and, looking up to heaven, said, 'Take away the atheists.'

The proconsul then urged him, saying, 'Swear, and I will release thee;—reproach Christ.'

Polycarp answered, 'Eighty and six years have I served him, and he never once wronged me; how then shall I blaspheme my King, Who hath saved me?'

The proconsul again urged him, 'Swear by the fortune of Cæsar.'

Polycarp replied, 'Since you still vainly strive to make me swear by the fortune of Cæsar, as you express it, affecting ignorance of my real character, hear me frankly declaring what I am—I am a

22

Christian—and if you desire to learn the Christian doctrine, assign me a day, and you shall hear.'

Hereupon the proconsul said, 'I have wild beasts; and I will expose you to them, unless you repent.'

'Call for them,' replied Polycarp; 'for repentance with us is a wicked thing, if it is to be a change from the better to the worse, but a good thing if it is to be a change from evil to good.'

'I will tame thee with fire,' said the proconsul, 'since you despise the wild beasts, unless you repent.'

Then said Polycarp, 'You threaten me with fire, which burns for an hour, and is soon extinguished; but the fire of the future judgment, and of eternal punishment reserved for the ungodly, you are ignorant of. But why do you delay? Do whatever you please.'

The proconsul sent the herald to proclaim thrice in the middle of the Stadium, 'Polycarp hath professed himself a Christian.' Which words were no sooner spoken, but the whole multitude, both of Gentiles and Jews, dwelling at Smyrna, with outrageous fury shouted aloud, 'This is the doctor of Asia, the father of the Christians, and the subverter of our gods, who hath taught many not to sacrifice nor adore.' They now called on Philip, the asiarch, to let loose a lion against Polycarp. But he refused, alleging that he had closed his exhibition. They then unanimously shouted, that he should be burnt alive. For his vision must needs be accomplished—the vision which he had when he was praying, and saw his pillow burnt. The people immediately gathered wood and other dry matter from the workshops and baths: in which service the Jews (with their usual malice) were particularly forward to help.

When they would have fastened him to the stake, he said, 'Leave me as I am; for he who giveth me strength to sustain the fire, will enable me also, without your securing me with nails, to remain without flinching in the pile.' Upon which they bound him without nailing him. So he said thus:—'O Father, I bless thee that thou hast counted me worthy to receive my portion among the number of martyrs.'

As soon as he had uttered the word 'Amen,' the officers lighted the fire. The flame, forming the appearance of an arch, as the sail of a vessel filled with wind, surrounded, as with a wall, the body of the martyr; which was in the midst, not as burning flesh, but as gold and silver refining in the furnace. We received also in our nostrils such a fragrance as proceeds from frankincense or some other precious perfume. At length the wicked people, observing that his body could not be consumed with the fire, ordered the confector to approach, and to plunge his sword into his body. Upon this such a quantity of blood gushed out, that the fire was extinguished. But the envious, malignant, and spiteful enemy of the just studied to prevent us from obtaining his poor body. For some persons suggested to Nicetes, to go to the proconsul, and entreat him not to deliver the body to the Christians, 'lest,' said they, 'leaving the crucified one, they should begin to worship *him*.' And they said these things upon the suggestions and arguments of the Jews, who also watched us when we were going to take the body from the pile. The centurion, perceiving the malevolence of the Jews, placed the body in the midst of the fire and burned it. Then we gathered up his bones—more precious than gold and jewels—and deposited them in a proper place.

In the same persecution suffered the glorious and most constant martyrs of Lyons and Vienne, two cities in France; giving a glorious testimony, and to all Christian men a spectacle or example of singular fortitude in Christ our Saviour. Their history is set forth by their own churches, where they did suffer:—

The whole fury of the multitude, the governor, and the soldiers, was spent on Sanctus of Vienne, the deacon, and on Maturus, a late convert indeed, but a magnanimous wrestler in spiritual things; and on Attalus of Pergamos, a man who had ever been a pillar and support of our church; and lastly on Blandina, through whom Christ showed that those things that appear unsightly and contemptible among men are most honourable in the presence of God, on account of love to His name exhibited in real energy, and not in boasting and pompous pretences. For—while we all feared, and among the rest while her mistress according to the flesh, who herself was one of the noble army of martyrs, dreaded that she would not be able to witness a good confession, because of the weakness of her body;—Blandina was endued with so much fortitude, that those who successively tortured her from morning to night were quite worn out with fatigue, owned themselves conquered and exhausted of their whole apparatus of tortures, and were amazed to see her still breathing whilst her body was torn and laid open. The blessed woman recovered fresh vigour in the act of confession; and it was an evident annihilation of all her pains, to say—'I am a Christian, and no evil is committed among us.'

Sanctus, having sustained in a manner more than human the most barbarous indignities, while the impious hoped to extort from him something injurious to the Gospel, through the duration and intenseness of his sufferings, resisted with so much firmness, that he would neither tell his own name, nor that of his nation or state, nor whether he was a freeman or a slave; but to every interrogatory he answered, 'I am a Christian.' This, he repeatedly owned, was to him both name, and country, and family, and everything.

The faithful, while they were dragged along, proceeded with cheerful steps; their countenances shone with much grace and glory; their bonds were as the most beautiful ornaments; and they themselves looked as brides adorned with their richest array, breathing the fragrance of Christ. They were put to death in various ways: or, in other words, they wove a chaplet of various odours and flowers, and presented it to the Father.

Maturus, Sanctus, Blandina, and Attalus, were led to the wild beasts into the amphitheatre to be the common spectacle of Gentile inhumanity. They were exposed to all the barbarities which the mad populace with shouts demanded, and above all to the hot iron chair, in which their bodies were roasted and emitted a disgusting smell. These after remaining alive a long time, expired at length.

Blandina, suspended from a stake, was exposed

as food to the wild beasts; she was seen suspended in the form of a cross and employed in vehement supplication. The sight inspired her fellow-combatants with much alacrity, while they beheld with their bodily eyes, in the person of their sister, the figure of Him Who was crucified for them. None of the beasts at that time touched her: she was taken down from the stake and thrown again into prison. Weak and contemptible as she might be deemed, yet when clothed with Christ, the mighty and invincible champion, she became victorious over the enemy in a variety of encounters, and was crowned with immortality.

Attalus also was vehemently demanded by the multitude, for he was a person of great reputation among us. He advanced in all the cheerfulness and serenity of a good conscience;—an experienced Christian, and ever ready and active in bearing testimony to the truth. He was led round the amphitheatre, and a tablet carried before him, inscribed 'This is Attalus the Christian.' The rage of the people would have had him dispatched immediately; but the governor, understanding that he was a Roman, ordered him back to prison: and concerning him and others, who could plead the same privilege of Roman citizenship, he wrote to the emperor and waited for his instructions. Cæsar sent orders that the confessors of Christ should be put to death. Roman citizens had the privilege of dying by decollation; the rest were exposed to wild beasts.

Now it was that our Redeemer was magnified in those who had apostatized. They were interrogated separate from the rest, as persons soon to be dismissed, and made a confession to the surprise of the Gentiles, and were added to the list of martyrs.

The blessed Blandina, last of all, as a generous mother having exhorted her children, and sent them before her victorious to the king, reviewing the whole series of their sufferings, hastened to undergo the same herself, rejoicing and triumphing in her exit, as if invited to a marriage supper, not as one going to be exposed to wild beasts. After she had endured stripes, the tearing of the beasts, and the iron chair, she was enclosed in a net, and thrown to a bull; and having been tossed some time by the animal, and proving quite superior to her pains, through the influence of hope, and the realising view of the objects of her faith and her fellowship with Christ, she at length breathed out her soul.

Now let us enter the story of that most constant and courageous martyr of Christ, St Lawrence, whose words and works deserve to be as fresh and green in Christian hearts, as is the flourishing laurel-tree. This thirsty hart, longing after the water of life, desirous to pass unto it through the strait door of bitter death, when on a time he saw his vigilant shepherd Sixtus, Bishop of Rome, led as a harmless lamb, of harmful tyrants, to his death, cried out with open mouth and heart invincible, saying, 'O dear father! whither goest thou, without the company of thy dear son? What crime is there in me that offendeth thy fatherhood? Hast thou proved me unnatural? Now try, sweet father, whether thou hast chosen a faithful minister or not? Deniest thou unto him the fellowship of thy blood?' These words with tears Saint Lawrence uttered, not because his master should suffer, but because he might not be suffered to taste of death's cup which he thirsted after.

Then Sixtus to his son shaped this answer: 'I forsake thee not, O my son, I give thee to wit, that a sharper conflict remaineth for thee. A feeble and weak old man am I, and therefore run the race of a lighter and easier death: but lusty and young art thou, and more lustily, yea more gloriously, shalt thou triumph over this tyrant. Thy time approacheth; cease to weep and lament; three days after thou shalt follow me. Why cravest thou to be partaker with me in my passion? I bequeath unto thee the whole inheritance.'

Let us draw near to the fire of martyred Lawrence, that our cold hearts may be warmed thereby. The merciless tyrant, understanding him to be not only a minister of the sacraments, but a distributor also of the Church riches, promised to himself a double prey, by the apprehension of one soul. First, with the rake of avarice to scrape to himself the treasure of poor Christians; then with the fiery fork of tyranny, so to toss and turmoil them, that they should wax weary of their profession. With furious face and cruel countenance, the greedy wolf-demanded where this Lawrence had bestowed the substance of the church: who, craving three day's respite, promised to declare where the treasure might be had. In the meantime, he caused a good number of poor Christians to be congregated. So, when the day of his answer was come, the persecutor strictly charged him to stand to his promise. Then valiant Lawrence, stretching out his arms over the poor, said: 'These are the precious treasure of the church; these are the treasure indeed, in whom the faith of Christ reigneth, in whom Jesus Christ hath His mansion-place. What more precious jewels can Christ have, than those in whom He hath promised to dwell? For so it is written, "I was hungry and ye gave me to eat; I was thirsty, and ye gave me to drink; I was harbourless and ye lodged me." And again; "Look, what ye have done to the least of these, the same have ye done to me." What greater riches can Christ our Master possess, than the poor people, in whom He loveth to be seen?'

O, what tongue is able to express the fury and madness of the tyrant's heart! Now he stamped, he stared, he ramped, he fared as one out of his wits: his eyes like fire glowed, his mouth like a boar foamed, his teeth like a hellhound grinned. Now, not a reasonable man, but a roaring lion, he might be called.

'Kindle the fire (he cried)—of wood make no spare. Hath this villain deluded the emperor? Away with him, away with him: whip him with scourges, jerk him with rods, buffet him with fists, brain him with clubs. Jesteth the traitor with the emperor? Pinch him with fiery tongs, gird him with burning plates, bring out the strongest chains, and the fire-forks, and the grated bed of iron: on the fire with it; bind the rebel hand and foot; and when the bed is fire-hot, on with him: roast him, broil him, toss him, turn him: on pain of our high displeasure do every man his office, O ye tormentors.'

The word was no sooner spoken, but all was done. After many cruel handlings, this meek lamb was laid, I will not say on his fiery bed of iron, but on his soft bed of down. So mightily God wrought with his martyr Lawrence, so miraculously God tempered His element the fire; not a bed of consuming pain, but a pallet of nourishing rest was it unto Lawrence.

Alban was the first martyr that ever in England suffered death for the name of Christ. At what time Dioclesian and Maximian the emperors had directed out their letters with all severity for the persecuting of the Christians, Alban, being then an infidel, received into his house a certain clerk, flying from the persecutors' hands, whom when Alban beheld continually, both day and night, to persevere in watching and prayer, suddenly by the great mercy of God he began to imitate the example of his faith and virtuous life; whereupon, by little and little, he being instructed by his wholesome exhortation, and leaving the blindness of his idolatry, became at length a perfect Christian.

And when the aforenamed clerk had lodged with him a certain time, it was informed the wicked prince, that this good man and confessor of Christ (not yet condemned to death) was harboured in Alban's house, or very near unto him. Whereupon immediately he gave in charge to the soldiers to make more diligent inquisition of the matter. As soon as they came to the house of Alban he, putting on the apparel wherewith his guest and master was apparelled, offered himself in the stead of the other to the soldiers; who, binding him, brought him forthwith to the judge.

It fortuned that at that instant when blessed Alban was brought unto the judge, they found the same judge at the altars offering sacrifice unto devils, who, as soon as he saw Alban, was straightways in a great rage, for that he would presume of his own voluntary will to offer himself to peril, and give himself a prisoner to the soldiers, for safeguard of his guest whom he harboured; wherefore he commanded him to be brought before the images of the devils whom he worshipped, saying: 'For that thou hadst rather hide and convey away a rebel, than deliver him to the officers, that (as a contemner of our gods) he might suffer punishment of his blasphemy; what punishment he should have had, thou for him shalt suffer the same, if I perceive thee any whit to revolt from our manner of worshipping.' But blessed Alban, who of his own accord had betrayed to the persecutors that he was a Christian, feared not at all the menaces of the prince; but being armed with the spiritual armour, openly pronounced that he would not obey his commandment.

Then said the judge, 'Of what stock or kindred art thou come?' Alban answered, 'What is that to you, of what stock I come? If you desire to hear the verity of my religion, I do you to wit, that I am a Christian, and apply myself altogether to that calling.' Then said the judge, 'I would know thy name, and see thou tell me the same without delay.' Then said he, 'My parents named me Alban, and I worship the true and living God, Who created all the world.' Then said the judge, fraught with fury, 'If thou wilt enjoy the felicity of prolonged life, do sacrifice (and that out of hand) to the mighty gods.' Alban replieth, 'These sacrifices which ye offer unto devils, can neither help them that offer the same, neither yet can they accomplish the desires and prayers of their suppliants.' The judge, when he heard these words, was passing angry, and commanded the tormentors to whip this holy confessor of God, endeavouring to overcome with stripes the constancy of his heart against which he had prevailed nothing with words. And he was cruelly beaten, yet suffered he the same patiently, nay rather joyfully, for the Lord's sake. Then when the judge saw that he would not with torments be overcome, nor be seduced from the Christian religion, he commanded him to be beheaded.

Now from England to return unto other countries where persecution did more vehemently rage.

Pitiless Galerius with his grand prefect Asclepiades invaded the city of Antioch, intending by force of arms to drive all Christians to renounce utterly their pure religion. The Christians were at that time congregated together, to whom one Romanus hastily ran, declaring that the wolves were at hand which would devour the Christian flock; 'But fear not,' said he, 'neither let this imminent peril disturb you, my brethren.' Brought was it to pass, by the great grace of God working in Romanus, that old men and matrons, fathers and mothers, young men and maidens, were all of one will and mind, most ready to shed their blood in defence of their Christian profession.

Word was brought unto the prefect, that the band of armed soldiers was not able to wrest the staff of faith out of the hand of the armed congregation, and all by reason that Romanus so mightily did encourage them, that they stuck not to offer their naked throats, wishing gloriously to die for the name of their Christ. 'Seek out that rebel,' quoth the prefect, 'and bring him to me, that he may answer for the whole sect.' Apprehended he was, and, bound as a sheep appointed to the slaughter-house, was presented to the emperor, who, with wrathful countenance beholding him, said: 'What! art thou the author of this sedition? Art thou the cause why so many shall lose their lives? By the gods I swear thou shalt smart for it, and first in thy flesh shalt thou suffer the pains whereunto thou hast encouraged the hearts of thy fellows.'

Romanus answered, 'Thy sentence, O prefect, I joyfully embrace; I refuse not to be sacrificed for my brethren, and that by as cruel means as thou mayest invent: and whereas thy soldiers were repelled from the Christian congregation, that so happened, because it lay not in idolaters and wor-shippers of devils, to enter into the holy house of God, and to pollute the place of true prayer.'

Then Asclepiades, wholly inflamed with this stout answer, commanded him to be trussed up, and his bowels drawn out. The executioners themselves more pitiful at heart than the prefect, said, 'Not so, sir, this man is of noble parentage; unlawful it is to put a nobleman to so unnoble a death.' 'Scourge him then with whips,' quoth the prefect, 'with knaps of lead at the ends.' Instead of tears, sighs, and groans, Romanus sang psalms all the time of his whipping, requiring them not to favour him for nobility's sake. 'Not the blood of my progenitors,' said he, 'but Christian profession maketh me noble. The wholesome words of the martyr were as oil to the fire of the prefect's fury. The more the martyr spake, the madder was he, insomuch that he commanded the martyr's sides to be lanced with knives, until the bones appeared white again.

The second time Romanus preached the living God, the Lord Jesus Christ His well-beloved Son, and eternal life through faith in His blood, Asclepiades commanded the tormentors to strike Romanus on the mouth, that his teeth being stricken out, his pronunciation at leastwise might be impaired. The commandment was obeyed, his face buffeted, his eyelids torn with their nails, his cheeks scotched with knives; the skin of his beard was plucked by little and little from the flesh; finally, his seemly face was wholly defaced. The meek martyr said, 'I thank thee, O prefect, that thou hast opened unto me many mouths, whereby I may preach my Lord and Saviour Christ. Look; how many wounds I have, so many mouths I have lauding and praising God.'

The prefect astonished with this singular constancy, commanded them to cease from the tortures. He threateneth cruel fire, he revileth the noble martyr, he blasphemeth God, saying, 'Thy crucified Christ is but a yesterday's God; the gods of the Gentiles are of most antiquity.'

Here again Romanus, taking good occasion, made a long oration of the eternity of Christ, of His human nature, of the death and satisfaction of Christ for all mankind. Which done, he said, 'Give me a child, O prefect, but seven years of age, which age is free from malice and other vices wherewith riper age is commonly infected, and thou shalt hear what he will say.' His request was granted.

A little boy was called out of the multitude, and

set before him. 'Tell me, my babe,' quoth the martyr, 'whether thou think it reason that we should worship one Christ, and in Christ one Father, or else that we worship many gods?'

Unto whom the babe answered, 'That certainly (whatsoever it be) which men affirm to be God, must needs be one; and that which pertains to that one, is unique: and inasmuch as Christ is unique, of necessity Christ must be the true God; for that there be many gods, we children cannot believe.'

The prefect hereat clean amazed, said, 'Thou young villain and traitor, where, and of whom learnedst thou this lesson?'

'Of my mother,' quoth the child, 'with whose milk I sucked in this lesson, that I must believe in Christ.' The mother was called, and she gladly appeared. The prefect commanded the child to be hoisted up and scourged. The pitiful beholders of this pitiless act, could not temper themselves from tears: the joyful and glad mother alone stood by with dry cheeks. Yea, she rebuked her sweet babe for craving a draught of cold water: she charged him to thirst after the cup that the infants of Bethlehem once drank of, forgetting their mothers' milk and paps; she willed him to remember little Isaac, who, beholding the sword wherewith, and the altar whereon, he should be sacrificed, willingly proffered his tender neck to the dint of his father's sword. Whilst this council was in giving, the butcherly tormentor plucked the skin from the crown of his head, hair and all. The mother cried, 'Suffer, my child! anon thou shalt pass to Him that will adorn thy naked head with a crown of eternal glory.' The mother counselleth, the child is counselled; the mother encourageth, the babe is encouraged, and receiveth the stripes with smiling countenance.

The prefect perceiving the child invincible, and himself vanquished, committeth the blessed babe to the stinking prison, commanding the torments of Romanus to be renewed and increased, as chief author of this evil.

Thus was Romanus brought forth again to new stripes, the punishments to be renewed and received again upon his old sores. No longer could the tyrant forbear, but needs he must draw nearer to the sentence of death. 'Is it painful to thee,' saith he, 'to tarry so long alive? A flaming fire, doubt thou not, shall be prepared for thee by and by, wherein thou and that boy, thy fellow in rebellion, shall be consumed into ashes.' Romanus and the babe were led to execution. When they were come to the place, the tormentors required the child of the mother, for she had taken it up in her arms; and she, only kissing it, delivered the babe. 'Farewell,' she said, 'my sweet child; and when thou hast entered the kingdom of Christ, there in thy blest estate remember thy mother.' And as the hangman applied his sword to the babe's neck, she sang on this manner:

> All laud and praise with heart and voice,
>   O Lord, we yield to thee:
> To whom the death of this thy saint,
>   We know most dear to be.

The innocent's head being cut off, the mother wrapped it up in her garment, and laid it on her breast. On the other side a mighty fire was made, whereinto Romanus was cast, whereupon a great storm arose and quenched the fire. The prefect at length being confounded with the fortitude and courage of the martyr, straitly commanded him to be brought back into the prison, and there to be strangled.

Chapter Two

CONSTANTINE THE GREAT

In the beginning of the tenth persecution, Dioclesian, being made emperor, took to him Maximian. These two, governing as emperors together, chose out two other Cæsars under them, to wit, Galerius and Constantius, the father of Constantine the Great.

Thus then Dioclesian, reigning with Maximian, in the nineteenth year of his reign began his furious persecution against the Christians, whose reign after the same continued not long. For it pleased God to put such a snaffle in the tyrant's mouth, that within two years after, he caused both him and Maximian to give over their imperial function, and so remain not as emperors any more, but as private persons.

They being now dispossessed, the imperial dominion remained with Constantius and Galerius, which two divided the whole monarchy between them: so that Galerius should govern the east countries, and Constantius the west parts. But Constantius, as a modest prince, refused Italy and Africa, contenting himself with France, Spain, and Britain, refusing the other kingdoms for the troublesome and difficult government of the same.

Galerius chose to him Maximian and Severus, as Cæsars. Likewise Constantius took Constantine his son Cæsar under him.

In the meantime, while Galerius with his two Cæsars were in Asia, the Roman soldiers set up for their emperor Maxentius, the son of Maximian who had before deposed himself. Against whom Galerius the emperor of the East sent his son Severus, which Severus in the same voyage was slain of Maxentius; in whose place then Galerius took Licinius.

And these were the emperors and Cæsars, who, succeeding after Dioclesian and Maximian, prosecuted the rest of that persecution, which Dioclesian and Maximian before began, during near the space of seven or eight years, which was to the year of our Lord 313; save only that Constantius, with his son Constantine, was no great doer therein, but rather a maintainer and a supporter of the Christians.

Which Constantius was a prince, very excellent, civil, meek, gentle, liberal, and desirous to do good unto those that had any private authority under him. And as Cyrus once said, that he got treasure for himself when he made friends rich, even so it is said that Constantius would oftentimes say that it were better that his subjects had the public wealth than he to have it hoarded in his own treasure-house. Also he was by nature sufficed with a little, insomuch that he used to eat and drink in earthen vessels (which thing was counted in Agathocles the Sicilian a great commendation); and if at any time cause required to garnish his table, he would send for plate and other furniture to his friends. In consequence of which virtues ensued great peace and tranquillity in all his provinces.

To these virtues he added a yet more worthy ornament, that is, devotion, love, and affection towards the Word of God. By which Word being guided, he neither levied any wars contrary to piety and Christian religion, neither aided he any others that did the same, neither destroyed he the churches, but commanded that the Christians should be preserved and defended, and kept safe from all contumelious injuries. And when in the other jurisdictions of the empire the churches were molested with persecution, he alone gave license unto the Christians to live after their accustomed manner.

Constantius minding at a certain time to try what sincere and good Christians he had yet in his court, called together all his officers and servants, feigning himself to choose out such as would do sacrifice to devils, and that those only should dwell there and keep their offices; and that those who would refuse to do the same, should be thrust out and banished the court. At this appointment, all the courtiers divided themselves into companies: the emperor marked who were the constantest and godliest from the rest. And when some said they would willingly do sacrifice, others openly and boldly refused to do the same; then the emperor sharply rebuked those who were so ready to do sacrifice, and judged them as false traitors unto God, accounting them unworthy to be in his court, who were such traitors to God; and forthwith commanded that they only should be banished the same. But greatly he commended those who refused to do sacrifice, and confessed God; affirming that they only were worthy to be about a prince; forthwith commanding that thenceforth they should be the trusty counsellors and defenders both of his person and kingdom; saying thus much more, that they only were worthy to be in office, whom he might make account of as his assured friends, and that he meant to have them in more estimation than the substance he had in his treasury.

Constantius died in the third year of the persecution, in the year of our Lord 306, and was buried at York. After whom succeeded Constantine, as a second Moses sent and set up of God, to deliver His people out of their so miserable captivity into liberty most joyful.

He, Constantine, was the good and virtuous child of a good and virtuous father; born in Britain. His mother was named Helena, daughter of king Coilus. He was a most bountiful and gracious prince, having a desire to nourish learning and good arts, and did oftentimes use to read, write, and study himself. He had marvellous good success and prosperous achieving of all things he took in hand, which then was (and truly) supposed to proceed of this, for that he was so great a favourer of the Christian faith. Which faith when he had once embraced, he did ever after most devoutly and religiously reverence.

As touching his natural disposition and wit, he was very eloquent, a good philosopher, and in disputation sharp and ingenious. He was accustomed to say that an emperor ought to refuse no labour for the utility of the common-weal. An empire was given by the determinate purpose of God ; and he to whom it was given, should so employ his diligence, as that he might be thought worthy of the same at the hands of the Giver.

I showed before how Maxentius, the son of Maximian, was set up at Rome by the prætorian soldiers to be emperor. Whereunto the senate, although they were not consenting, yet, for fear, they were not resisting. Maximian his father, who had before deprived himself, hearing of this, took heart again to resume his dignity, and laboured to persuade Dioclesian to do the same: but when he could not move him thereunto, he repaireth to Rome, thinking to wrest the empire out of his son's hands. But when the soldiers would not suffer that, of a crafty purpose he flieth to Constantine in France, under pretence to complain of Maxentius his son, but in very deed to kill Constantine. That conspiracy being detected by Fausta, the daughter of Maximian, whom Constantine had married, Constantine through the grace of God was preserved, and Maximian retired back: in his flight he was apprehended, and put to death.

Maxentius all this while reigned at Rome with tyranny and wickedness intolerable, much like to another Pharaoh or Nero; for he slew the most part of his noblemen, and took from them their goods. And sometimes in his rage he would destroy great multitudes of the people of Rome by his soldiers. Also he left no mischievous nor lascivious act unattempted.

He was also much addicted to the art magical, which to execute he was more fit than for the imperial dignity. Often he would invocate devils in a secret manner, and by the answers of them he sought to repel the wars which he knew Constantine prepared against him. And to the end he might the better perpetrate his mischievous and wicked attempts, he feigned himself in the beginning of his reign to be a favourer of the Christians; and thinking to make the people of Rome his friends, he commanded that they should cease from persecuting the Christians. He himself abstained from no contumelious vexation of them, till that he began at the last to show himself an open persecutor of them.

The citizens and senators of Rome being much grieved and oppressed by the grievous tyranny and unspeakable wickedness of Maxentius sent their complaints with letters unto Constantine, with much suit and most hearty petitions, desiring him to help and release their country and city of Rome; who, hearing and understanding their miserable and pitiful state, and grieved therewith not a little, first sendeth by letters to Maxentius, desiring and exhorting him to restrain his corrupt doings and great cruelty. But when no letters nor exhortations would prevail, at length, pitying the woful case of the Romans, he gathered together his army in Britain and France, therewith to repress the violent rage of that tyrant.

Thus Constantine, sufficiently appointed with strength of men but especially with strength of God, entered his journey coming towards Italy, which was about the last year of the persecution, 313 A.D. Maxentius, understanding of the coming of Constantine, and trusting more to his devilish art of magic than to the good-will of his subjects, which he little deserved, durst not show himself out of the city, nor encounter him in the open field, but with privy garrisons laid wait for him by the way in sundry straits, as he should come; with whom Constantine had divers skirmishes, and by the power of the Lord did ever vanquish them and put them to flight.

Notwithstanding, Constantine yet was in no great comfort, but in great care and dread in his mind (approaching now near unto Rome) for the magical charms and sorceries of Maxentius, wherewith he had vanquished before Severus, sent by Galerius against him. Wherefore, being in great doubt and perplexity in himself, and revolving many things in his mind, what help he might have against the operations of his charming, Constantine, in his journey drawing toward the city, and casting up his eyes many times to heaven, in the south part, about the going down of the sun, saw a great brightness in heaven, appearing in the similitude of a cross, giving this inscription, *In hoc vince*, that is, 'In this overcome.'

Eusebius Pamphilus doth witness that he had heard the said Constantine himself oftentimes report, and also to swear this to be true and certain, which he did see with his own eyes in heaven, and also his soldiers about him. At the sight whereof when he was greatly astonied, and consulting with his men upon the meaning thereof, behold, in the night season in his sleep, Christ appeared to him with the sign of the same cross which he had seen before, bidding him to make the figuration thereof, and to carry it in his wars before him, and so should he have the victory.

Wherein is to be noted, good reader, that this sign of the cross, and these letters added withal *In hoc vince*, was given to him of God, not to induce any superstitious worship or opinion of the cross, as though the cross itself had any such power or strength in it, to obtain victory; but only to bear the meaning of another thing, that is, to be an admonition to him to seek and inspire to the knowledge and faith of Him Who was crucified upon the cross, for the salvation of him and of all the world, and so to set forth the glory of His name.

The day following this vision, Constantine caused a cross after the same figuration to be made of gold and precious stone, and to be borne before him instead of his standard; and so with much hope of victory, and great confidence, as one armed from heaven, he speedeth himself toward his enemy. Against whom Maxentius, being constrained perforce to issue out of the city, sendeth all his power to join with him in the field beyond the river Tiber; where Maxentius, craftily breaking down the Bridge called 'Pons Milvius,' caused another deceitful bridge to be made of boats and wherries, being joined together and covered over with boards and planks, in manner of a bridge, thinking therewith to take Constantine as in a trap.

But herein came to pass, that which in the seventh Psalm is written. 'He made a pit and digged it, and is fallen into the ditch which he made; his mischief shall return upon his own head, and his violent dealing shall come down upon his own pate:' which here in this Maxentius was rightly verified; for after the two hosts did meet, he, being not able to sustain the force of Constantine fighting under the cross of Christ against him, was put to such a flight, and driven to such an exigence, that, in retiring back upon the same bridge which he did lay for Constantine (for haste, thinking to get the city), he was overturned by the fall of his horse into the bottom of the flood; and there with the weight of his armour he was drowned: and his host drowned in the Red Sea. Pharaoh not unaptly seemeth to bear a prophetical figuration of this Maxentius.

For as the children of Israel were in long thraldom and persecution in Egypt till the drowning of their last persecutor; so was this Maxentius the last persecutor in the Roman monarchy of the Christians; whom this Constantine, fighting under the cross of Christ did vanquish, setting the Christians at liberty; who before had been persecuted now three hundred years in Rome.

In histories we read of many victories and great conquests gotten, yet we never read, nor ever shall, of any victory so wholesome, so commodious, so opportune to mankind as this was; which made an end of so much bloodshed, and obtained so much liberty and life to the posterity of so many generations.

Constantine so established the peace of the Church, that for the space of a thousand years we read of no set persecution against the Christians, unto the time of John Wickliff.

So happy, so glorious was this victory of Constantine, surnamed the Great. For the joy and gladness whereof, the citizens who had sent for him before, with exceeding triumph brought him into the city of Rome, where he was most honourably received, and celebrated the space of seven days together; having, moreover, in the market-place, his image set up, holding in his right hand the sign of the cross, with this inscription: 'With this wholesome sign, the true token of fortitude, I have rescued and delivered our city from the yoke of the tyrant.'

Constantine, with his fellow Licinius eftsoons set forth their general proclamation not constraining any man to any religion, but giving liberty to all men, both for the Christians to persist in their profession without any danger, and for other men freely to adjoin with them, whosoever pleased. Which thing was very well taken, and highly allowed of the Romans and all wise men.

I doubt not, good reader, but thou dost right well consider with thyself the marvellous working of God's mighty power ; to see so many emperors confederate together against the Lord and Christ His anointed, who, having the subjection of the whole world under their dominion, did bend their whole might and devices to extirpate the name of Christ, and of all Christians. Wherein, if the power of man could have prevailed, what could they not do? or what could they do more than they did? If policy or devices could have served, what policy was there lacking ? If torments or pains of death could have helped, what cruelty of torment by man could be invented which was not attempted? If laws, edicts, proclamations, written not only in tables, but engraven in brass, could have stood, all this was practised against the weak Christians. And yet, notwithstanding, to see how no counsel can stand against the Lord, note how all these be gone, and yet Christ and his Church doth stand.

Chapter Three

THE LIFE OF JOHN WICKLIFF

ALTHOUGH it be manifest that there were divers
before Wickliff's time, who have wrestled and
laboured in the same cause and quarrel that our
countryman Wicliff hath done, whom the Holy
Ghost hath from time to time raised and stirred up
in the Church of God, something to work against
the bishop of Rome, to weaken the pernicious
superstition of the friars, and to vanquish and overthrow the great errors which daily did grow and
prevail in the world, yet notwithstanding, forsomuch
as they are not many in number, neither very famous
or notable, we will begin with the story of John
Wickliff; at whose time this furious fire of persecution seemed to take his first original and beginning.
Through God's providence stepped forth into the
arena the valiant champion of the truth, John Wickliff,
our countryman, whom the Lord raised up here in
England, to detect more fully and amply the poison
of the Pope's doctrine and false religion.

Wickliff, being the public reader of divinity in the
University of Oxford, was, for the rude time wherein
he lived, famously reputed for a great clerk, a deep
schoolman, and no less expert in all kinds of philosophy; the which doth not only appear by his own
most famous and learned writings, but also by the
confession of Walden, his most cruel and bitter
enemy, who in a certain epistle written unto Pope
Martin V. saith, ' that he was wonderfully astonished

at his most strong arguments, with the places of authority which he had gathered, with the vehemency and force of his reasons.'

It appeareth that this Wickcliff flourished about A.D. 1371, Edward III. reigning in England. This is out of all doubt, that at what time all the world was in most desperate and vile estate, and the lamentable ignorance and darkness of God's truth had overshadowed the whole earth, this man stepped forth like a valiant champion, unto whom that may justly be applied which is spoken of one Simon, the son of Onias : ' Even as the morning star being in the midst of a cloud, and as the moon being full in her course, and as the bright beams of the sun ; so doth he shine and glister in the temple and Church of God.'

In these days the whole state of religion was depraved and corrupted : the name only of Christ remained amongst Christians, but His true and lively doctrine was as far unknown to the most part as His name was common to all men. As touching faith, consolation, the end and use of the law, the office of Christ, our impotency and weakness, the Holy Ghost, the greatness and strength of sin, true works, grace and free justification by faith, the liberty of a Christian man, there was almost no mention.

The world, forsaking the lively power of God's spiritual Word, was altogether led and blinded with outward ceremonies and human traditions; in these was all the hope of obtaining salvation fully fixed; insomuch that scarcely any other thing was seen in the temples or churches, taught or spoken of in sermons, or finally intended or gone about in their whole life, but only heaping up of certain shadowy ceremonies upon ceremonies; neither was there any end of this their heaping.

The Church did fall into all kind of extreme tyranny; whereas the poverty and simplicity of Christ were changed into cruelty and abomination of life. With how many bonds and snares of ceremonies were the consciences of men, redeemed by Christ to liberty, ensnared and snarled! The Christian people were wholly carried away as it were by the nose, with mere decrees and constitutions of men, even whither it pleased the bishops to lead them, and not as Christ's will did direct them. The simple and unlearned people, being far from all knowledge of the holy Scripture, thought it quite enough for them to know only those things which were delivered them by their pastors; and they, on the other part, taught in a manner nothing else but such things as came forth of the court of Rome; whereof the most part tended to the profit of their order, more than to the glory of Christ.

What time there seemed to be no spark of pure doctrine remaining, this aforesaid Wickliff, by God's providence, sprang up, through whom the Lord would first waken and raise up again the world, which was drowned and whelmed in the deep streams of human traditions.

This Wickliff, perceiving the true doctrine of Christ's Gospel to be adulterated and defiled with so many filthy inventions and dark errors of bishops and monks, after long debating and deliberating with himself (with many secret sighs, and bewailing in his mind the general ignorance of the whole world), could no longer abide the same, and at the last determined with himself to help and to remedy such things as he saw to be wide, and out of the way.

This holy man took great pains, protesting, as they said, openly in the schools, that it was his principal purpose to call back the Church from her idolatry, especially in the matter of the sacrament of the body and blood of Christ. But this boil or sore could not be touched without the great grief and pain of the whole world : for, first of all, the whole glut of monks and begging friars was set in a rage and madness, who, even as hornets with their sharp stings, did assail this good man on every side; fighting, as is said, for their altars, paunches, and bellies. After them the priests and bishops, and then after them the archbishop, being then Simon Sudbury, took the matter in hand; who, for the same cause, deprived him of his benefice, which then he had in Oxford. At the last, when their power seemed not sufficient to withstand the truth which was then breaking out, they ran unto the lightnings and thunderbolts of the bishop of Rome, as it had been unto the last refuge of most force and strength. Notwithstanding, the said Wickliff, being somewhat friended and supported by the king, bore out the malice of the friars and of the archbishop; John of Gaunt, Duke of Lancaster, the king's son, and Lord Henry Percy, being his special maintainers.

The opinions for which Wickliff was deprived, were these : That the Pope hath no more power to excommunicate any man, than hath another. That if it be given by any person to the Pope to excommunicate, yet to absolve the same is as much in the power of another priest, as in his. He affirmed,

moreover, that neither the king, nor any temporal
lord, could give any perpetuity to the Church, or
to any ecclesiastical person; for that when such
ecclesiastical persons do sin habitually, the temporal
powers may meritoriously take away from them
what before hath been bestowed upon them. And
that he proved to have been practised before here
in England by William Rufus; 'which thing' (said
he) 'if he did lawfully, why may not the same also
be practised now? If he did it unlawfully, then
doth the Church err, and doth unlawfully in praying
for him.'

Beside these opinions he began something nearly
to touch the matter of the sacrament, proving that
in the said sacrament the accidents of bread remained
not without the subject, or substance, and that the
simple and plain truth doth appear in the Scriptures,
whereunto all human traditions, whatsoever they be,
must be referred. The truth, as the poet speaketh
very truly, had gotten John Wickliff great displeasure
and hatred at many men's hands; especially of the
monks and richest sort of priests.

Albeit, through the favour and supportation of
the Duke of Lancaster and Lord Henry Percy, he
persisted against their wolfish violence and cruelty:
till at last, about A.D. 1377, the bishops, still urging
and inciting their archbishop Simon Sudbury, who
before had deprived him, and afterward prohibited
him not to stir any more in those sorts of matters,
had obtained, by process and order of citation, to
have him brought before them.

The Duke, having intelligence that Wickliff
should come before the bishops, fearing that he,
being but one, was too weak against such a

multitude, calleth to him, out of the orders of friars, four bachelors of divinity, out of every order one, to join them with Wickliff also, for more surety. When the day was come, assigned to the said Wickliff to appear, which day was Thursday, the nineteenth of February, he went, accompanied with the four friars aforesaid, and with them also the Duke of Lancaster, and Lord Henry Percy, Lord Marshal of England; the said Lord Percy going before them to make room and way where Wickliff should come.

Thus Wickliff, through the providence of God, being sufficiently guarded, was coming to the place where the bishops sat; whom, by the way, they animated and exhorted not to fear or shrink a whit at the company of the bishops there present, who were all unlearned, said they, in respect of him, neither that he should dread the concourse of the people, whom they would themselves assist and defend, in such sort as he should take no harm.

With these words, and with the assistance of the nobles, Wickliff, in heart encouraged, approached to the church of St Paul in London, where a main press of people was gathered to hear what should be said and done. Such was there the frequency and throng of the multitude, that the lords, for all the puissance of the High Marshal, with great difficulty could get way through; insomuch that the Bishop of London, whose name was William Courtney, seeing the stir that the Lord Marshal kept in the church among the people, speaking to the Lord Percy, said that if he had known before what masteries he would have kept in the church, he would have stopped him out from coming there; at which words of the bishop the duke, disdaining not a little, answered that he would keep such mastery there, though he said 'nay.'

At last, after much wrestling, they pierced through and came to Our Lady's Chapel, where the dukes and barons were sitting together with the archbishops and other bishops; before whom Wickliff, according to the manner, stood, to know what should be laid unto him. To whom first spake the Lord Percy, bidding him to sit down, saying that he had many things to answer to, and therefore had need of some softer seat. But the Bishop of London, cast eftsoons into a fumish chafe by those words, said he should not sit there. Neither was it, said he, according to law or reason, that he, who was cited there to appear to answer before his ordinary, should sit down during the time of his answer, but that he should stand. Upon these words a fire began to kindle between them; insomuch that they began so to rate and revile one the other, that the whole multitude, therewith disquieted, began to be set on a hurry.

Then the duke, taking the Lord Percy's part, with hasty words began also to take up the bishop. To whom the bishop again, nothing inferior in reproachful checks and rebukes, did render and requite not only to him as good as he brought, but also did so far excel in this railing art of scolding, that the duke blushed and was ashamed, because he could not overpass the bishop in brawling and railing, and, therefore, he fell to plain threatening; menacing the bishop, that he would bring down the pride, not only of him, but also of all the prelacy of England. 'Thou,' said he, 'bearest thyself so brag upon thy parents, who shall not be able to help thee; they shall have enough to do to help themselves'; for his parents were the Earl and Countess of Devonshire. To whom the bishop answered, that his confidence was not in his parents, nor in any man else, but only in God.

Then the duke softly whispering in the ear of him next by him, said that he would rather pluck the bishop by the hair of his head out of the church, than he would take this at his hand. This was not spoken so secretly, but that the Londoners overheard him. Whereupon, being set in a rage, they cried out, saying that they would not suffer their bishop so contemptuously to be abused. But rather they would lose their lives, than that he should so be drawn out by the hair. Thus that council, being broken with scolding and brawling for that day, was dissolved before nine o'clock.

After King Edward III. succeeded his son's son, Richard II., who was no great disfavourer of the way and doctrine of Wickliff. But the bishops now seeing the aged king to be taken away, during the time of whose old age all the government of the realm depended upon the Duke of Lancaster, and seeing the said duke, with the Lord Percy, the Lord Marshal, give over their offices, and remain in their private houses without intermeddling, thought now the time to serve them to have some vantage against John Wickliff; who hitherto, under the protection of the aforesaid duke and Lord Marshal, had some rest and quiet. Notwithstanding being by the bishops forbid to deal in doctrine any more, he continued yet with his fellows going barefoot and in long frieze gowns, preaching diligently unto the people. Out of whose sermons these articles were collected.

Articles collected out of Wickliff's sermons.

The holy eucharist, after the consecration, is not the very body of Christ.

The Church of Rome is not the head of all churches more than any other church is; nor that Peter had any more power given of Christ than any other apostle had.

The Pope of Rome hath no more in the keys of the Church than hath any other within the order of priesthood.

The Gospel is a rule sufficient of itself to rule the life of every Christian man here, without any other rule.

All other rules, under whose observances divers religious persons be governed, do add no more perfection to the Gospel, than doth the white colour to the wall.

Neither the Pope, nor any other prelate of the church, ought to have prisons wherein to punish transgressors.

Wickliff, albeit he was commanded by the bishops and prelates to keep silence, yet could not so be suppressed, but that through the vehemency of the truth he burst out afterwards much more fiercely. For he, having obtained the goodwill and favour of certain noblemen, attempted again to stir up his doctrine amongst the common people. Then began the Pharisees to swarm together striving against the light of the Gospel, which began to shine abroad; neither was the Pope himself behind with his part, for he never ceased with his bulls and letters to stir up them who otherwise, of their own accord, were but too furious and mad.

Accordingly, in the year of our Lord 1377, being the first year of King Richard II., Pope Gregory sendeth his bull directed unto the University of Oxford, rebuking them sharply, imperiously, and like a Pope, for suffering so long the doctrine of John Wickliff to take root, and not plucking it up with the crooked sickle of their catholic doctrine. Which bull, the proctors and masters of the University, joining together in consultation, stood long in doubt, deliberating with themselves whether to receive it with honour, or to refuse and reject it with shame.

The copy of this wild bull, sent to them from the Pope, was this : —

'It hath been intimated to us by many trustworthy persons that one John Wickliff, rector of Lutterworth, in the diocese of Lincoln, professor of divinity, hath gone to such a pitch of detestable folly, that he feareth not to teach, and publicly preach, or rather to vomit out of the filthy dungeon of his breast, certain erroneous and false propositions and conclusions, savouring even of heretical pravity, tending to weaken and overthrow the *status* of the whole Church, and even the secular government. These opinions he is circulating in the realm of England, so glorious for power and abundance of wealth, but still more so for the shining purity of its faith, and wont to produce men illustrious for their clear and sound knowledge of the Scriptures, ripe in gravity of manners, conspicuous for devotion,

58

and bold defenders of the catholic faith; and some of Christ's flock he hath been defiling therewith, and misleading from the straight path of the sincere faith into the pit of perdition. Wherefore, being unwilling to connive at so deadly a pest, we strictly charge that by our authority you seize or cause to be seized the said John, and send him under trusty keeping to our venerable brethren the Archbishop of Canterbury and the Bishop of London, or either of them.'

I find, moreover, two other letters of the Pope concerning the same matter, the one directing that in case Wickliff could not be found, he should be warned by public citation to appear before the Pope at Rome within three months; the other exhorting the bishops that the King and the nobles of England should be admonished not to give any credit to the said John Wickliff, or to his doctrine.

The letters, being received from the Pope, the Archbishop of Canterbury and other bishops took no little heart; for, being encouraged by them, and pricked forward by their own fierceness and cruelty, it is to be marvelled at, with what boldness and stomach they did openly profess, before their provincial council, that all fear or favour set apart, no person, neither high nor low, should let them, neither would they be seduced by the entreaty of any man, neither by any threatenings or rewards, but that they would follow straight and upright justice and equity, yea, albeit that danger of life should follow thereupon. But these so fierce brags and stout promise, with the subtle practices of these bishops, who thought themselves so sure before, the Lord, against Whom no determination of man's counsel can prevail, by a small occasion did lightly confound and overthrow. For the day of the examination being come, a certain personage of the prince's court, and yet of no great noble birth, named Lewis Clifford, entering in among the bishops, commanded them that they should not proceed with any definite sentence against John Wickliff. With which words all they were so amazed, and their combs so cut, that they became mute and speechless. And thus, by the wondrous work of God's providence, John Wickliff escaped the second time out of the bishops' hands.

This good man ceased not to proceed in his godly purpose, labouring as he had begun; unto whom also, as it happened by the providence of God, this was a great help and stay, for that in the same year the aforesaid Pope Gregory XI. who was the stirrer up of all this trouble against him, turned up his heels and died. Whose death was not a little happy to Wickliff; for immediately after his decease there fell a great dissension between the Romish and the French Popes, and others succeeding them, one striving against another, that the schism thereof endured the space of thirty-nine years, until the time of the Council of Constance (A.D. 1417).

About the same time also, about three years after, there fell a cruel dissension in England, between the common people and the nobility, the which did not a little disturb and trouble the commonwealth. In this tumult Simon of Sudbury, Archbishop of Canterbury, was taken by the rustical and rude people, and was beheaded; in whose place succeeded William Courtney, who was no less diligent in rooting out heretics. Notwithstanding, Wickliff's sect daily grew to greater force, until the time that William Berton, Chancellor of Oxford, about A.D. 1381, had the whole rule of that University: who, calling together eight monastical doctors and four others, and putting the common seal of the University unto certain writings, set forth an edict, declaring that no man, under a grievous penalty, should be so hardy hereafter to associate themselves with any of Wickliff's abettors or favourers; and unto Wickliff himself he threatened the greater excommunication and farther imprisonment, and to all his fautors, unless that they after three-days' admonition or warning, canonical and peremptory (as they call it), did repent and amend. The which thing when Wickliff understood, forsaking the Pope and all the clergy, he thought to appeal unto the King's majesty; but the Duke of Lancaster coming between forbade him, saying that he ought rather to submit himself unto the censure and judgment of his ordinary. Whereby Wickliff being beset with troubles and vexations, as it were in the midst of the waves, was forced once again to make confession of his doctrine.

Here is not to be passed over the great miracle of God's divine admonition or warning; for when the archbishop and suffragans, with the other doctors of divinity and lawyers, with a great company of babbling friars and religious persons, were gathered together to consult touching John Wickliff's books, when they were gathered together at the Black-Friars in London to begin their business upon St Dunstan's day, after dinner, about two of the clock, the very hour and instant that they should go forward, a wonderful and terrible earthquake fell throughout all England : whereupon divers of the suffragans, being affrighted by the strange and wonderful demonstration, doubting what it should mean, thought it good to leave off from their determinate purpose. But the archbishop (as chief captain of that army, more rash and bold than wise) interpreting the chance which had happened clean contrary to another meaning or purpose, did confirm and strengthen their hearts and minds, which were almost daunted with fear, stoutly to go forward in their attempted enterprise ; who then discoursing Wickliff's articles, not according unto the sacred canons of the holy Scripture, but unto their own private affections and men's traditions, gave sentence that some of them were simply and plainly heretical, others were erroneous, others irreligious, some seditious and not consonant to the Church of Rome.

Besides the earthquake aforesaid, there happened another strange and wonderful chance, sent by God, and no less to be marked than the other, if it be true, that was reported by John Huss's enemies. These enemies of his, amongst other principal points of his accusation, laid this to his charge at the Council of Constance; that he should say openly unto the people as touching Wickliff, that at what time a great number of religious men and doctors were gathered together in a certain church to dispute against Wickliff, suddenly, the door of the church was broken open with lightning, in such sort, that his enemies hardly escaped without hurt. This thing, albeit that it were objected against Huss by his adversaries, yet, forsomuch as he did not deny the same, neither, if he so said, it seemeth that he would speak it without some ground or reason, I have not thought it good to leave clean out of memory.

Of like credit is this also, which is reported of Wickliff, that when he was lying very sick at London, certain friars came unto him to counsel him; and when they had babbled much unto him touching the catholic church, the acknowledging of his errors, and the bishop of Rome, Wickliff, being moved with the foolishness and absurdity of their talk, with a stout stomach, setting himself upright in his bed, repeated this saying out of the Psalms [cxviii. 17], "I shall not die, but I shall live, and declare the works of the Lord."

The Mandate of the Archbishop of Canterbury directed to the Bishop of London, against John Wickliff and his Adherents.

It is come to our hearing, that although, by the canonical sanctions, no man, being forbidden or not sent, ought to usurp to himself the office of preaching, publicly or privily, without the authority of the apostolic see or of the bishop of the place; yet notwithstanding, certain, being sons of perdition under the veil of great sanctity, are brought into such a doating mind, that they take upon them authority to preach, and are not afraid to affirm, and teach, and generally, commonly, and publicly to preach, as well in the churches as in the streets, and also in many other profane places of our said province, certain propositions and conclusions, heretical, erroneous, and false, condemned by the Church of God, and repugnant to the determinations of holy church; who also infect therewith very many good Christians, causing them lamentably to err from the catholic faith, without which there is no salvation.

We therefore admonish and warn that no man henceforth, of what estate or condition soever, do hold, teach, preach, or defend the aforesaid heresies and errors, or any of them; nor that he hear or hearken to any one preaching the said heresies or errors, or any of them; nor that he favour or adhere to him, either publicly or privily; but that immediately he shun and avoid him, as he would avoid a serpent putting forth pestiferous poison; under pain of the greater curse.

And furthermore, we command our fellow-brethren, that of such presumptions they carefully and diligently inquire, and do proceed effectually against the same.

The chancellor the same time in Oxford was Master Robert Rygge; who, as it seemeth, favouring Wickliff's part, as much as he could or durst, many times dissembled and cloked certain matters, and oftentimes (as opportunity would serve) holpe forward the cause of the Gospel, which was then in great danger. When the time was come, that there must needs be sermons made unto the people, he committed the whole doings thereof to such as he knew to be greatest favourers of John Wickliff. The two proctors were John Huntman and Walter Dish; who then, as far as they durst, favoured the cause of John Wickliff. Insomuch that the same time and year, which was A.D. 1382, when certain public sermons should be appointed customably at the feast of the Ascension and of Corpus Christi to be preached in the cloister of St Frideswide (now called Christ's Church), before the people, by the chancellor aforesaid and the proctors, the doings hereof the chancellor and proctors had committed to Philip Reppyngdon and Nicholas Hereford.

Hereford, beginning, was noted to defend John Wickliff openly, to be a faithful, good, and innocent man; for the which no small ado with outcries was among the friars. This Hereford, after he had long favoured and maintained Wickliff's part, grew in suspicion amongst the enemies of the truth; for as soon as he began somewhat liberally and freely to utter any thing which tended to the defence of Wickliff, by-and-by the Carmelites and all the orders of religion were on his top, and laid not a few heresies unto his charge, the which they had strained here and there out of his sermons, through the industry of one Peter Stokes, a Carmelite, a kind of people prone to mischief, uproars, debate, and dissension, as though they were born for that purpose. Much like thing do divers writers write of the nature of certain spiders; that whatsoever pleasant juice is in herbs, they suck it out, and convert it into poison. But these cowled merchants in this behalf do pass all the spiders, for whatsoever is worst and most pestilent in a man, that do they hunt out for, and with their teeth even, as it were, gnaw it out; and of the opinions which be good, and agreeable with verity, they do make schisms and heresies.

After this, the feast of Corpus Christi drew near, upon which day it was looked for that Reppyngdon should preach, who in the schools had shown forth and uttered that which he had long hidden and dissembled, protesting openly that in all moral matters he would defend Wickliff; but as touching the sacrament, he would as yet hold his peace, until such time as the Lord should illuminate the hearts and minds of the clergy. When the friars understood that this man should preach shortly, these Babylonians, fearing lest that he would scarce civilly or gently rub the galls of their religion, convented with the Archbishop of Canterbury, that the same day, a little before Philip should preach, Wickliff's conclusions, which were privately condemned, should be openly defamed in the presence of the whole University; the doing of which matter was committed to Peter Stokes, friar, standard-bearer and chief champion against Wickliff.

The chancellor having received the archbishop's letters and perceived the malicious enterprise of the Carmelite, was wonderfully moved against him, and falling out with him and his like (not without cause) for troubling the state of the University, said that neither the bishop nor the archbishop had any power over that University, nor should not have, in the determination of any heresies. And afterward taking deliberation, calling together the proctors, with other regents and non-regents, he did openly affirm that he would by no means help the Carmelite in his doings.

These things thus done, Reppyngdon at the hour appointed proceeded to his sermon; in the which, he was reported to have uttered 'that in all moral matters he would defend Master Wickliff as a true catholic doctor. Moreover, that the Duke of Lancaster was very earnestly affected and minded in this matter, and would that all such should be received under his protection'; besides many things more, which touched the praise and defence of Wickliff.

When the sermon was done, Reppyngdon entered into St Frideswide's Church, accompanied with many of his friends, who, as the enemies surmised, were privily weaponed under their garments. Friar Stokes, the Carmelite, suspecting all this to be against him, and being afraid of hurt, kept himself within the sanctuary of the church, not daring to put out his head. The chancellor and Reppyngdon, friendly saluting one another in the church-porch, sent away the people, and so departed every man home to his own house. There was not a little joy throughout the whole University for that sermon.

John Wickliff returning again within short space, either from his banishment, or from some other place where he was secretly kept, repaired to his parish of Lutterworth, where he was parson; and there, quietly departing this mortal life, slept in peace in the Lord, in the end of the year 1384, upon Silvester's day. It appeareth that he was well aged before he departed, 'and that the same thing pleased him in his old age, which did please him being young.'

This Wickliff, albeit in his life-time he had many grievous enemies, yet was there none so cruel to him, as the clergy itself. Yet, notwithstanding, he had many good friends, men not only of the meaner sort, but also of the nobility, amongst whom these men are to be numbered, John Clenbon, Lewes Clifford, Richard Stury, Thomas Latimer, William Nevil, and John Montague, who plucked down all the images in his church. Besides all these, there was the Earl of Salisbury, who, for contempt in him noted towards the sacrament, in carrying it home to his house, was enjoined by Ralph Ergom, Bishop of Salisbury, to make in Salisbury a cross of stone, in which all the story of the matter should be written: and he, every Friday during his life, to come to the cross barefoot, and bareheaded in his shirt, and there kneeling upon his knees do penance for his deed.

And for the residue, we will declare what cruelty they used not only against the books and articles of John Wickliff, but also in burning his body and bones, commanding them to be taken up many years after he was buried; as appeareth by the decree of the synod of Constance, A.D. 1415, 'This holy synod declareth, determineth, and giveth sentence, that John Wickliff was a notorious heretic, and that he died obstinate in his heresy; cursing alike him and condemning his memory. This synod also decreeth and ordaineth that his body and bones, if they might be discerned from the bodies of other faithful people, should be taken out of the ground, and thrown away far from the burial of any church, according as the canons and laws enjoin.' This wicked and malicious sentence of the synod would require here a diligent apology, but that it is so foolish and vain, and no less barbarous, that it seemeth more worthy of derision and disdain, than by any argument to be confuted.

What Heraclitus would not laugh, or what Democritus would not weep, to see these so sage and reverend Catos occupying their heads to take up a poor man's body, so long dead and buried; and yet, peradventure, they were not able to find his right bones, but took up some other body, and so of a catholic made a heretic! Albeit, herein

Wickliff had some cause to give them thanks, that they would at least spare him till he was dead, and also give him so long respite after his death, forty-one years[1] to rest in his sepulchre before they ungraved him, and turned him from earth to ashes; which ashes they also took and threw into the river. And so was he resolved into three elements, earth, fire, and water, thinking thereby utterly to extinguish and abolish both the name and doctrine of Wickliff for ever. Not much unlike the example of the old Pharisees and sepulchre-knights, who, when they had brought the Lord unto the grave, thought to make him sure never to rise again. But these and all others must know that, as there is no counsel against the Lord, so there is no keeping down of verity, but it will spring up and come out of dust and ashes, as appeared right well in this man; for though they digged up his body, burnt his bones, and drowned his ashes, yet the Word of God and the truth of his doctrine, with the fruit and success thereof, they could not burn.

[1] The decree of the synod was not carried out until after the lapse of several years from its meeting.

Chapter Four

SIR JOHN OLDCASTLE, LORD COBHAM

AFTER that the true servant of Jesus Christ, John Wickliff, a man of very excellent life and learning, had, for the space of more than twenty-six years, most valiantly battled with the great Antichrist of Europe, or Pope of Rome, and his diversely disguised host of anointed hypocrites, to restore the Church to the pure estate that Christ left her in at His ascension, he departed hence most Christianly in the hands of God, the year of our Lord 1384, and was buried in his own parish church at Lutterworth, in Leicestershire.

No small number of godly disciples left that good man behind him, to defend the lowliness of the Gospel against the exceeding pride, ambition, simony, avarice, hypocrisy, sacrilege, tyranny, idolatrous worshippings, and other filthy fruits, of those stiff-necked pharisees; against whom Thomas Arundel, the Archbishop of Canterbury (as fierce as ever was Pharaoh, Antiochus, Herod, or Caiaphas) collected, in Paul's church at London, a universal synod of all the papistical clergy of England, in the year of our Lord 1413 (as he had done divers others before), to withstand their most godly enterprise.

The principal cause of the assembling thereof,

was to repress the growing and spreading of the Gospel, and especially to withstand the noble and worthy Lord Cobham, who was then noted to be a principal favourer, receiver, and maintainer of those whom the bishop named Lollards; especially in the dioceses of London, Rochester, and Hereford, setting them up to preach whom the bishops had not licensed, and sending them about to preach: holding also and teaching opinions of the sacraments, of images, of pilgrimage, of the keys and church of Rome, repugnant to the received determination of the Romish Church. It was concluded among them, that, without any further delay, process should be awarded out against him, as against a most pernicious heretic.

Some of that fellowship who were of more crafty experience than the others, thought it not best to have the matter so rashly handled, but by some preparation made thereunto beforehand: considering the said Lord Cobham was a man of great birth, and in favour at that time with the King, their counsel was to know first the King's mind. This counsel was well accepted, and thereupon the archbishop, Thomas Arundel, with his other bishops, and a great part of the clergy, went straitways unto the King then remaining at Kennington, and there laid forth most grievous complaints against the said Lord Cobham, to his great infamy and blemish: being a man right godly. The King gently heard those blood-thirsty prelates, and far otherwise than became his princely dignity: notwithstanding requiring, and instantly desiring them, that in respect of his noble stock and knighthood, they should yet favourably deal with him; and that they would, if it were possible, without all rigour or extreme handling, reduce him again to the Church's unity. He promised them also, that in case they were contented to take some deliberation, he himself would seriously commune the matter with him.

Anon after, the King sent for the said Lord Cobham, and as soon as he was come, he called him secretly, admonishing him betwixt him and him, to submit himself to his mother the Holy Church, and, as an obedient child, to acknowledge himself culpable.

Unto whom the Christian knight made this answer: 'You, most worthy prince,' saith he, 'I am always prompt and willing to obey, forasmuch as I know you a Christian king, and the appointed minister of God, bearing the sword to the punishment of evil doers, and for safeguard of them that be virtuous. Unto you, next my eternal God, owe I my whole obedience, and submit thereunto, as I have done ever, all that I have, either of fortune or nature, ready at all times to fulfil whatsoever ye shall in the Lord command me. But, as touching the Pope and his spirituality, I owe them neither suit nor service, forasmuch as I know him, by the Scriptures, to be the great Antichrist, the son of perdition, the open adversary of God, and the abomination standing in the holy place.'

When the King had heard this, with such like sentences more, he would talk no longer with him, but left him so utterly.

And as the archbishop resorted again unto the King for an answer, he gave him his full authority to cite him, examine him, and punish him, according to their devilish decrees, which they called 'The Laws of Holy Church.' But forasmuch as the Lord

Cobham did not appear at the day appointed, the archbishop condemned him of most deep contumacy. After that, when he had been falsely informed by his hired spies, and other glozing glaverers, that the said Lord Cobham had laughed him to scorn, disdained all his doings, maintained his old opinions, contemned the Church's power, the dignity of a bishop, and the order of priesthood (for of all these was he then accused), in his moody madness, without just proof, did he openly excommunicate him.

This most constant servant of the Lord, and worthy knight, Sir John Oldcastle, the Lord Cobham, beholding the unpeaceable fury of Antichrist thus kindled against him, perceiving himself compassed on every side with deadly dangers, took paper and pen in hand, and wrote a confession of his faith, both signing and sealing it with his own hand: wherein he answered to the four chief articles that the archbishop laid against him. That done, he took the copy with him, and went therewith to the King, trusting to find mercy and favour at his hand.

The King would in no case receive it, but commanded it to be delivered unto them that should be his judges. Then desired he, in the King's presence, that a hundred knights and esquires might be suffered to come in upon his purgation, who he knew would clear him of all heresies. Moreover he offered himself, after the law of arms, to fight for life or death with any man living, Christian or heathen, in the quarrel of his faith; the King and the lords of his council excepted. Finally, with all gentleness, he protested before all that were present that he would refuse no manner of correction that

73

should, after the laws of God, be ministered unto him; but that he would at all times, with all meekness, obey it.

Notwithstanding all this the King suffered him to be summoned personally in his own privy chamber. Then said the Lord Cobham to the King, that he had appealed from the archbishop to the Pope of Rome, and therefore he ought, he said, in no case to be his judge. And having his appeal there at hand ready written, he showed it with all reverence to the King; wherewith the King was then much more displeased than afore, and said angrily to him, that he should not pursue his appeal; but rather he should tarry in hold, till such time as it were of the Pope allowed. And then, would he or nild he, the archbishop should be his judge.

Thus was there nothing allowed that the good Lord Cobham had lawfully required; but, forasmuch as he would not be sworn in all things to submit himself to the Church, and so take what penance the archbishop would enjoin him, he was arrested at the King's commandment, and led forth to the Tower of London.

When the day of examination was come, which was the 23rd day of September, the Saturday after the feast of St Matthew, Thomas Arundel, the Archbishop, sat in Caiaphas' room, in the chapter-house of Paul's, with Richard Clifford, Bishop of London, and Henry Bolingbrook, Bishop of Winchester. Sir Robert Morley, knight, and lieutenant of the Tower, brought before him the said Lord Cobham, and there left him for the time; unto whom the archbishop said these words: 'Sir John, in the last general convocation of the clergy of this our province, ye were detected of certain heresies, and, by sufficient witnesses, found culpable: whereupon ye were, by form of spiritual law, cited, and would in no case appear. Upon your rebellious contumacy ye were both privately and openly excommunicated. Notwithstanding we neither yet showed ourselves unready to have given you absolution (nor yet do to this hour), would ye have meekly asked it.'

Unto whom the Lord Cobham said that he desired no absolution; but he would gladly, before him and his brethren, make rehearsal of that faith which he held and intended always to stand to. And then he took out of his bosom a certain writing concerning the articles whereof he was accused, and read it before them.

'As for images, I understand that they be not of belief, but that they were ordained since the belief of Christ was given by sufferance of the Church, to represent and bring to mind the passion of our Lord Jesus Christ, and martyrdom and good living of other saints: and that whoso it be, that doth the worship to dead images that is due to God, or putteth such hope or trust in help of them, as he should do to God, or hath affection in one more than in another, he doth in that, the greatest sin of idol worship.

'Also I suppose this fully, that every man in this earth is a pilgrim toward bliss, or toward pain; and that he that knoweth not, ne will not know, ne keep the holy commandments of God in his living here (albeit that he go on pilgrimages to all the world, and he die so), he shall be damned: he that knoweth the holy commandments of God, and

75

keepeth them to his end, he shall be saved, though he never in his life go on pilgrimage, as men now use, to Canterbury, or to Rome, or to any other place.'

Then counselled the archbishop with the other two bishops and with divers of the doctors, what was to be done; commanding him, for the time, to stand aside. In conclusion, by their assent and information, he said thus unto him: 'Come hither, Sir John: ye must declare us your mind more plainly. As thus, whether ye hold, affirm, and believe, that in the sacrament of the altar, after the consecration rightly done by a priest, remaineth material bread, or not? Moreover, whether ye do hold, affirm, and believe, that, as concerning the sacrament of penance (where a competent number of priests are), every Christian man is necessarily bound to be confessed of his sins to a priest ordained by the church, or not?'

This was the answer of the good Lord Cobham: that none otherwise would he declare his mind, nor yet answer unto his articles, than was expressly in his writing there contained.

Then said the archbishop again unto him: 'Sir John, beware what ye do; for if ye answer not clearly to those things that are here objected against you, the law of holy church is that we may openly proclaim you a heretic.'

Unto whom he gave this answer: 'Do as ye shall think best.' Wherewith the bishops and prelates were amazed and wonderfully disquieted.

At last the archbishop again declared unto him, what the Holy Church of Rome, following the saying of St Augustine, St Jerome, St Ambrose, and of the holy doctors, had determined in these matters: no manner of mention once made of Christ! 'which determination,' saith he, 'ought all Christian men both to believe and to follow.'

Then said the Lord Cobham unto him, that he would gladly both believe and observe whatsoever holy Church of Christ's institution had determined, or yet whatsoever God had willed him either to believe or to do: but that the Pope of Rome, with his cardinals, archbishops, bishops, and other prelates of that church, had lawful power to determine such matter as stood not with His word thoroughly; that, would he not (he said) at that time affirm. With this the Archbishop bade him to take good advisement till the Monday next following (which was the twenty-fifth day of September), and then justly to answer, specially unto this point: Whether there remained material bread in the sacrament of the altar after the words of consecration, or not?

The Lord Cobham perceived that their uttermost malice was purposed against him, and therefore he put his life into the hands of God, desiring his only Spirit to assist him in his next answer. When the said twenty-fifth day of September was come Thomas Arundel, the Archbishop of Canterbury, commanded his judicial seat to be removed from the chapter-house of Paul's to the Dominic friars within Ludgate at London. And as he was there set, with a great sort more of priests, monks, canons, friars, parish-clerks, bell-ringers, and pardoners, Sir Robert Morley, knight, and lieutenant of the Tower, brought the good Lord Cobham, leaving him among them as a lamb among wolves.

Then said the archbishop unto him: 'Sir John, we sent you a writing concerning the faith of the blessed sacrament, clearly determined by the Church of Rome, our mother, and by the holy doctors.'

Then he said unto him: 'I know none holier than is Christ and His apostles. And as for that determination, I wot it is none of theirs; for it standeth not with the Scriptures, but manifestly against them.'

Then said one of the lawyers: 'What is your belief concerning Holy Church.'

The Lord Cobham answered: 'My belief is, that all the Scriptures of the sacred Bible are true. All that is grounded upon them I believe thoroughly, for I know it is God's pleasure that I should so do; but in your lordly laws and idle determinations have I no belief. For ye be no part of Christ's Holy Church, as your open deeds do show; but ye are very Antichrists, obstinately set against His holy law and will. The laws that ye have made are nothing to His glory, but only for your vain glory and abominable covetousness. And as for your superiority, were ye of Christ, ye should be meek ministers, and no proud superiors.'

Then said Doctor Walden unto him: 'Swift judges always are the learned scholars of Wickliff!'

Unto him the Lord Cobham thus answered: 'As for that virtuous man Wickliff, I shall say here, before God and man, that before I knew that despised doctrine of his, I never abstained from sin. But since I learned therein to fear my Lord God, it hath otherwise, I trust, been with me: so much grace could I never find in all your glorious instructions.'

Then said Dr Walden yet again unto him: 'It were not well with me (so many virtuous men living, and so many learned men teaching the Scripture, being also so open, and the examples of fathers so plenteous), if I then had no grace to amend my life, till I heard the devil preach!'

The Lord Cobham said: 'Your fathers, the old Pharisees, ascribed Christ's miracles to Beelzebub, and His doctrine to the devil; and you, as their children, have still the selfsame judgment concerning His faithful followers. They that rebuke your vicious living must needs be heretics, and that must your doctors prove, when you have no Scripture to do it.' Then said he to them all: 'To judge you as you be, we need go no further than to your own proper acts. Where do you find in all God's law, that ye should thus sit in judgment on any Christian man, or yet give sentence upon any other man unto death, as ye do here daily? No ground have ye in all the Scripture so lordly to take it upon you, but in Annas and Caiaphas, who sat thus upon Christ, and upon His apostles after His ascension. Of them only have ye taken it to judge Christ's members as ye do; and neither of Peter nor John.'

Then said some of the lawyers: 'Yes, forsooth, Sir, for Christ judged Judas.'

The Lord Cobham said, 'No! Christ judged him not, but he judged himself, and thereupon went forth and so did hang himself: but indeed Christ said: "Woe unto him, for that covetous act of his," as He doth yet still unto many of you. For since the venom of Judas was shed into the Church, ye never followed Christ, neither yet have ye stood in the perfection of God's law.'

Then the archbishop asked him, What he meant by that venom?

The Lord Cobham said: 'Your possessions and lordships. For then[1] cried an angel in the air, as your own chronicles mention, Woe, woe, woe, this day is venom shed into the Church of God. Before that time all the bishops of Rome were martyrs, in a manner: and since that time we read of very few. But indeed since that same time, one hath put down another, one hath poisoned another, one hath cursed another, and one hath slain another, and done much more mischief besides, as all the chronicles tell. And let all men consider well this, that Christ was meek and merciful; the Pope is proud and a tyrant: Christ was poor and forgave; the Pope is rich and a malicious manslayer.'

Then a doctor of law, called Master John Kemp, plucked out of his bosom a copy of the bill which they had before sent him into the Tower by the archbishop's council, thinking thereby to make shorter work with him. 'My Lord Cobham,' saith this doctor, 'we must briefly know your mind concerning these four points here following. The first of them is this':—and then he read upon the bill: "The faith and determination of Holy Church touching the blessed sacrament of the altar is this; That after the sacramental words be once spoken by a priest in his mass, the material bread, that was before bread, is turned into Christ's very body, and the material wine is turned into Christ's blood. And so there remaineth, in the sacrament of the

[1] When Constantine endowed the Church.

80

altar, from thenceforth no material bread, nor material wine, which were there before the sacramental words were spoken": Sir, believe you not this?'

The Lord Cobham said: 'This is not my belief; but my faith is, as I said to you before, that in the worshipful sacrament of the altar is Christ's very body in form of bread.'

Then read the doctor again: 'The second point is this: Holy Church hath determined that every Christian man, living here bodily upon earth, ought to be shriven of a priest ordained by the Church, if he may come to him. Sir, what say you to this?'

The Lord Cobham answered and said: 'A diseased or sore wounded man hath need to have a sure wise chirurgeon and a true, knowing both the ground and the danger of the same. Most necessary were it, therefore, to be first shriven unto God, who only knoweth our diseases, and can help us.'

Then read the doctor again: 'The third point is this: Christ ordained St Peter the apostle to be His vicar here in earth, whose see is the Church of Rome, and He granted that the same power which He gave unto Peter should succeed unto all Peter's successors, whom we now call popes of Rome: by whose special power, in churches particular, be ordained prelates and archbishops, parsons, curates, and other degrees besides, to whom Christian men ought to obey after the laws of the Church of Rome. This is the determination of Holy Church. Sir, believe ye not this?'

To this he answered and said: 'He that followeth Peter most nigh in pure living, is next unto him in succession; but your lordly order esteemeth not

greatly the lowly behaviour of poor Peter, whatsoever ye prate of him, neither care ye greatly for the
humble manners of them that succeeded him till
the time of Silvester, who, for the more part, were
martyrs.'

With that, one of the other doctors asked him:
'Then what do ye say of the Pope?'

The Lord Cobham answered: 'He and you
together make whole the great Antichrist, of whom
he is the great head; you bishops, priests, prelates,
and monks, are the body; and the begging friars
are the tail.'

Then read the doctor again: 'The fourth point
is this: Holy Church hath determined, that it is
meritorious to a Christian man to go on pilgrimage
to holy places, and there specially to worship the
holy relics and images of saints, apostles, martyrs,
confessors, and all other saints besides, approved by
the Church of Rome. Sir, what say you to this?'

Whereunto the Lord Cobham answered: 'I owe
them no service by any commandment of God, and
therefore I mind not to seek them for your covetousness. It were best ye swept them fair from
cobwebs and dust, and so laid them up for catching
of scathe, or else to bury them fair in the ground,
as ye do other aged people, who are God's images.
It is a wonderful thing that saints now being dead
should become so covetous and needy, and thereupon so bitterly beg, who all their life-time hated
all covetousness and begging. But this I say unto
you, and I would all the world should mark it, that
with your shrines and idols, your feigned absolutions
and pardons, ye draw unto you the substance,
wealth, and chief pleasures of all Christian realms.'

Then said the archbishop unto him: 'Sir John, ye must either submit yourself to the ordinance of Holy Church, or else throw yourself (no remedy) into most deep danger. We require you to have no other manner of opinion in these matters, than the universal faith and belief of the Holy Church of Rome is. And so, like an obedient child, return again to the unity of your mother.'

The Lord Cobham said expressly before them all: 'I will no otherwise believe in these points than what I have told you here before. Do with me what you will.'

And with that the archbishop stood up and read a bill of his condemnation, all the clergy and laity vailing their bonnets: 'Forasmuch as we have found Sir John Oldcastle, knight, and Lord Cobham, not only to be an evident heretic in his own person, but also a mighty maintainer of other heretics against the faith and religion of the holy and universal Church of Rome; and that he, as the child of iniquity and darkness, hath so hardened his heart, that he will in no case attend unto the voice of his pastor; his faults also aggravated or made double through his damnable obstinacy, we commit him to the secular jurisdiction. Furthermore, we excommunicate and denounce accursed, not only this heretic here present, but so many else besides as shall hereafter, in favour of his error, either receive him or defend him, counsel him or help him, or any other way maintain him, as very fautors, receivers, defenders, counsellors, aiders, and maintainers of condemned heretics.

'And we give straight commandment that ye cause this condemnation and definitive sentence of excommunication concerning both this heretic and his fautors, to be published throughout all dioceses, in cities, towns, and villages, by your curates and parish priests, at such times as they shall have most recourse of people. Let the curate everywhere go into the pulpit, and there open, declare, and expound his process, in the mother-tongue, in an audible and intelligible voice, that it may be perceived of all men: and that upon the fear of this declaration also the people may fall from their evil opinions conceived now of late by seditious preachers.'

After the archbishop had read the bill of his condemnation before the whole multitude, the Lord Cobham said with a most cheerful countenance: 'Though ye judge my body, which is but a wretched thing, yet am I certain and sure, that ye can do no harm to my soul, no more than could Satan unto the soul of Job. He that created that, will of His infinite mercy and promise save it. I have, therein, no manner of doubt.'

He fell down upon his knees, and before them all prayed for his enemies, holding up both his hands and his eyes towards heaven, and saying, 'Lord God Eternal! I beseech Thee, of Thy great mercy sake, to forgive my pursuers, if it be Thy blessed will.'

After this, the bishops and priests were in great discredit both with the nobility and commons; for that they had so cruelly handled the good Lord Cobham. The prelates feared this to grow to further inconvenience towards them, wherefore they drew their heads together, and consented to use another practice somewhat contrary to that they had done before. They caused it to be blown abroad by their fee'd servants, friends, and babbling Sir Johns, that the said Lord Cobham was become a good man, and had lowly submitted himself in all things unto Holy Church, utterly changing his opinion concerning the sacrament. And thereupon, they counterfeited an abjuration in his name, that the people should take no hold of his opinion by any thing they had heard of him before, and so to stand the more in awe of them, considering him so great a man, and by them subdued.

When the clergy perceived that policy would not help, but made more and more against them, then sought they out another false practice: they went unto the King with a most grievous complaint, that in every quarter of the realm, by reason of Wickliff's opinions, and the said Lord Cobham, were wonderful contentions, rumours, tumults, uproars, confederations, dissensions, divisions, differences, discords, harms, slanders, schisms, sects, seditions, perturbations, perils, unlawful assemblies, variances, strifes, fightings, rebellious rufflings, and daily insurrections. The Church, they said, was hated. The diocesans were not obeyed. The ordinaries were not regarded. The spiritual officers, as suffragans, archdeacons, chancellors, doctors, commissaries, officials, deans, lawyers, scribes, and somners, were everywhere despised. The laws and liberties of Holy Church were trodden under foot. The Christian faith was ruinously decayed. God's service was laughed to scorn. The spiritual jurisdiction, authority, honour, power, policy, laws, rites, ceremonies, curses, keys, censures, and canonical sanctions of the Church, were had in utter contempt, so that all, in a manner, was come to naught.

And the cause of this was, that the heretics and lollards of Wickliff's opinion were suffered to preach abroad so boldly, to gather conventicles unto them, to keep schools in men's houses, to make books, compile treatises, and write ballads, to teach privately in angles and corners, as in woods, fields, meadows, pastures, groves, and in caves of the ground.

This would be, said they, a destruction to the commonwealth, a subversion to the land, and an utter decay of the King's estate royal, if remedy were not sought in time. And this was their policy, to couple the King's authority with what they had done in their former council, of craft, and so to make it, thereby, the stronger. For they perceived themselves very far too weak else, to follow against their enemies, what they had so largely enterprised. Upon this complaint, the King immediately called a parliament at Leicester. It might not, in those days, be holden at Westminster, for the great favour that the Lord Cobham had, both in London and about the city.

Thus were Christ's people betrayed every way, and their lives bought and sold. For, in the said parliament, the King made this most blasphemous and cruel act, to be a law for ever: that whatsoever they were that should read the Scriptures in the mother-tongue (which was then called Wickliff's learning), they should forfeit land, cattle, body, life, and goods, from their heirs for ever, and so be condemned for heretics to God, enemies to the crown, and most arrant traitors to the land. Besides this, it was enacted, that never a sanctuary, nor privileged ground within the realm, should hold them, though they were still permitted both to thieves and murderers. And if, in any case they would not give over, or were, after their pardon, relapsed, they should suffer death in two manner of kinds: that is; they should first be hanged for treason against the King, and then be burned for heresy against God.

Then had the bishops, priests, monks, and friars a world somewhat to their minds. Many were taken in divers quarters, and suffered most cruel death. And many fled out of the land into Germany, Bohemia, France, Spain, Portugal, and into the welds of Scotland, Wales, and Ireland; working there many marvels.

Sentence of death being given, the Lord Cobham was sent away, Sir Robert Morley carrying him again unto the Tower, where, after he had remained a certain space, in the night season (it is not known by what means), he escaped out, and fled into Wales. A great sum of money was proclaimed by the King, to him that could take the said Sir John Oldcastle, either quick or dead: who confederated with the Lord Powis (who was at that time a great governor in Wales), feeding him with lordly gifts and promises. About the end of four years, the Lord Powis, whether for greediness of the money, or for hatred of the true and sincere doctrine of Christ, seeking all manner of ways how to play the part of Judas, and outwardly pretending him great amity and favour, at length obtained his bloody purpose, and most cowardly and wretchedly took him, and brought the Lord Cobham bound, up to London; which was about the year of our Lord 1417, and about the month of December; at which there was a parliament assembled in London. It was adjudged, that he should be taken as a traitor to the King and the realm; that he should be carried to the Tower, and from thence drawn through London, unto the new gallows in St Giles without Temple-Bar, and there to be hanged, and burned hanging.

Upon the day appointed, the Lord Cobham was brought out of the Tower with his arms bound behind him, having a very cheerful countenance. Then was he laid upon a hurdle, as though he had been a most heinous traitor to the crown, and so drawn forth into St Giles's field. As he was come to the place of execution, and was taken from the hurdle, he fell down devoutly upon his knees, desiring Almighty God to forgive his enemies. Then stood he up and beheld the multitude, exhorting them in most godly manner to follow the laws of God written in the Scriptures, and to beware of such teachers as they see contrary to Christ in their conversation and living. Then was he hanged up by the middle in chains of iron, and so consumed alive in the fire, praising the name of God so long as his life lasted; the people, there present, showing great dolour. And this was done A.D. 1418.

How the priests that time fared, blasphemed, and accursed, requiring the people not to pray for him, but to judge him damned in hell, for that he departed not in the obedience of their Pope, it were too long to write.

Thus resteth this valiant Christian knight, Sir

John Oldcastle, under the altar of God, which is Jesus Christ, among that godly company, who, in the kingdom of patience, suffered great tribulation with the death of their bodies, for His faithful word and testimony.

Chapter Five

THE MARTYRDOM OF JOHN HUSS

By the occasion of Queen Anne, who was a Bohemian, and married to King Richard II., the Bohemians coming to the knowledge of Wickliff's books here in England, began first to taste and savour Christ's Gospel, till at length, by the preaching of John Huss, they increased more and more in knowledge, insomuch that Pope Alexander V. hearing thereof, began to stir coals, and directeth his bull to the Archbishop of Prague, requiring him to look to the matter, and to provide that no person in churches, schools, or other places, should maintain that doctrine; citing also John Huss to appear before him. To whom the said John answering, declared that mandate or bull of the Pope utterly to repugn against the manifest examples and doings both of Christ and of His apostles, and to be prejudicial to the liberty of the Gospel, in binding the Word of God not to have free course; and, therefore, from this mandate of the Pope he appealed to the same Pope better advised. But, while he was prosecuting his appeal, Pope Alexander died.

After Alexander succeeded Pope John XXIII., who also, playing his part like a Pope, sought by all means possible to keep under the Bohemians, first beginning to work his malice upon the aforesaid John Huss, their preacher who, at the same time preaching at Prague in the temple of Bethlehem, because he seemed rather willing to teach the

Gospel of Christ than the traditions of bishops, was accused for a heretic.

The Pope committed the whole matter to Cardinal de Columna; who, when he had heard the accusation, appointed a day to John Huss, that he should appear in the court of Rome: which thing done, Wenceslaus, King of the Romans and of Bohemia, at the request specially of his wife Sophia and of the whole nobility of Bohemia, as also at the earnest suit and desire of the town and University of Prague, sent his ambassadors to Rome, to desire the Pope to quit and clearly deliver John Huss from that citation and judgment; and that if the Pope did suspect the kingdom of Bohemia to be infected with any heretical or false doctrine, he should send his ambassadors, who might correct and amend same, and that all this should be done at the sole cost and charges of the King of Bohemia: and to promise in his name, that he would assist the Pope's legates with all his power and authority, to punish all such as should be taken or found in any erroneous doctrine.

In the mean season, also, John Huss, before his day appointed, sent his lawful and meet procurators unto the court of Rome, and with most firm and strong reasons did prove his innocency; whereupon he so trusted, that he thought he should have easily obtained, that he should not have been compelled, by reason of the great danger, to appear the day appointed. But, when the Cardinal de Columna, unto whose will and judgment the whole matter was committed, would not admit any defence or excuse, John Huss's procurators appealed unto the Pope: yet, notwithstanding, this last refuge did not so much prevail with Cardinal de Columna, but that he would openly excommunicate John Huss as an obstinate heretic, because he came not at his day appointed to Rome.

Notwithstanding, forsomuch as his proctors had appealed unto the Pope, they had other judges appointed unto them, as the Cardinals of Aquileia and of Venice, with certain others; which judges, after they had deferred the matter by the space of a year and a half, returned to the sentence and judgment of Cardinal de Columna, and, confirming the same, commanded John Huss's procurators, that they should leave off to defend him any more, for they would suffer it no longer: whereupon, when his procurators would not cease their instant suit, certain of them were cast into prison, and grievously punished; the others, leaving their business undone, returned into Bohemia.

The Bohemians little cared for all this; but, as they grew more in knowledge, so the less they regarded the Pope, complaining daily against him and the archbishop for stopping the Word of God and the Gospel of Christ to be preached, saying, that by their indulgences, and other practices of the court of Rome, they sought their own profit, and not that of Jesus Christ; that they plucked from the sheep of Christ the wool and milk, and did not feed them, either with the Word of God, or with good examples; teaching, moreover, and affirming, that the commandments of the Pope and prelates are not to be obeyed but so far as they follow the doctrine and life of Christ and of His apostles. They derided also and scorned the Pope's jurisdiction, because of the schism that was then in the church, when there were three Popes together, one striving against another for the papacy.

It happened by the occasion of Ladislaus, King of Naples, who was ravaging the Pope's towns and territories, that Pope John, raising up war against the said Ladislaus, gave full remission of sins to all those who would war on his side to defend the Church. When the bull of the Pope's indulgence was come to Prague, and there published, the King Wenceslaus, who then favoured that Pope, gave commandment that no man should attempt any thing against the said Pope's indulgences.

But Huss, with his followers, not able to abide the impiety of those pardons, began to speak against them, of which company were three certain artificers, who, hearing the priest preaching of these indulgences, did openly speak against them, and called the Pope Antichrist. Wherefore they were brought before the senate, and committed to ward: but the people, joining themselves together in arms, came to the magistrates, requiring them to be let loose. The magistrates, with gentle words and fair promises, satisfied the people, so that every man returning home to his own house, the tumult was assuaged: but the artisans, whose names were John, Martin, and Stascon, being in prison, were notwithstanding there beheaded. The martyrdom of th hree being known to the people, they took the bodies, and with great solemnity brought them unto the church of Bethlehem: at whose funeral divers priests favouring that side, did sing on this wise; 'These be the saints, who, for the testament of God, gave their bodies.' And so their bodies were sumptuously interred in the church of Bethlehem, John Huss

93

preaching at the funeral, much commending them for their constancy.

Thus this city of Prague was divided. The prelates, with the greatest part of the clergy and most of the barons who had any thing to lose, did hold with the Pope. On the contrary part, the commons, with part of the clergy and students of the University, went with John Huss. Wenceslaus the King, fearing lest this would grow to a tumult, being moved by the doctors and prelates and council of his barons, thought best to remove John Huss out of the city. And further to cease this dissension risen in the Church, he committed the matter to the disposition of the doctors and the clergy. They, consulting together, did set forth a decree, confirmed by the sentence of the King, containing eighteen articles for the maintenance of the Pope and of the see of Rome, against the doctrine of Wickliff and John Huss.

John Huss, thus departing out of Prague, went to his country, where he, being protected by the lord of the soil, continued preaching, to whom resorted a great concourse of people; neither yet was he so expelled out of Prague, but that sometimes he resorted to his church at Bethlehem, and there preached unto the people.

Moreover, against the said decree of the doctors John Huss answered with contrary articles as followeth.

The Objections of John Huss against the Decree of the Doctors.

False it is that they say the Pope and his cardinals to be the true and manifest successors of

Peter and of the apostles, neither that any other successors of Peter and of the apostles can be found upon the earth besides them: whereas all bishops and priests be successors of Peter and of the apostles.

Not the Pope, but Christ only, is the head; and not the cardinals, but all Christ's faithful people, be the body of the Catholic Church.

If the Pope be a reprobate, it is plain that he is no head, no nor member even, of the Holy Church of God, but of the devil and of his synagogue.

Neither is it true, that we ought to stand in all things to the determination of the Pope and of the cardinals, but so far forth as they do agree with the holy Scripture of the Old and New Testament.

The Church of Rome is not that place where the Lord did appoint the principal see of His whole Church: for Christ, Who was the head priest of all, did first sit in Jerusalem, and Peter did sit first in Antioch, and afterward in Rome. Also other Popes did sit, some at Bologna, some at Perugia, some at Avignon.

The prelates are falsifiers of the holy Scriptures who affirm and say, that we must obey the Pope in all things. For why? it is known that many Popes have been heretics, and one Pope was also a woman.

They fondly and childishly argue that the processes made against Master John Huss ought to be obeyed, because, forsooth, the whole body of the clergy of Prague have received them. By the same reason they may argue also, that we must obey the devil, because our first parents, Adam and Eve, obeyed him.

Unto these objections of John Huss the catholic doctors did answer in a long tedious process, the scope whereof principally tended to defend the principality of the Pope, and to maintain obedience to him above all other potentates in the world. Like as Christ is King of all Kings, and yet Charles may be King of France; so say they, Christ may be the universal head, and yet the Pope may be head under Him of the whole Church. While Christ walked here on earth in His bodily presence, He was Pope Himself and chief bishop, and so head of the Church here militant on earth. But because after He departed out of the world His body, which is the Church militant upon the earth, should not be headless, therefore He left Peter and his successors to His Church for a head in His place, unto the consummation of the world.

Thus then Master John Huss, being driven out of Prague, and, moreover, being so excommunicated, that no mass must be said where he was present, the people began mightily to grudge and to cry out against the prelates and other popish priests, accusing them as being simoniacs, covetous, proud; sparing not to lay open their vices, to their great ignominy and shame, and much craving reformation to be had of the clergy.

The King, seeing the inclination of the people, being also not ignorant of the wickedness of the clergy, under pretence of reforming the Church, began to require greater exactions upon such priests and men of the clergy as were known to be wicked livers. Whereupon they that favoured John Huss, complained of all, whomsoever they knew to be of the catholic faction, or enemies to John Huss; by reason whereof the priests of the popish clergy were brought, such as were faulty, into great distress, and such as were not faulty, into great fear, insomuch that they were glad to fall in, at least not to fall out, with the Protestants, being afraid to displease them. By this means Master Huss began to take some more liberty unto him, and to preach in his church at Bethlehem, and none to control him: by the same means the people received some comfort, and the King much gain.

Thus the popish clergy, while they went about to persecute John Huss, were enwrapped themselves in great tribulation, and afflicted on every side, as well of laymen, as of the evangelical clergy; nay, the women also and children were against them because of the interdict against John Huss.

The more the Pope's clergy were pinched, the more grudge and hatred redounded to John Huss, although he was no cause thereof, but only their own wicked deservings. And to help the matter forward, the Pope writeth letters to Wenceslaus, King of Bohemia, who was brother to Sigismund, the emperor, for the suppressing of John Huss and of his doctrine. 'We hear that in divers places under your dominion, there be certain who do follow and preach the errors of that arch-heretic Wickliff, whose books have been long since condemned in the general Roman council to be erroneous, heretical, and swerving from the catholic faith. Wherefore we do exhort your worship effectuously to show forth your regal power, both for the glory of God and defence of the catholic faith, as it becometh a catholic prince; whereby this heresy may be rooted out.'

During all this time of Pope John, there were three Popes reigning together, neither was yet the schism ceased, which had continued the space, already, of thirty-six years; by reason whereof a General Council was holden at Constance in A.D. 1414, being called by Sigismund the Emperor, and Pope John XXXIII. These three Popes were John, whom the Italians set up; Gregory, whom the Frenchmen set up; Benedict, whom the Spaniards placed. In this schismatical ambitious conflict every one defended his Pope, to the great disturbance of Christian nations. This Council endured three years and five months. Many great and profitable things to the glory of God and public profit might have been coucluded, if the rotten flesh of the churchmen could have bidden the salt of the Gospel, and if they had loved the truth.

Pope John was deposed by the decree of the Council, more than three and forty most grievous and heinous crimes being proved against him: as that he had hired Marcilius Parmensis, a physician, to poison Alexander, his predecessor; further, that he was a heretic, a simoniac, a liar, a hypocrite, a murderer, an enchanter, and a dice-player. Finally, what crime is it that he was not infected withal?

In this Council of Constance nothing was decreed or enacted worthy of memory, but this only, that the Pope's authority is under the Council, and that the Council ought to judge the Pope. And, as touching the communion in both kinds (bread and wine), although the Council did not deny but that it was used by Christ and His apostles, yet notwithstanding, by the same Council it was decreed to the contrary.

Which Council, although it was principally thought to be assembled for quieting of the schism between the three Popes; yet, notwithstanding, a great part thereof was for the cause of the Bohemians, and especially for John Huss. For before the Council began, the Emperor Sigismund sent certain gentlemen, Bohemians, who were of his own household, giving them in charge to bring John Huss, bachelor of divinity, unto the said Council. The meaning and intent thereof was, that John Huss should purge and clear himself of the blame which they had laid against him: and, for the better assurance, the Emperor did not only promise him safe conduct, that he might come freely unto Constance, but also that he should return again into Bohemia, without fraud or interruption; he promised also to receive him under his protection, and under safeguard of the whole empire.

John Huss, seeing so many fair promises and the assurance which the Emperor had given to him, sent answer, that he would come unto the Council. But before he departed out of the realm of Bohemia, and especially out of the town of Prague, he did write certain bills and caused them to be fastened upon the gates of the cathedral churches and parish churches, cloisters and abbeys, signifying unto them all, that he would go to the General Council at Constance there to declare his faith which he hath hitherto holden, and even at the present doth hold, and by God's help will defend and keep even unto death; wherefore, if any man have any suspicion of his doctrine, that he should declare it before the Lord Conrad, Archbishop of Prague; or, if he had rather, at the General Council, for there he would render unto every one, and before them all, an account and reason of his faith.

About the ides of October, 1414, John Huss, being accompanied with two noble gentlemen, Wenceslaus of Duba, and John of Clum, departed from Prague, and took his journey towards Constance. In all cities as he passed by, a great number of people did come unto him, and he was very gently received and entertained through all the towns of Germany, not only of his hosts, but of the citizens generally, and oftentimes of the curates; insomuch that the said Huss did confess, in a certain epistle, that he found in no place so great enemies as in Bohemia. And if it happened that there were any bruit or noise before of his coming, the streets were always full of people who were desirous to see and gratify him; especially at Nuremberg, where there were many curates who came unto him, desiring him that they might talk with him secretly, unto whom he answered: that he loved much rather to show forth his mind openly before all men than in hugger-mugger, for he would keep nothing close or hidden. So, after dinner, until it was night, he spake before the priests, senators, and divers other citizens, insomuch that they had him in great estimation and reverence.

The twentieth day after that he parted out of the town of Prague, which was the third day of November, he came unto Constance, and lodged at an honest matron's house, being a widow named Faithful, in St Gale's Street.

The morrow after, the noble men, Lord John de Clum, and Lord Henry Latzemboge, went to speak with the Pope, and certified him that John Huss was come, desiring that he would grant the said John Huss liberty to remain in Constance, without any trouble, or vexation, or interruption. Unto whom the Pope answered—that even if John Huss had killed his brother, yet would he go about, as much as in him lay, that no outrage or hurt should be done unto him during his abode in the city of Constance.

In this meantime, the greatest adversary that John Huss had, named Master Stephen Paletz, who was also a Bohemian born, was come unto Constance. The said Paletz did associate unto him one Michael de Causis, who was the first and bitterest accuser of the said John Huss. Paletz had been familiarly conversant with John Huss from his youth upward; but after that there was a bull brought unto Prague from Pope John XXIII. against the king of Apulia, named Ladislaus, the said John Huss withstood it openly, forsomuch as he saw that it was wicked and nought. Paletz, albeit that he had confessed at a certain banquet, in the presence of the said John Huss, that the said bull was contrary to all equity and right, yet, notwithstanding, forsomuch as he was bound unto the Pope by means of certain benefices received at his hand, he maintained and defended the said bull against John Huss.

As for Michael de Causis, the companion of Master Paletz, he was sometime the curate of New Prague: but he, not being content therewith, and seeking after a further prey, imagined a new device how to attain unto it; for he made a semblance that he had found out a new invention, whereby the mines of gold in Gilowy, which were perished and lost, might be set on work again. By this means he did so much with the King Wenceslaus, that he did put a great sum of money into his hands, to do that withal which he had promised. This honest man, after he had laboured certain days about it, perceiving that he brought nothing to pass, and that he was utterly in despair of his purpose, conveyed himself privily out of the realm of Bohemia with the rest of the money, and withdrew himself, as a worthy bird for such a nest, to the court of Rome.

These two jolly roisters, Stephen Paletz and Michael de Causis, drew out certain articles against the said Huss, saying, that they had gathered them out of his own writings, and especially out of his treatise which he had written of the Church. They trotted up and down, hither and thither, taking great pains to show the said articles unto the cardinals, bishops and monks, giving them to understand, that there were other matters of greater importance, which the said John Huss had committed against the holy constitutions, and other ordinances of the Pope and the church; which, if need were, they said they would propound before the Council. Through the kindling of this their fire, they did so incense the cardinals and the priests, that they all, with one mind, thought to cause the good man to be laid hands on.

The twenty-sixth day after the said Huss was come to Constance (during all which time he was occupied in reading, writing, and familiar talk with his friends), the cardinals, through the instigation of Paletz, and Michael de Causis, sent two bishops, to wit, the Bishops of Augsburg and of Trent, and with them the borough-master of Constance, and a certain knight, to the place where John Huss lodged, about dinner-time; who should make report unto him that they were sent by the Pope and his cardinals, to advertise him that he should come to render some knowledge of his doctrine before them as he had oftentimes desired, and that they were ready to hear him.

Unto whom John Huss answered, 'I am not come for any such intent, as to defend my cause particularly before the Pope and his cardinals, but that I would willingly appear before the whole Council, and there answer for my defence openly, without any fear or doubt, unto all such things as shall be required of me. Notwithstanding, forasmuch as you require me so to do, I will not refuse to go with you before the cardinals; and if it happen that they evil entreat or handle me, yet I trust in my Lord Jesus, that He will so comfort and strengthen me, that I shall desire much rather to die for His glory's sake, than to deny the verity which I have learned by His holy Scriptures.'

Wherefore it came to pass that, the bishops being instant upon him, and not showing any outward semblance that they bare any malice against him in their hearts (albeit they had privily laid garrisons both in the house where they were assembled, and also in other houses), John Huss took his horse which he had at his lodging, and went unto the court of the Pope and the cardinals.

When he was come thither, and had saluted the cardinals, they began to speak to him in this sort: 'We have heard many reports of you, which, if they be true, are in no case to be suffered; for men say, that you have taught great and manifest errors against the doctrine of the true Church; and that you have sowed your errors abroad through all the realm of Bohemia, by a long space of time; wherefore we have caused you to be called hither before us, that we might know how the matter standeth.'

Unto whom John Huss answered in few words: 'Reverend fathers! you shall understand that I am thus minded and affectioned, that I should rather choose to die, than I should be found culpable of one only error, much less of many and great errors. I am ready to receive correction, if any man can prove any errors in me.' The cardinals answered him that his sayings pleased them very well; and upon that they went away, leaving the said John Huss with Lord John de Clum, under the guard of the armed men, until four of the clock in the afternoon.

After that time the cardinals assembled again in the Pope's court, to take counsel what they should do with John Huss. Stephen Paletz and Michael de Causis, with divers others of their adherents, made earnest suit that he should not be let go at liberty again, and having the favour of the judges on their part, they bragged up and down in a manner as they had been mad men, and mocked the said John Huss, saying, 'Now we will hold thee well enough; thou art under our power and jurisdiction, and shalt not depart until such time as thou hast paid the uttermost farthing.'

A little before night, they sent the provost of the Roman court unto Lord John de Clum, to show him that he might return to his lodging; but as for John Huss, they had otherwise provided for him. When Lord John de Clum heard this news, he was wonderfully displeased, forasmuch as through their crafts, subtleties, and glosing words, they had so trained this good man into their snares; whereupon he went unto the Pope, declaring unto him all that was done; most humbly beseeching him, that he would call to remembrance the promise which he had made unto him and Lord Henry Latzemboge, and that he would not so lightly break his faith. The Pope answered, that all these things were done without his consent or commandment; and said further to Lord de Clum apart, 'What reason is it that you should impute this deed unto me, seeing that you know well enough that I myself am in the hands of these cardinals and Bishops?'

So the said Lord de Clum returned very pensiveful and sorry; he complained very sore, both privily and openly, of the outrage that the Pope had done; but all profited nothing. After this, the said John Huss was led to the house of the precentor of the church of Constance, where he was kept prisoner by the space of eight days; from thence he was carried unto the Jacobites, hard by the river Rhine, and was shut up in the prison of the abbey.

After he had been enclosed there a certain time he fell sore sick of an ague, by means of the stench of the place, and became so weak, that they despaired of his life. And for fear lest this good man should die in prison, the Pope sent unto him certain of his physicians to cure him. In the midst of his sickness his accusers made importunate suit to the principals of the Council, that the said John Huss might be condemned, and presented unto the Pope these articles:

He doth err about the sacraments of the Church,

and especially about the sacrament of the body of Christ, forasmuch as he hath openly preached, that it ought to be ministered openly unto the people under both kinds, that is to say, the body and blood. Moreover, it is affirmed by divers, that he hath taught both in the schools and in the church, or at the least that he doth hold this opinion, that after the words of consecration pronounced upon the altar, there remaineth still material bread in the sacrament.

He doth err as touching the ministers of the Church, forasmuch as he saith, that they cannot consecrate or minister the sacraments when they are in mortal sin. Moreover he saith, that other men beside priests may minister the sacrament.

He doth not allow and admit that the church signifieth the Pope, cardinals, archbishops, and the clergy underneath them.

He saith, that the Church hath no power of the keys, when the Pope, cardinals, and all other of the priests and clergy are in deadly sin.

He holdeth opinion that every man hath authority to invest and appoint any man to the cure of souls. This is evident by his own doings, forasmuch as many in the kingdom of Bohemia by their defenders and favourers, or rather by himself, were appointed and put into parish churches, which they have long ruled and kept, not being appointed by the apostolic see, neither yet by the ordinary of the city of Prague.

He holdeth opinion, that a man, being once ordained a priest or deacon, cannot be forbidden or kept back from the office of preaching. This is likewise manifest by his own doings, forasmuch as he himself could never be letted from preaching, neither by the apostolic see, nor yet by the Archbishop of Prague.

Moreover, when there were questions moved amongst the divines of the University of Prague upon the forty-five articles of John Wickliff, and they had called a convocation, and all the divines of Bohemia had concluded that every one of those articles was either heretical, seditious, or erroneous; he alone held the contrary opinion, that none of those articles were either heretical, seditious, or erroneous, as afterwards he did dispute, hold, and teach, in the common schools of Prague; whereby it is evidently enough foreseen, that he doth affirm those articles of Wickliff, which are not only condemned in England, but also by the whole Church.

Upon this accusation, they appointed three commissioners or judges; the Patriarch of Constantinople, the Bishop of Castel-a-mare, and the Bishop of Lebus; the which prelates heard the accusation and the witness which was brought in by certain babbling priests of Prague, confirmed by their oaths, and afterwards recited the said accusation unto the said Huss in the prison, at such time as his ague was fervent and extremely upon him.

Upon this, John Huss required to have an advocate to answer for him; which was plainly and utterly denied him. And the reason that the masters commissioners brought against it was this: that the plain canon doth forbid that any man should be a defender of him who is suspected of heresy. The vanity and folly of the witnesses was such, that if they had not been both the accusers and judges themselves, there should have needed no confutation.

Thus John Huss remained in the prison of the convent of the Franciscans, until the Wednesday before Palm Sunday; and in the mean season, to employ his time, he wrote certain books of the ten commandments, of the love and knowledge of God, of matrimony, of penance, of the three enemies of mankind, of the prayer of our Lord, and of the supper of our Lord.

The same day Pope John XXIII. changed his apparel, and conveyed himself secretly out of Constance, fearing the judgment by which afterwards he was deprived of his papal dignity by reason of most execrable and abominable forfeits and doings. This was the cause that John Huss was transported and carried unto another prison; for the Pope's servants, who had the keeping of John Huss, understanding that their master was fled, delivered up the keys of the prison unto the Emperor Sigismund, and to the cardinals, and followed their master the Pope. Then, by the consent of the Council, the said John Huss was put into the hands of the Bishop of Constance, who sent him to a castle on the other side of the river Rhine, not very far from Constance, where he was shut up in a tower with fetters on his legs, that he could scarce walk in the day-time, and at night he was fastened up to a rack against the wall hard by his bed.

In the mean season, certain noblemen and gentlemen of Poland and Bohemia did all their endeavour to purchase his deliverance, having respect to the good renown of all the realm, which was wonderfully defamed and slandered by certain naughty persons. The matter was grown unto this point, that all they who were in the town of Constance, who seemed to bear any favour unto John Huss, were made as mocking stocks, and derided of all men, yea, even of the slaves and base people. Wherefore they took counsel and concluded together to present their request in writing unto the whole Council, the fourteenth day of May, A.D. 1415; the tenor here ensueth:—

'When Master John Huss was freely of his own accord come unto Constance, under safe-conduct, he was grievously imprisoned before he was heard, and at this present is tormented both with fetters, and also with hunger and thirst. Master John Huss, neither being convicted nor condemned, no not so much as once heard, is taken and imprisoned, and is so weakened with thin and slender diet, that it is to be feared, lest that, his power and strength being hereby consumed and wasted, he should be put in danger of his wit or reason.

'Wherefore, we do wholly and most earnestly desire and require your reverences that both for the honour of the safe-conduct of our lord the King, and also for the preservation and increase of the worthy fame and renown both of the kingdom of Bohemia, and your own also, you will make a short end about the affairs of Master John Huss.'

The said barons and lords also presented a supplication unto the emperor: 'We most humbly require and desire your princely majesty, that you would interpose your good offices with the said most reverend fathers and lords, that they may effectually hear us in this our just petition.'

But what answer the emperor made hereunto, we could never understand or know; but by the process of the matter a man may easily judge, that this good emperor was led even unto this point, through the obstinate mischief of the cardinals and bishops, to break and falsify his promise and faith: and this was their reason whereby he was driven thereunto, that no defence could or might be given either by safe-conduct, or by any other means, unto him who was suspected or judged to be a heretic.

When John Huss was brought forth again before the whole assembly, a strange and shameful matter happened. They had scarcely read one article, and brought forth a few witnesses, but, as he was about to open his mouth to answer, all this mad herd began so to cry out upon him, that he had not leisure to speak one only word. The noise and trouble was so great and so vehement, that a man might well have called it a bruit of wild beasts, and not of men; much less was it to be judged a congregation of men gathered together, to determine so grave and weighty matters.

Some did outrage in words against him, and others spitefully mocked him; so that he, seeing himself overwhelmed with these rude and barbarous noises, and that it profited nothing to speak, determined finally with himself to hold his peace. From that time forward, all the whole rout of his adversaries thought that they had won the battle of him, and cried out all together; 'Now he is dumb, now he is dumb: this is a certain sign and token, that he doth consent and agree unto these his errors.' Finally, the matter came to this point, that certain of the most moderate and honest among them, seeing this disorder, determined to proceed no further, but that all should be put off until another time. Through their advice, the prelates and others parted from the Council for that present, and appointed to meet there again on the day after the morrow, to proceed in judgment.

On that day, which was the seventh of June, somewhere about seven of the clock, the sun a little before having been almost wholly eclipsed, this same flock assembled in the cloister of the friars minor, and by their appointment John Huss was brought before them, accompanied with a great number of armed men. Thither went also the emperor, whom the noble men, Lords Wenceslaus de Duba and John de Clum, did follow, to see what the end would be.

Then was read a certain article of accusation, in the which it was alleged, that John Huss had taught, and obstinately defended, certain erroneous articles of Wickliff's. To confirm their article, there was alleged that John Huss did withstand the condemnation of Wickliff's articles, the which had been first made at Rome. And afterward also, when the Archbishop of Prague, with other learned men, held a convocation at Prague for the same matter, he answered, that he durst not agree thereunto, for offending of his conscience, and especially for these articles: that Silvester the Pope, and Constantine, did err in bestowing great gifts and rewards upon the Church: also, that the Pope or priest, being in mortal sin, cannot consecrate nor baptize. 'This article,' said Huss, 'I have thus limited, so as I should say, that he doth unworthily consecrate or baptize, for that, when he is in deadly sin, he is an unworthy minister of the sacraments of God.' He did not consent that Wickliff's articles should be condemned, before sufficient reasons were alleged out of the holy Scripture for their condemnation.

'And of the same mind,' saith John Huss, 'are a great many other doctors and masters of the University of Prague; for when Sbinco the archbishop commanded all Wickliff's books to be gathered together in the whole city of Prague, and to be brought unto him, I myself brought also certain books of Wickliff's, which I gave unto the archbishop, desiring him, that if he found any error or heresy in them, he would note and mark them, and I myself would publish them openly. But the archbishop, albeit that he showed me no error nor heresy in them, burned my books, together with those that were brought unto him. He obtained a bull from the Pope that all Wickliff's books, for the manifold errors contained in them (whereof there were none named), should be taken out of all men's hands. The archbishop, using the authority of this bull, thought that he should bring to pass, that the King of Bohemia and the nobles should consent to the condemnation of Wickliff's books; but therein he was deceived. Yet nevertheless, calling together certain divines, he gave them in commission to sit upon Wickliff's books, and to proceed against them by a definitive sentence in the canon law. These men, by a general sentence, judged all those books worthy to be burned; which when the doctors, masters and scholars of the University heard report of, they, all together, with one consent and accord (none excepted but only they, who before were chosen by the archbishop to sit in judgment), determined to make supplication unto the King to stay the matter. The King, granting their request, sent by and by certain unto the archbishop to examine the matter. There he denied that he would decree any thing, as touching Wickliff's books, contrary unto the King's will and pleasure. Whereupon, albeit that he had determined to burn them the next day after, yet for fear of the King, the matter was passed over. In the meantime Pope Alexander V. being dead, the archbishop, fearing lest the bull which he had received of the Pope, would be no longer of any force or effect, privily calling unto him his adherents, and shutting the gates of his court round about him, being guarded with a number of armed soldiers, consumed and burned all Wickliff's books. Besides this great injury, the archbishop by means of this bull aforesaid, committed another no less intolerable ; for he gave commandment, that no man after that time, under pain of excommunication, should teach any more in chapels. Whereupon I did appeal unto the Pope ; who being dead, and the cause of my matter remaining undetermined, I appealed likewise unto his successor John XXIII. : before whom when, by the space of two years, I could not be admitted by my advocates to defend my cause, I appealed unto the high judge Christ.'

When John Huss had spoken these words, it was demanded of him, whether he had received absolution of the Pope or no? He answered, 'no.' Then again, whether it were lawful for him to appeal unto Christ or no? Whereunto John Huss answered : 'Verily I do affirm here before you all, that there is no more just or effectual appeal, than that appeal which is made unto Christ, forasmuch as the law doth determine, that to appeal, is no other thing than in a cause of grief or wrong done by an inferior judge, to implore and require aid and remedy at a higher judge's hand. Who is then a higher judge than Christ? Who, I say, can know or judge the matter more justly, or with more equity? when in Him there is found no deceit, neither can He be deceived; or, who can better help the miserable and oppressed than He?' While John Huss, with a devout and sober countenance, was speaking and pronouncing those words, he was derided and mocked by all the whole Council.

Then was there rehearsed another article of his accusation in this manner; that John Huss, to confirm the heresy which he had taught the common people out of Wickliff's books, said that he wished his soul to be in the same place where John Wickliff's soul was. Whereunto John Huss answered, that a dozen years before any books of divinity of John Wickliff's were in Bohemia, he did see certain works of philosophy of his, which, he said, did marvellously delight and please him. And when he understood the good and godly life of the said Wickliff, he spake these words.

This done, the said John Huss was committed to the custody of the Archbishop of Riga. But before he was led away, the Cardinal of Cambray, calling him back again in the presence of the emperor, said, 'John Huss, I have heard you say, that if you had not been willing of your own mind to come unto Constance, neither the emperor himself, nor the King of Bohemia, could have compelled you to do it.'

Unto whom John Huss answered: 'Under your license, most reverend father! I did say, that there were in Bohemia a great number of gentlemen and noblemen, who did favour and love me, who also might easily have kept me in some sure and secret place, that I should not have been constrained to come unto this town of Constance, neither at the will of the emperor, neither of the King of Bohemia.'

With that the Cardinal of Cambray even for very anger began to change his colour, and despitefully said: 'Do you not see the unshamefastness of the man here?'

And as they were murmuring and whispering on all parts, the Lord John de Clum, ratifying and confirming that which John Huss had spoken, said, that John Huss had spoken very well; 'for on my part' said he, 'who, in comparison of a great many others, am but of small force in the realm of Bohemia, yet always, if I would have taken it in hand, I could have defended him easily by the space of one year, even against all the force and power of both these great and mighty kings. How much better might they have done it who are of more force or puissance than I am, and have stronger castles and places than I have?'

After the Lord de Clum had spoken, the Cardinal of Cambray said, 'Let us leave this talk; and I tell you, John Huss! and counsel you, that you submit yourself unto the sentence and mind of the Council, as you did promise in the prison; and if you will do so, it shall be greatly both for your profit and honour.'

And the emperor himself began to tell him the same tale, saying, 'forasmuch as divers have told us, that we may not, or ought not, of right to defend any man who is a heretic, or suspected of heresy;

therefore, now, we give you counsel that you be not obstinate to maintain any opinion, but that you do submit yourself unto the authority of the holy Council, which thing if you do, we will give order that the Council shall suffer you to depart in peace, with an easy penance. Which thing if you, contrariwise, refuse to do, the presidents of the Council shall proceed against you. And, for our part, be ye well assured, that we will sooner make the fire with our own hands, to burn you withal, than we will suffer any longer that you shall maintain or use this stiffness of opinions, which you have hitherto used.'

The morrow after, which was the eighth day of June, the company assembled at the convent of the Franciscans. Thither was John Huss brought; and in his presence there were read the articles, which, they said, were drawn out of his books. Huss acknowledged all those that were faithfully and truly collected and gathered, to be his; of which sort there were but very few.

The Articles drawn from the books of John Huss, with his Answers to the same.

'Peter never was, neither is the head of the holy universal Church.'

Answer. This article was drawn out of these words of my book: 'All men do agree in this point, that Peter had received of the Rock of the Church (which is Christ), humility, poverty, steadfastness of faith, and consequently blessedness. Not as though the meaning of our Lord Jesus Christ was, when He said, "Upon this Rock I will build My

Church," that He would build every militant Church upon the person of Peter, for Christ should build His church upon the Rock which is Christ Himself, from whence Peter received his steadfastness of faith, forasmuch as Jesus Christ is the only head and foundation of every church, and not Peter.'

'If he that is called the vicar of Jesus Christ, do follow Christ in his life, then he is his true vicar. But, if so be he do walk in contrary paths and ways, then is he the messenger of Antichrist, and the enemy and adversary of St Peter, and of our Lord Jesus Christ, and also the vicar of Judas Iscariot.'

Answer. The words of my book are these: 'If he who is called the vicar of St Peter, walk in the ways of Christian virtues aforesaid, we do believe verily that he is the true vicar, and true Bishop of the Church which he ruleth; but if he walk in contrary paths and ways, then is he the messenger of Antichrist, contrary both to St Peter, and to our Lord Jesus Christ. And therefore St Bernard, in his fourth book, did write in this sort unto Pope Eugene: "Thou delightest and walkest in great pride and arrogancy, being gorgeously and sumptuously arrayed; what fruit or profit do thy flock or sheep receive by thee? If I durst say it, these be rather the pastures and feedings of devils than of sheep. St Peter and St Paul did not so; wherefore thou seemest by these thy doings to succeed Constantine, and not St Peter."' It followeth after, in my book, 'That if the manner and fashion of his life and living be contrary to that which St Peter used, or that he be given to avarice and covetousness, then is he the vicar of Judas Iscariot, who loved and chose the reward of iniquity, and did set out to sale the Lord Jesus Christ.'

'The papal dignity hath his original from the Emperors of Rome.'

Answer. Mark well what my words are: 'The pre-eminence and institution of the Pope is sprung and come of the emperor's power and authority; for Constantine granted this privilege unto the Bishop of Rome, and others after him confirmed the same: that like as Augustus, for the outward and temporal goods bestowed upon the Church, is counted always the most high King above all others; so the Bishop of Rome should be called the principal father above all other bishops.'

'No man would reasonably affirm (without revelation) either of himself or of any other, that he is the head of any particular Church.'

Answer. I confess it to be written in my book.

'The Pope's power as vicar is but vain and nothing worth, if he do not confirm and address his life according to Jesus Christ, and follow the manners of St Peter.'

Answer. It is thus in my book; 'That it is meet and expedient that he who is ordained vicar, should address and frame himself, in manners and conditions, to the authority of Him who did put him in place.'

'The cardinals are not the manifest and true successors of the other apostles of Jesus Christ, if they live not according to the fashion of the apostles, keeping the commandments and ordinances of the Lord Jesus.'

Answer. It is thus written in my book.

'A heretic ought not to be committed to the

118

secular powers to be put to death, for it is sufficient only that he abide and suffer the ecclesiastical censure.'

Answer. These are my words, 'They might be ashamed of their cruel sentence and judgment, especially forasmuch as Jesus Christ, Bishop both of the Old and New Testament, would not judge such as were disobedient by civil judgment, neither condemn them to bodily death.' A heretic ought first to be instructed and taught with Christian love and gentleness by the holy Scriptures. But if there were any, who, after gentle and loving admonitions and instructions, would not cease from their stiffness of opinions, but obstinately resist against the truth, such, I say, ought to suffer corporal or bodily punishment.

As soon as John Huss had spoken those things, the judges read in his book a certain clause, wherein he seemed grievously to inveigh against them who delivered a heretic unto the secular power, not being confuted or convicted of heresy: and compared them unto the high priests, Scribes and Pharisees, who said unto Pilate, 'It is not lawful for us to put any man to death,' and delivered Christ unto him: and yet notwithstanding, according unto Christ's own witness, they were greater murderers than Pilate. 'For he,' said Christ, 'who hath delivered Me unto thee, hath committed the greatest offence.' Then the cardinals and bishops made a great noise, and demanded of John Huss, saying: 'Who are they that thou dost compare unto the Pharisees?'

Then he said, 'All those who deliver up any innocent unto the civil sword, as the Scribes and Pharisees delivered Jesus Christ unto Pilate.'

'He that is excommunicated by the Pope, if he refuse and forsake the judgment of the Pope and the General Council, and appealeth unto Jesus Christ, after he hath made his appellation, all the excommunications and curses of the Pope cannot annoy or hurt him.'

Answer. I did make my complaint in my book, that they had both done me, and such as favoured me, great wrong; and that they refuse to hear me in the Pope's court. For after the death of one Pope, I did appeal to his successor, and all that did profit me nothing. And, therefore, last of all, I have appealed to the Head of the Church, my Lord Jesus Christ; for He is much more excellent and better than any Pope, to discuss and determine matters and causes, forasmuch as He cannot err, neither yet deny justice to him that doth ask or require it in a just cause; neither can He condemn the innocent.

'The minister of Christ, living according to His law, and having the knowledge and understanding of the Scriptures, and an earnest desire to edify the people, ought to preach; notwithstanding the pretended excommunication of the Pope. And moreover, if the Pope, or any other ruler, do forbid any priest or minister, so disposed, to preach, that he ought not to obey him.'

Answer. These are my words: 'That albeit the excommunication were either threatened or come out against him, in such sort that a Christian ought not to do the commandments of Christ, it appeareth by the words of St Peter, and the other apostles, that we ought rather to obey God than man.' Whereupon it followeth, that the minister of Christ, living according unto this law, ought to preach, notwithstanding any pretended excommunication; for God hath commanded us to preach and testify unto the people. Whereby it is evident, that if the Pope, or any other ruler of the Church, do command any minister disposed to preach, not to preach, they ought not to obey him.'

They objected unto him, that he had said, that such kind of excommunications were rather blessings.

'Verily,' said John Huss, 'even so I do now say again, that every excommunication, by which a man is unjustly excommunicated, is unto him a blessing before God. No Christian ought to doubt, but that a man sufficiently instructed in learning is more bound to counsel and instruct the ignorant, to teach those who are in doubt, to chastise those who are unruly, and to remit and forgive those that do him injury, than to do any other works of mercy.'

'There is no spark of appearance, that there ought to be one head in the spiritualty, to rule the Church, which should be always conversant with the militant Church.'

Answer. I do grant it. Christ is the Head of the spiritualty, ruling and governing the militant Church by much more and greater necessity than Cæsar ought to rule the temporalty; forasmuch as Christ Who sitteth on the right hand of God the Father, doth necessarily rule the militant Church as head.

'Christ would better rule His Church by His true apostles, dispersed throughout the whole world, without such monstrous heads.'

Answer. It is in my book as here followeth: 'We do verily believe that Christ Jesus is the head over every Church, ruling the same without lack or default, pouring upon the same a continual motion and sense. The Church, in the time of the apostles, was far better ruled and governed than now is. And what doth hinder, that Christ should not now rule the same better by His true disciples, without such monstrous heads as have been of late?'

When the articles were read over, together with their testimonies, the Cardinal of Cambray calling unto John Huss, said: 'Thou hast heard what grievous and horrible crimes are laid against thee, and what a number of them there are; and now it is thy part to devise with thyself what thou wilt do. Two ways are set before thee by the Council. First, that thou do meekly submit thyself unto the judgment of the Council, that whatsoever shall be there determined, thou wilt patiently bear, and suffer the same. Which thing if thou wilt do, we will treat and handle thee with as great humanity, love, and gentleness, as we may. But if as yet thou art determined to defend any of those articles which we have propounded unto thee, and dost desire or require to be further heard thereupon, we will not deny thee power and license thereunto: but this thou shalt well understand, that here are such manner of men, so clear in understanding and knowledge, and having such firm and strong reasons and arguments against thy articles, that I fear it will be to thy great hurt, detriment and peril.'

Unto whom, with a lowly countenance, John Huss answered: Most reverend fathers! I have often said that I came hither of mine own free will, not to the intent obstinately to defend any thing, but that if in any thing I should seem to have conceived a perverse or evil opinion, I would meekly and patiently be content to be reformed and taught. Whereupon I desire that I may have yet further liberty to declare my mind; whereof, except I shall allege most firm and strong reasons, I will willingly submit myself, as you require.'

Then said the Cardinal of Cambray: 'Forasmuch, then, as thou dost submit thyself unto the grace of this Council, this is decreed—First, that thou shalt humbly and meekly confess thyself to have erred in these articles which are alleged and brought against thee: Secondly, that thou shalt promise by an oath, that from henceforth thou shalt not hold, or teach, any of these articles: And last of all, that thou shalt openly recant all these articles.'

Upon which sentence, when many others had spoken their minds at length, John Huss said: 'I most humbly desire you all, even for His sake Who is the God of us all, that I be not compelled to do the thing which my conscience doth strive against, or which I cannot do without danger of eternal damnation: that is, that I should make revocation, by oath, to all the articles which are alleged against me. But if there be any man who can teach me contrariwise unto them, I will willingly perform that which you desire.'

Then said the Cardinal of Florence, 'John Huss, you shall have a form of abjuration, which shall be gentle, and tolerable enough, written and delivered unto you, and then you will easily and soon determine with yourself, whether you will do it or no.'

But John Huss constantly answered as before, insomuch that they said he was obstinate and stubborn. Thus they were all so grievous and troublesome unto him that he waxed faint and weary, for he had passed all the night before without sleep, through the pain of his teeth.

The Archbishop of Riga, unto whom John Huss was committed, commanded, that he should be carried again safely to prison. Then John de Clum following him, did not a little comfort him. No tongue can express what courage he received by the short talk which he had with him, when, in so great a broil and grievous hatred, he saw himself forsaken of all men.

After that John Huss was carried away, the emperor began to exhort the presidents of the Council in this manner following: 'You have heard the manifold and grievous crimes which are laid against John Huss, which are not only proved by manifest and strong witnesses, but also confessed by him; of which, every one of them, by my judgment and advice, hath deserved and is worthy of death. Therefore, except he do recant them all, I judge and think meet that he be punished with fire.'

The day before his condemnation, which was the sixth of July, the Emperor Sigismund sent unto him four bishops, accompanied with Lords Wenceslaus de Duba and John de Clum, that they should learn of him what he did intend to do.

When he was brought out of prison unto them, John de Clum began first to speak unto him, saying, 'Master John Huss, I am a man unlearned, neither am I able to counsel you, being a man of understanding: notwithstanding I do require you, if you know yourself guilty of any of those errors which are laid against you, that you will not be ashamed to alter your mind: if contrariwise, I would not that you should do any thing against your conscience, but rather suffer any punishment, than deny that which you have known to be the truth.'

Unto whom John Huss, turning himself, with lamentable tears said: 'Verily, I do take the Most High God for my witness, that I am ready with my heart and mind, if the Council can teach me any better by the holy Scripture, to alter my purpose.'

Then one of the bishops who sat by, said unto him, that he would never be so arrogant, that he would prefer his own mind before the judgment of the whole Council.

To whom John Huss answered: 'If he who is the least in all this Council can convict me of error, I will, with an humble heart and mind, perform whatsoever the Council shall require of me.'

'Mark,' said the bishops, 'how obstinately he doth persevere in his errors.'

And when they had thus talked, they commanded the keepers to carry him again to prison.

The next day after, which was Saturday, the sixth day of July, there was a general session holden of the princes and lords, both of the ecclesiastical and temporal estates, in the head church of the city of Constance, the Emperor Sigismund being president in his imperial robes and habit; in the midst whereof there was made a certain high place, being square about like a table, and hard by it there was a desk of wood, on which the vestments pertaining unto priesthood were laid for this cause, that before John Huss should be delivered over unto the civil power, he should be openly spoiled of his priestly ornaments.

When John Huss was brought thither, he fell down upon his knees and prayed a long time.

The proctor of the Council required that they might proceed unto the definitive sentence. Then a certain bishop, who was appointed one of the judges, repeated those articles which we have before remembered. John Huss went about briefly, with a word or two, to answer unto every one of them; but as often as he was about to speak, the Cardinal of Cambray commanded him to hold his peace, saying, 'Hereafter you shall answer all together, if you will.' Then said John Huss: 'How can I at once answer all these things which are alleged against me, when I cannot remember them all?' Then said the Cardinal of Florence: 'We have heard thee sufficiently.'

But when John Huss, for all that, would not hold his peace, they sent the officers who should force him thereunto. Then began he to entreat, pray, and beseech them, that they would hear him, that such as were present might not credit or believe those things to be true which were reported of him. But when all this would nothing prevail, he, kneeling down upon his knees, committed the whole matter unto God, and the Lord Jesus Christ. 'O Lord Jesu Christ! Whose Word is openly condemned here in this Council, unto Thee again I do appeal, Who when Thou wast evil entreated of Thine enemies, didst appeal unto God Thy Father, committing Thy cause unto a most just Judge; that by Thy example, we also being oppressed with manifest wrongs and injuries, should flee unto Thee.'

When he had spoken these words, one of them, who was appointed judge, read the definitive sentence against him:

'Forasmuch as one John Huss, the disciple of John Wickliff, hath taught, preached, and affirmed the articles of Wickliff, which were condemned by the Church of God; especially resisting in his open sermons, and also with his adherents and accomplices in the schools, the condemnation of the said articles of Wickliff, and hath declared him, the said Wickliff, for the favour and commendation of his doctrine, before the whole multitude of the clergy and people, to be a catholic man, and a true evangelical doctor.

'Wherefore, this most sacred and holy Council of Constance, doth condemn and reprove all those books which the said John Huss wrote; and doth decree, that they all shall be solemnly and openly burned in the presence of the clergy and people of the city of Constance, and elsewhere; adding, moreover, that all his doctrine is worthy to be despised and eschewed of all faithful Christians. This sacred Synod doth straitly command, that diligent inquisition be made for such treatises and works; and that such as are found, be consumed with fire.

'Wherefore, this most sacred and holy synod, determineth, pronounceth, declareth, and decreeth that John Huss was and is a true and manifest heretic, and that he hath preached openly errors and heresies, despising the keys of the Church, and ecclesiastical censures. In the which his error, he hath continued with a mind altogether indurate and hardened by the space of many years, much offending the faithful Christians by his obstinacy and stubbornness, when he made his appeal unto the Lord Jesus Christ, as the Most High Judge.

'Whereupon the said synod judgeth him to be condemned as a heretic; and reproveth the said appeal as injurious, offensive, and done in derision unto the ecclesiastical jurisdiction; and judgeth the said Huss not only to have seduced the Christian people by his writings and preachings, neither to have been a true preacher of the Gospel of Christ, but also to have been an obstinate and stiffnecked person, such a one as doth not desire to return again to the lap of our holy mother the Church, neither to abjure the errors and heresies which he hath openly preached and defended. Wherefore this most sacred Council decreeth that the said John Huss shall be deposed and degraded from his priestly orders and dignity.'

While these things were thus read, John Huss, albeit he was forbidden to speak, notwithstanding, did often interrupt them; and especially when he was reproved of obstinacy, he said with a loud voice: I was never obstinate, but, as always heretofore, even so now again I desire to be taught by the holy Scriptures.' When his books were condemned, he said, 'Wherefore have you condemned those books, when you have not proved that they are contrary to the Scriptures?' And oftentimes looking up unto heaven, he prayed.

When the sentence and judgment were ended, kneeling down upon his knees, he said: 'Lord Jesus Christ! forgive mine enemies, by whom Thou knowest that I am falsely accused, and that they have used false witness and slanders against me; forgive them, I say, for Thy great mercy's sake.' This his prayer, the greater part, and especially the chief of the priests, did deride and mock.

At last the seven bishops who were chosen out to degrade him of his priesthood, commanded him to put on the garments pertaining unto priesthood. When he came to the putting on of the albe, he called to his remembrance the white vesture which Herod put on Jesus Christ to mock Him withal. So, likewise, in all other things he did comfort himself by the example of Christ. When he had now put on all his priestly vestures, the bishops exhorted him that he should yet alter his purpose, and provide for his honour and salvation. Then he, being full of tears, spake unto the people in this sort.

'These lords and bishops do exhort and counsel me, that I should here confess before you all that I have erred; which thing to do, if it were such as might be done with the infamy and reproach of man only, they might peradventure easily persuade me thereunto; but now truly I am in the sight of the Lord my God, without Whose great ignominy and grudge of mine own conscience, I can by no means do that which they require of me. With what countenance then should I behold the heavens? With what face should I look upon them whom I have taught, whereof there is a great number, if, through me, it should come to pass that those things, which they have hitherto known to be most certain and sure, should now be made uncertain? Should I, by this my example, astonish or trouble so many souls, so many consciences, endued with the most firm and certain knowledge of the Scriptures and Gospel of our Lord Jesu Christ and His most pure doctrine, armed against all the assaults of Satan? I will never do it, neither commit any such kind of offence, that I should seem more to esteem this vile carcase appointed unto death, than their health and salvation.'

Then one of the bishops took away the chalice from him which he held in his hand, saying; 'O cursed Judas! why hast thou forsaken the counsel and ways of peace? We take away from thee this chalice of thy salvation.'

But John Huss received this curse in this manner: 'I trust unto God, the Father omnipotent, and my Lord Jesus Christ, for Whose sake I do suffer these things, that He will not take away the chalice of His redemption, but have a steadfast and firm hope that this day I shall drink thereof in His kingdom.'

Then followed the other bishops in order, who every one of them took away the vestments from him which they had put on, each one of them giving him their curse. Whereunto John Huss answered: that he did willingly embrace and hear those blasphemies for the name of our Lord Jesus Christ.

At last they came to the rasing of his shaven crown; but before the bishops would go in hand with it, there was a great contention between them, with what instrument it should be done; with a razor, or with a pair of shears. In the mean season, John Huss, turning himself toward the emperor, said: 'I marvel that forasmuch as they be all of like cruel mind, yet they cannot agree upon their kind of cruelty.' At last they agreed to cut off the skin of the crown of his head with a pair of shears.

And when they had done that, they added these words: 'Now hath the Church taken away all her ornaments and privileges from him. Now there resteth nothing else, but that he be delivered over unto the secular power.'

But before they did that, there yet remained

another knack of reproach; for they caused to be made a certain crown of paper, almost a cubit deep, on which were painted three devils of wonderfully ugly shape, and this title set over their heads, 'Heresiarcha.' Which when he saw, he said: 'My Lord Jesus Christ, for my sake, did wear a crown of thorns; why should not I then, for His sake, again wear this light crown, be it ever so ignominious? Truly I will do it, and that willingly.' When it was set upon his head, the bishop said: 'Now we commit thy soul unto the devil.' 'But I,' said John Huss, lifting his eyes up towards the heavens, 'do commend into Thy hands, O Lord Jesu Christ! my spirit which Thou hast redeemed.'

These contumelious opprobries thus ended, the bishops, turning themselves towards the emperor, said: 'This most sacred synod of Constance leaveth now John Huss, who hath no more any office in the Church of God, unto the civil judgment and power.'

Then the emperor commanded Louis, Duke of Bavaria, who stood before him in his robes, holding the golden apple with the cross in his hand, that he should receive John Huss of the bishops, and deliver him unto them who should do the execution; by whom as he was led to the place of execution, before the church doors he saw his books burning, whereat he smiled and laughed. And all men that passed by he exhorted, not to think that he should die for any error or heresy, but only for the hatred and ill-will of his adversaries, who had charged him with most false and unjust crimes. All the whole city in a manner, being in armour, followed him.

The place appointed for the execution was before the Gottlieben gate, between the gardens and the gates of the suburbs. When John Huss was come thither, kneeling down upon his knees, and lifting his eyes up unto heaven, he prayed, and said certain Psalms, and especially the thirty-first and fifty-first Psalms. And they who stood hard by, heard him oftentimes in his prayer, with a merry and cheerful countenance, repeat this verse: 'Into Thy hands, O Lord! I commend my spirit,' which thing when the lay-people beheld who stood next unto him, they said: 'What he hath done before, we know not; but now we see and hear that he doth speak and pray very devoutly and godly.' A certain priest sitting on horseback, in a green gown, drawn about with red silk, said: 'He ought not to be heard, because he is a heretic.' In the meantime, while John Huss prayed, as he bowed his neck backwards to look upward unto heaven, the crown of paper fell off from his head upon the ground. Then one of the soldiers, taking it up again, said: 'Let us put it again upon his head, that he may be burned with his masters the devils, whom he hath served.'

When, by the commandment of the tormentors, he was risen up from the place of his prayer, with a loud voice he said: 'Lord Jesu Christ! help me, that with a constant and patient mind, I may suffer this cruel and ignominious death, whereunto I am condemned for the preaching of Thy most Holy Gospel and Word.' Then, as before, he declared the cause of his death unto the people. In the mean season the hangman stripped him of his garments, and turning his hands behind his back, tied him fast unto the stake with ropes that were made wet. And whereas, by chance, he was turned towards the east, certain cried out that he should not look towards the east, for he was a heretic: so he was turned towards the west. Then was his neck tied with a chain unto the stake, which chain when he beheld, smiling he said, that he would willingly receive the same for Jesus Christ's sake, Who, he knew, was bound with a far worse chain. Under his feet they set two faggots, admixing straw withal, and so from the feet up to the chin, he was enclosed round about with wood.

But before the wood was set on fire, Louis, Duke of Bavaria, and another gentleman with him, who was the son of Clement, came and exhorted John Huss, that he would yet be mindful of his salvation, and renounce his errors. To whom he said: 'What error should I renounce, when I know myself guilty of none? For this was the principal end and purpose of my doctrine, that I might teach all men repentance and remission of sins, according to the verity of the Gospel of Jesus Christ: wherefore, with a cheerful mind and courage, I am here ready to suffer death.' When he had spoken these words, they left him, and shaking hands together, departed.

Then was the fire kindled, and John Huss began to sing with a loud voice: 'Jesu Christ! the Son of the living God! have mercy upon me.' And when he began to say the same the third time, the wind drove the flame so upon his face, that it choked him. Yet, notwithstanding, he moved awhile after, by the space that a man might almost say three times the Lord's Prayer. When all the wood was consumed, the upper part of the body was left hanging in the chain, which they threw down stake and all, and making a new fire, burned it, the head being first cut in small gobbets, that it might the sooner be consumed unto ashes. The heart, which was found amongst the bowels, being well beaten with staves and clubs, was at last pricked upon a sharp stick, and roasted at a fire apart until it was consumed. Then, with great diligence gathering the ashes together, they cast them into the river Rhine, that the least remnant of that man should not be left upon the earth, whose memory, notwithstanding, cannot be abolished out of the minds of the godly, neither by fire, neither by water, neither by any kind of torment.

This godly servant and martyr of Christ was burned at Constance, the sixth day of the month of July, A.D. 1415.

Chapter Six

GOD'S SERVANT, WILLIAM TYNDALE

We have now to enter into the story of the good martyr of God, William Tyndale; which William Tyndale, as he was a special organ of the Lord appointed, and as God's mattock to shake the inward roots and foundation of the Pope's proud prelacy, so the great prince of darkness, with his impious imps, having a special malice against him, left no way unsought how craftily to entrap him, and falsely to betray him, and maliciously to spill his life, as by the process of his story here following may appear.

William Tyndale, the faithful minister of Christ, was born about the borders of Wales, and brought up from a child in the University of Oxford, where he, by long continuance, increased as well in the knowledge of tongues, and other liberal arts, as especially in the knowledge of the Scriptures, whereunto his mind was singularly addicted; insomuch that he, lying then in Magdalen hall, read privily to certain students and fellows of Magdalen college some parcel of divinity; instructing them in the knowledge and truth of the Scriptures. His manners and conversation being correspondent to the same, were such, that all they that knew him, reputed him to be a man of most virtuous disposition, and of life unspotted.

Thus he, in the University of Oxford, increasing

more and more in learning, and proceeding in degrees of the schools, spying his time, removed from thence to the University of Cambridge, where he likewise made his abode a certain space. Being now further ripened in the knowledge of God's Word, leaving that University, he resorted to one Master Welch, a knight of Gloucestershire, and was there schoolmaster to his children, and in good favour with his master. As this gentleman kept a good ordinary commonly at his table, there resorted to him many times sundry abbots, deans, archdeacons, with divers other doctors, and great beneficed men; who there, together with Master Tyndale sitting at the same table, did use many times to enter communication, and talk of learned men, as of Luther and of Erasmus; also of divers other controversies and questions upon the Scripture.

Then Master Tyndale, as he was learned and well practised in God's matters, spared not to show unto them simply and plainly his judgment, and when they at any time did vary from Tyndale in opinions, he would show them in the book, and lay plainly before them the open and manifest places of the Scriptures, to confute their errors, and confirm his sayings. And thus continued they for a certain season, reasoning and contending together divers times, till at length they waxed weary, and bare a secret grudge in their hearts against him.

Not long after this, it happened that certain of these great doctors had invited Master Welch and his wife to a banquet; where they had talk at will and pleasure, uttering their blindness and ignorance without any resistance or gainsaying. Then Master

Welch and his wife, coming home, and calling for Master Tyndale, began to reason with him about those matters whereof the priests had talked at their banquet. Master Tyndale, answering by the Scriptures, maintained the truth, and reproved their false opinions. Then said the Lady Welch, a stout and a wise woman (as Tyndale reported), 'Well,' said she, 'there was such a doctor who may dispend a hundred pounds, and another two hundred pounds, and another three hundred pounds: and what! were it reason, think you, that we should believe you before them?'

Master Tyndale gave her no answer, and after that (because he saw it would not avail), he talked but little in those matters. At that time he was about the translation of a book called *Enchiridion Militis Christiani*, which he delivered to his master and lady; after they had well perused the same, the doctorly prelates were no more so often called to the house, neither had they the cheer and countenance when they came, as before they had: which thing they well perceiving, and supposing no less but it came by the means of Master Tyndale, refrained themselves, and at last utterly withdrew, and came no more there.

As this grew on, the priests of the country, clustering together, began to grudge and storm against Tyndale, railing against him in alehouses and other places, affirming that his sayings were heresy; and accused him secretly to the chancellor, and others of the bishop's officers.

It followed not long after this, that there was a sitting of the bishop's chancellor appointed, and warning was given to the priests to appear, amongst whom Master Tyndale was also warned to be there. And whether he had any misdoubt by their threatenings, or knowledge given him that they would lay some things to his charge, it is uncertain; but certain this is (as he himself declared), that he doubted their privy accusations; so that he by the way, in going thitherwards, cried in his mind heartily to God, to give him strength fast to stand in the truth of His Word.

When the time came for his appearance before the chancellor, he threatened him grievously, reviling and rating him as though he had been a dog, and laid to his charge many things whereof no accuser could be brought forth, notwithstanding that the priests of the country were there present. Thus Master Tyndale, escaping out of their hands, departed home, and returned to his master again.

There dwelt not far off a certain doctor, that had been chancellor to a bishop, who had been of old, familiar acquaintance with Master Tyndale, and favoured him well; unto whom Master Tyndale went and opened his mind upon divers questions of the Scripture: for to him he durst be bold to disclose his heart. Unto whom the doctor said, 'Do you not know that the Pope is very Antichrist, whom the Scripture speaketh of? But beware what you say; for if you shall be perceived to be of that opinion, it will cost you your life.'

Not long after, Master Tyndale happened to be in the company of a certain divine, recounted for a learned man, and, in communing and disputing with him, he drave him to that issue, that the said great doctor burst out into these blasphemous words, 'We were better to be without God's laws than the

Pope's.' Master Tyndale, hearing this, full of godly zeal, and not bearing that blasphemous saying, replied, 'I defy the Pope, and all his laws;' and added, that if God spared him life, ere many years he would cause a boy that driveth the plough, to know more of the Scripture than he did.

The grudge of the priests increasing still more and more against Tyndale, they never ceased barking and rating at him, and laid many things sorely to his charge, saying that he was a heretic. Being so molested and vexed, he was constrained to leave that country, and to seek another place; and so coming to Master Welch, he desired him, of his good will, that he might depart from him, saying: 'Sir, I perceive that I shall not be suffered to tarry long here in this country, neither shall you be able, though you would, to keep me out of the hands of the spiritualty; what displeasure might grow to you by keeping me, God knoweth; for the which I should be right sorry.'

So that in fine, Master Tyndale, with the good will of his master, departed, and eftsoons came up to London, and there preached awhile, as he had done in the country.

Bethinking himself of Cuthbert Tonstal, then Bishop of London, and especially of the great commendation of Erasmus, who, in his annotations, so extolleth the said Tonstal for his learning, Tyndale thus cast with himself, that if he might attain unto his service, he were a happy man. Coming to Sir Henry Guilford, the King's comptroller, and bringing with him an oration of Isocrates, which he had translated out of Greek into English, he desired him to speak to the said Bishop of

London for him; which he also did; and willed him moreover to write an epistle to the bishop, and to go himself with him. This he did, and delivered his epistle to a servant of his, named William Hebilthwait, a man of his old acquaintance. But God, who secretly disposeth the course of things, saw that was not the best for Tyndale's purpose, nor for the profit of His Church, and therefore gave him to find little favour in the bishop's sight; the answer of whom was this: his house was full; he had more than he could well find: and he advised him to seek in London abroad, where, he said, he could lack no service.

Being refused of the bishop he came to Humphrey Mummuth, alderman of London, and besought him to help him: who the same time took him into his house, where the said Tyndale lived (as Mummuth said) like a good priest, studying both night and day. He would eat but sodden meat by his good will, nor drink but small single beer. He was never seen in the house to wear linen about him, all the space of his being there.

And so remained Master Tyndale in London almost a year, marking with himself the course of the world, and especially the demeanour of the preachers, how they boasted themselves, and set up their authority; beholding also the pomp of the prelates, with other things more, which greatly misliked him; insomuch that he understood, not only that there was no room in the bishop's house for him to translate the New Testament, but also that there was no place to do it in all England.

Therefore, having by God's providence, some aid ministered unto him by Humphrey Mummuth, and certain other good men, he took his leave of the realm, and departed into Germany, where the good man, being inflamed with a tender care and zeal of his country, refused no travail nor diligence, how, by all means possible, to reduce his brethren and countrymen of England to the same taste and understanding of God's holy Word and verity, which the Lord had endued him withal. Whereupon, considering in his mind, and conferring also with John Frith, Tyndale thought with himself no way more to conduce thereunto, than if the Scripture were turned into the vulgar speech, that the poor people might read and see the simple plain Word of God. He perceived that it was not possible to establish the lay people in any truth, except the Scriptures were so plainly laid before their eyes in their mother tongue, that they might see the meaning of the text; for else, whatsoever truth should be taught them, the enemies of the truth would quench it, either with reasons of sophistry, and traditions of their own making, founded without all ground of Scripture; or else juggling with the text, expounding it in such a sense as it were impossible to gather of the text, if the right meaning thereof were seen.

Master Tyndale considered this only, or most chiefly, to be the cause of all mischief in the Church, that the Scriptures of God were hidden from the people's eyes; for so long the abominable doings and idolatries maintained by the pharisaical clergy could not be espied; and therefore all their labour was with might and main to keep it down, so that either it should not be read at all, or if it were, they would darken the right sense with the mist of their sophistry, and so entangle those who rebuked or despised their abominations; wresting the Scripture unto their own purpose; contrary unto the meaning of the text, they would so delude the unlearned lay people, that though thou felt in thy heart, and wert sure that all were false that they said, yet couldst thou not solve their subtle riddles.

For these and such other considerations this good man was stirred up of God to translate the Scripture into his mother tongue, for the profit of the simple people of his country; first setting in hand with the New Testament, which came forth in print about A.D. 1529. Cuthbert Tonstal, Bishop of London, with Sir Thomas More, being sore aggrieved, devised how to destroy that false erroneous translation, as they called it.

It happened that one Augustine Packington, a mercer, was then at Antwerp, where the bishop was. This man favoured Tyndale, but showed the contrary unto the bishop. The bishop, being desirous to bring his purpose to pass, communed how that he would gladly buy the New Testaments. Packington hearing him say so, said, 'My lord! I can do more in this matter, than most merchants that be here, if it be your pleasure; for I know the Dutchmen and strangers that have bought them of Tyndale, and have them here to sell; so that if it be your lordship's pleasure, I must disburse money to pay for them, or else I cannot have them: and so I will assure you to have every book of them that is printed and unsold.' The Bishop, thinking he had God 'by the toe,' said, 'Do your diligence, gentle Master Packington! get them for me, and I will pay whatsoever they cost; for I intend to burn and destroy them all at Paul's Cross.' This Augustine Packington went unto William Tyndale, and declared the whole matter, and so, upon compact made between them, the Bishop of London had the books, Packington had the thanks, and Tyndale had the money.

After this, Tyndale corrected the same New Testaments again, and caused them to be newly imprinted, so that they came thick and threefold over into England. When the bishop perceived that, he sent for Packington, and said to him, 'How cometh this, that there are so many New Testaments abroad? you promised me that you would buy them all.' Then answered Packington, 'Surely, I bought all that were to be had: but I perceive they have printed more since. I see it will never be better so long as they have letters and stamps: wherefore you were best to buy the stamps too, and so you shall be sure:' at which answer the bishop smiled, and so the matter ended.

In short space after, it fortuned that George Constantine was apprehended by Sir Thomas More, who was then Chancellor of England, as suspected of certain heresies. Master More asked of him, saying, 'Constantine! I would have thee be plain with me in one thing that I will ask; and I promise thee, I will show thee favour in all other things, whereof thou art accused. There is beyond the sea, Tyndale, Joye, and a great many of you: I know they cannot live without help. There are some that succour them with money; and thou, being one of them, hadst thy part thereof, and therefore knowest from whence it came. I pray thee, tell me, who be they that help them thus?'

'My lord,' quoth Constantine, 'I will tell you truly: it is the Bishop of London that hath holpen us, for he hath bestowed among us a great deal of money upon New Testaments to burn them; and that hath been, and yet is, our only succour and comfort.' 'Now by my troth,' quoth More, 'I think even the same; for so much I told the bishop before he went about it.'

After that, Master Tyndale took in hand to translate the Old Testament, finishing the five books of Moses, with sundry most learned and godly prologues most worthy to be read and read again by all good Christians. These books being sent over into England, it cannot be spoken what a door of light they opened to the eyes of the whole English nation, which before were shut up in darkness.

At his first departing out of the realm he took his journey into Germany, where he had conference with Luther and other learned men; after he had continued there a certain season, he came down into the Netherlands, and had his most abiding in the town of Antwerp.

The godly books of Tyndale, and especially the New Testament of his translation, after that they began to come into men's hands, and to spread abroad, wrought great and singular profit to the godly; but the ungodly (envying and disdaining that the people should be anything wiser than they, and, fearing lest by the shining beams of truth, their works of darkness should be discerned), began to stir with no small ado.

At what time Tyndale had translated Deuteronomy, minding to print the same at Hamburg, he sailed thitherward; upon the coast of Holland, he suffered shipwreck, by which he lost all his books, writings, and copies, his money and his time, and so was compelled to begin all again. He came in another ship to Hamburg, where, at his appointment, Master Coverdale tarried for him, and helped him in the translating of the whole five books of Moses, from Easter till December, in the house of a worshipful widow, Mistress Margaret Van Emmerson, A.D. 1529; a great sweating sickness being at the same time in the town. So, having dispatched his business at Hamburg, he returned to Antwerp.

When God's will was, that the New Testament in the common tongue should come abroad, Tyndale, the translator thereof, added to the latter end a certain epistle, wherein he desired them that were learned to amend, if ought were found amiss. Wherefore if there had been any such default deserving correction, it had been the part of courtesy and gentleness, for men of knowledge and judgment to have showed their learning therein, and to have redressed what was to be amended. But the clergy, not willing to have that book prosper, cried out upon it, that there were a thousand heresies in it, and that it was not to be corrected, but utterly to be suppressed. Some said it was not possible to translate the Scriptures into English; some, that it was not lawful for the lay people to have it in their mother tongue; some, that it would make them all heretics. And to the intent to induce the temporal rulers unto their purpose, they said that it would make the people to rebel against the king.

All this Tyndale himself, in his prologue before the first book of Moses, declareth; showing further what great pains were taken in examining that translation, and comparing it with their own imaginations, that with less labour, he supposeth, they might have translated a great part of the Bible: showing moreover, that they scanned and examined every title and point in such sort, and so narrowly, that there was not one *i* therein, but if it lacked a prick over his head, they did note it, and numbered it unto the ignorant people for a heresy.

So great were then the froward devices of the English clergy (who should have been the guides of light unto the people), to drive the people from the knowledge of the Scripture, which neither they would translate themselves, nor yet abide it to be translated of others; to the intent (as Tyndale saith) that the world being kept still in darkness, they might sit in the consciences of the people through vain superstition and false doctrine, to satisfy their ambition, and insatiable covetousness, and to exalt their own honour above King and Emperor.

The bishops and prelates never rested before they had brought the King to their consent; by reason whereof, a proclamation in all haste was devised and set forth under public authority, that the Testament of Tyndale's translation was inhibited —which was about A.D. 1537. And not content herewith, they proceeded further, how to entangle him in their nets, and to bereave him of his life; which how they brought to pass, now it remaineth to be declared.

In the registers of London it appeareth manifest how that the bishops and Sir Thomas More having before them such as had been at Antwerp, most studiously would search and examine all things belonging to Tyndale, where and with whom he hosted, whereabouts stood the house, what was his stature, in what apparel he went, what resort he had; all which things when they had diligently learned then began they to work their feats.

William Tyndale, being in the town of Antwerp, had been lodged about one whole year in the house of Thomas Pointz, an Englishman, who kept a house of English merchants. Came thither one out of England, whose name was Henry Philips, his father being customer of Poole, a comely fellow, like as he had been a gentleman, having a servant with him: but wherefore he came, or for what purpose he was sent thither, no man could tell.

Master Tyndale divers times was desired forth to dinner and supper amongst merchants; by means whereof this Henry Philips became acquainted with him, so that within short space Master Tyndale had a great confidence in him, and brought him to his lodging, to the house of Thomas Pointz; and had him also once or twice with him to dinner and supper, and further entered such friendship with him, that through his procurement he lay in the same house of the said Pointz; to whom he showed moreover his books, and other secrets of his study, so little did Tyndale then mistrust this traitor.

But Pointz, having no great confidence in the fellow, asked Master Tyndale how he came acquainted with this Philips. Master Tyndale answered, that he was an honest man, handsomely learned, and very conformable. Pointz, perceiving that he bare such favour to him, said no more, thinking that he was brought acquainted with him by some friend of his. The said Philips, being in the town three or four days, upon a time desired Pointz to walk with him forth of the town to show him the commodities thereof, and in walking together without the town, had communication of divers things, and some of the King's affairs; by which talk Pointz as yet suspected nothing. But after, when the time was past, Pointz perceived this to be the mind of Philips, to feel whether the said Pointz might, for lucre of money, help him to his purpose, for he perceived before that Philips was monied, and would that Pointz should think no less. For he had desired Pointz before to help him to divers things; and such things as he named, he required might be of the best, 'for,' said he, 'I have money enough.'

Philips went from Antwerp to the court of Brussels, which is from thence twenty-four English miles, whence he brought with him to Antwerp, the procuror-general, who is the emperor's attorney, with certain other officers.

Within three or four days, Pointz went forth to the town of Barrois, being eighteen English miles from Antwerp, where he had business to do for the space of a month or six weeks; and in the time of his absence Henry Philips came again to Antwerp, to the house of Pointz, and coming in, spake with his wife, asking whether Master Tyndale were within. Then went he forth again and set the officers whom he brought with him from Brussels, in the street, and about the door. About noon he came again, and went to Master Tyndale, and desired him to lend him forty shillings; 'for,' said he, 'I lost my purse this morning, coming over at the passage

148

between this and Mechlin.' So Master Tyndale took him forty shillings, which was easy to be had of him, if he had it; for in the wily subtleties of this world he was simple and inexpert. Then said Philips, 'Master Tyndale! you shall be my guest here this day.' 'No,' said Master Tyndale, 'I go forth this day to dinner, and you shall go with me, and be my guest, where you shall be welcome.'

So when it was dinner-time, Master Tyndale went forth with Philips, and at the going forth of Pointz's house, was a long narrow entry, so that two could not go in a front. Master Tyndale would have put Philips before him, but Philips would in no wise, but put Master Tyndale before, for that he pretended to show great humanity. So Master Tyndale, being a man of no great stature, went before, and Philips, a tall comely person, followed behind him; who had set officers on either side of the door upon two seats, who might see who came in the entry. Philips pointed with his finger over Master Tyndale's head down to him, that the officers might see that it was he whom they should take. The officers afterwards told Pointz, when they had laid him in prison, that they pitied to see his simplicity. They brought him to the emperor's attorney, where he dined. Then came the procuror-general to the house of Pointz, and sent away all that was there of Master Tyndale's, as well his books as other things; and from thence Tyndale was had to the castle of Filford, eighteen English miles from Antwerp.

Then incontinent, by the help of English merchants, were letters sent, in favour of Tyndale, to the court of Brussels. Also, not long after, letters were directed out of England to the council at Brussels, and sent to the merchant-adventurers, to Antwerp, commanding them to see that with speed they should be delivered. Such of the merchants as were there at that time, being called together, required the said Pointz to take in hand the delivery of those letters, in favour of Master Tyndale, to the Lord of Barrois and others; which Lord of Barrois (as it was told Pointz by the way) at that time was departed from Brussels. Pointz did ride after the next way, and overtook him at Achon, where he delivered to him his letters; which when he had received and read, he made no direct answer, but somewhat objecting, said, there were of their countrymen that were burned in England not long before (as indeed there were Anabaptists burned in Smithfield); and so Pointz said to him, 'Howbeit,' said he, 'whatsoever the crime was, if his lordship or any other nobleman had written, requiring to have had them, he thought they should not have been denied.'

'Well,' said he, 'I have no leisure to write, for the princess is ready to ride.'

Then said Pointz, 'If it shall please your lordship, I will attend upon you unto the next baiting-place'; which was at Maestricht.

'If you so do,' said the lord, 'I will advise myself by the way what to write.'

So Pointz followed him from Achon to Maestricht, which are fifteen English miles asunder; and there he received letters of him, one to the council, another to the company of the merchant-adventurers, and another also to the Lord Cromwell in England.

So Pointz rode from thence to Brussels, and then

and there delivered to the council the letters out of England, with the Lord of Barrois' letters also, and received eftsoons answer into England of the same by letters which he brought to Antwerp to the English merchants, who required him to go with them into England. And he, very desirous to have Master Tyndale out of prison, let not to take pains, with loss of time in his own business, and diligently followed with the said letters, which he delivered to the council, and was commanded by them to tarry until he had other letters. A month after, the letters being delivered him, he returned, and delivered them to the emperor's council at Brussels, and tarried for answer for the same.

Philips, being there, followed the suit against Master Tyndale, and hearing that he should be delivered to Pointz, and fearing lest he should be put from his purpose, he knew no other remedy but to accuse Pointz, saying, that he was a dweller in the town of Antwerp, a succourer of Tyndale, and one of the same opinion; and that all this was only his own labour and suit, and no man's else, to have Master Tyndale at liberty. Thus Pointz was delivered to the keeping of two serjeants at arms.

Master Tyndale, still remaining in prison, was proffered an advocate and a procuror; the which he refused, saying that he would make answer for himself. He had so preached to them who had him in charge, and such as was there conversant with him in the Castle, that they reported of him, that if he were not a good Christian man, they knew not whom they might take to be one.

At last, after much reasoning, when no reason would serve, although he deserved no death, he was condemned by virtue of the emperor's decree, made in the assembly at Augsburg. Brought forth to the place of execution, he was tied to the stake, strangled by the hangman, and afterwards consumed with fire, at the town of Filford, A.D. 1536; crying at the stake with a fervent zeal, and a loud voice, 'Lord! open the King of England's eyes.'

Such was the power of his doctrine, and the sincerity of his life, that during the time of his imprisonment (which endured a year and a half), he converted, it is said, his keeper, the keeper's daughter, and others of his household.

As touching his translation of the New Testament, because his enemies did so much carp at it, pretending it to be full of heresies, he wrote to John Frith, as followeth, 'I call God to record against the day we shall appear before our Lord Jesus, that I never altered one syllable of God's Word against my conscience, nor would do this day, if all that is in earth, whether it be honour, pleasure, or riches, might be given me.'

Chapter Seven

THE HISTORY OF MARTIN LUTHER

MARTIN LUTHER, after he was grown in years, being born at Eisleben in Saxony, A.D. 1483, was sent to the University, first of Magdeburg, then of Erfurt. In this University of Erfurt, there was a certain aged man in the convent of the Augustines with whom Luther, being then of the same order, a friar Augustine, had conference upon divers things, especially touching remission of sins; which article the said aged Father opened unto Luther; declaring, that God's express commandment is, that every man should particularly believe his sins to be forgiven him in Christ: and further said, that this interpretation was confirmed by St Bernard: 'This is the testimony that the Holy Ghost giveth thee in thy heart, saying, Thy sins are forgiven thee. For this is the opinion of the apostle, that man is freely justified by faith.'

By these words Luther was not only strengthened, but was also instructed of the full meaning of St Paul, who repeateth so many times this sentence, 'We are justified by faith.' And having read the expositions of many upon this place, he then perceived, as well by the discourse of the old man, as by the comfort he received in his spirit, the vanity of those interpretations, which he had read before, of the schoolmen. And so, by little and little, reading and comparing the sayings and examples of the prophets and apostles, with continual invocation of God, and excitation of faith by force of prayer, he perceived that doctrine most evidently. Thus continued he his study at Erfurt the space of four years in the convent of the Augustines.

About this time one Staupitius, a famous man, who had ministered his help to further the erection of a University in Wittenberg, being anxious to promote the study of divinity in this new University, when he had considered the spirit and towardness of Luther, called him from Erfurt, to place him in Wittenberg, A.D. 1508 and of his age the twenty-sixth. In the meanwhile Luther intermitted no whit his study in theology. Three years after, he went to Rome, and returning the same year, he was graded doctor at the expense of the Elector Frederic, Duke of Saxony: for he had heard him preach; well understanded the quickness of his spirit; diligently considered the vehemency of his words; and had in singular admiration those profound matters which in his sermons he ripely and exactly explained. This degree Staupitius, against his will, enforced upon him ; saying merrily unto him, that God had many things to bring to pass in his Church by him. And though these words were spoken merrily, yet it came so to pass anon after.

After this, Luther began to expound the Epistle to the Romans, and the Psalms: where he showed the difference betwixt the Law and the Gospel; and confounded the error that reigned then in the schools and sermons, viz., that men may merit remission of sins by their own works, and that they be just before God by outward discipline; as the

Pharisees taught. Luther diligently reduced the minds of men to the Son of God: as John Baptist demonstrated the Lamb of God that took away the sins of the world, even so Luther, shining in the Church as the bright daylight after a long and dark night, expressly showed, that sins are freely remitted for the love of the Son of God, and that we ought faithfully to embrace this bountiful gift

His life was correspondent to his profession; and it plainly appeared that his words were no lip-labour, but proceeded from the very heart. This admiration of his holy life much allured the hearts of his auditors.

All this while Luther altered nothing in the ceremonies, but precisely observed his rule among his fellows. He meddled in no doubtful opinions, but taught this only doctrine, as most principal of all other, to all men, opening and declaring the doctrine of repentance, of remission of sins, of faith, of true comfort to be sought in the cross of Christ. Every man received good taste of this sweet doctrine, and the learned conceived high pleasure to behold Jesus Christ, the prophets and apostles, to come forth into light out of darkness.

It happened, moreover, about this time, that many were provoked by Erasmus's learned works to study the Greek and Latin tongues; who, having thus opened to them a more pleasant sort of learning than before, began to have in contempt the monks' barbarous and sophistical learning. Luther began to study the Greek and Hebrew tongues to this end, that having drawn the doctrine of the very fountains, he might form a more sound judgment.

As Luther was thus occupied in Germany, which

was A.D. 1516, Leo X., who had succeeded after Julius II., was Pope of Rome, who, under pretence of war against the Turk, sent his pardons abroad through all Christian dominions, whereby he gathered together innumerable riches and treasure; the gatherers and collectors whereof persuaded the people, that whosoever would give ten shillings, should at his pleasure deliver one soul from the pains of purgatory; but if it were but one jot less than ten shillings, it would profit them nothing.

This Pope's merchandise came also to Germany, through the means of a certain Dominic friar named Tetzel, who most impudently caused the Pope's indulgences to be sold about the country. Whereupon Luther, much moved with the blasphemous sermons of this shameless friar, and having his heart earnestly bent with ardent desire to maintain true religion, published certain propositions concerning indulgences, and set them openly on the temple that joineth to the castle of Wittenberg, the morrow after the feast of All Saints, A.D. 1517.

This beggarly friar, hoping to obtain the Pope's blessing, assembled certain monks and sophistical divines of his convent, and forthwith commanded them to write something against Luther. And while he would not himself be dumb, he began to thunder against Luther; crying, 'Luther is a heretic, and worthy to be persecuted with fire.' He burned openly Luther's propositions, and the sermon which he wrote of indulgences. This rage and fumish fury of this friar enforced Luther to treat more amply of the cause, and to maintain the truth. And thus rose the beginnings of this controversy.

The good Duke Frederic was one, of all the princes of our time, that loved best quietness and common tranquillity; so he neither encouraged nor supported Luther, but often discovered outwardly the heaviness and sorrow which he bare in his heart, fearing greater dissensions. But being a wise prince, and following the counsel of God's rule, and well deliberating thereupon, he thought with himself, that the glory of God was to be preferred above all things: neither was he ignorant what blasphemy it was, horribly condemned of God, obstinately to repugn the truth. Wherefore he did as a godly prince should do, he obeyed God, committing himself to His holy grace and omnipotent protection. And although Maximilian the Emperor, Charles King of Spain, and Pope Julius, had given commandment to the said Duke Frederic, that he should inhibit Luther from all place and liberty of preaching; yet the duke, considering with himself the preaching and writing of Luther, and weighing diligently the testimonies and places of the Scripture by him alleged, would not withstand the thing which he judged sincere. And yet neither did he this, trusting to his own judgment, but was very anxious to hear the judgment of others, who were both aged and learned; in the number of whom was Erasmus, whom the duke desired to declare to him his opinion touching the matter of Martin Luther; protesting, that he would rather the ground should open and swallow him, than he would bear with any opinions which he knew to be contrary to manifest truth.

Erasmus began jestingly and merrily to answer the duke's request, saying, that in Luther were two great faults; first, that he would touch the bellies of monks; the second, that he would touch the Pope's crown! Then, opening his mind plainly to the duke, he said, that Luther did well in detecting errors, that reformation was very necessary in the Church: adding moreover, that the effect of his doctrine was true.

Furthermore, the same Erasmus, in the following year, wrote to the Archbishop of Mentz a certain epistle touching the cause of Luther: 'The world is burdened with men's institutions, and with the tyranny of begging friars. Once it was counted a heresy when a man repugned against the Gospels. Now he that dissenteth from Thomas Aquinas is a heretic: whatsoever doth not like them, whatsoever they understand not, that is heresy. To know Greek is heresy; or to speak more finely than they do, that is heresy.'

The godly and faithful Christians, closed in monasteries, understanding images ought to be eschewed, began to abandon that wretched thraldom in which they were detained.

Luther held especially in contempt these horned bishops of Rome, who arrogantly and impudently affirmed, that St Peter had not the charge alone to teach the Gospel, but also to govern commonweals, and exercise civil jurisdiction. He exhorted every man to render unto God that appertained unto God, and to Cæsar that belonged unto Cæsar; and said, that all should serve God. After that Tetzel, the aforesaid friar, with his fellow-monks and friarly fellows, had cried out with open mouth against Luther, in maintaining the Pope's indulgences; and that Luther again, in defence of his cause, had set up propositions against the open abuses of the same, marvel it was to see how soon these propositions were sparkled abroad in sundry and far places, and how greedily they were caught up in the hands of divers both far and near.

Not long after steppeth up one Silvester de Priero, a Dominic friar, who first began to publish abroad a certain impudent and railing dialogue against Luther. Unto whom he answered out of the Scriptures.

Then was Martin Luther cited, the seventh of August, by one Hierome, Bishop of Ascoli, to appear at Rome. About which time Thomas Cajetan, Cardinal, the Pope's legate, was then lieger at the city of Augsburg, who before had been sent down in commission, with certain mandates from Pope Leo, unto that city. The University of Wittenberg, understanding of Luther's citation, eftsoons directed letters to the Pope, in Luther's behalf. Also another letter they sent to Carolus Miltitius, the Pope's chamberlain, being a German born. Furthermore, good Frederic ceased not to solicit, that the cause of Luther might be freed from Rome, and removed to Augsburg, in the hearing of the Cardinal. Cajetan, at the suit of the duke, wrote unto the Pope; from whom he received this answer:—

That he had cited Luther to appear personally before him at Rome, by Hierome, Bishop of Ascoli, auditor of the chamber; which bishop diligently had done what was commanded him: but Luther, abusing and contemning the gentleness offered, did not only refuse to come, but also became more bold and stubborn, continuing or rather increasing in his former heresy, as by his writings did appear.

Wherefore he would that the Cardinal should cite and call up the said Luther to appear at the city of Augsburg before him; adjoining withal, the aid of the princes of Germany, and of the emperor, if need required; so that when the said Luther should appear, he should lay hand upon him, and commit him to safe custody: and after, he should be brought up to Rome. And if he perceived him to come to any knowledge or amendment of his fault, he should release him and restore him to the Church again; or else he should be interdicted, with all other his adherents, abettors, and maintainers, of whatsoever state or condition they were, whether they were dukes, marquisses, earls or barons. Against all which persons and degrees, he willed him to extend the same curse and malediction (only the person of the emperor excepted); interdicting, by the censure of the Church, all such lands, lordships, towns, tenements, and villages, as should minister any harbour to the said Luther, and were not obedient unto the see of Rome. Contrariwise, to all such as showed themselves obedient, he should promise full remission of all their sins.

Likewise the Pope directed other letters also at the same time to Duke Frederic, with many grievous words, complaining against Luther.

The Cardinal, thus being charged with injunctions from Rome, according to his commission, sendeth with all speed for Luther to appear at Augsburg before him.

About the beginning of October, Martin Luther, yielding his obedience to the Church of Rome, came to Augsburg at the cardinal's sending (at the charges of the noble prince elector, and also with his letters of commendation), where he remained three days before he came to his speech; for so it was provided by his friends, that he should not enter talk with the cardinal, before a sufficient warrant or safe-conduct was obtained of the Emperor Maximilian. This being obtained, eftsoons he entered, offering himself to the speech of the cardinal, and was there received of the cardinal very gently; who, according to the Pope's commandment, propounded unto Martin Luther three things, to wit,

I. That he should repent and revoke his errors.

II. That he should promise, from that time forward, to refrain from the same.

III. That he should refrain from all things that might by any means trouble the Church.

When Martin Luther required to be informed wherein he had erred, the legate answered that he had held and taught that the merits of Christ are not the treasure of indulgences or pardons, and that faith is necessary to him that receiveth the sacrament. Furthermore Luther protested that the merits of Christ are not committed unto men: that the Pope's voice is to be heard when he speaketh agreeable to the Scriptures: that the Pope may err: and that he ought to be reprehended. Moreover he showed, that in the matter of faith, not only the General Council, but also every faithful Christian is above the Pope, if he lean to better authority and reason.

But the cardinal would hear no Scriptures; he disputed without Scriptures; he devised glosses and expositions of his own head. Luther, being rejected from the speech and sight of the cardinal, after six days' waiting, departed by the advice of his friends, and returned unto Wittenberg; leaving an appellation to the Bishop of Rome from the cardinal, which he caused openly to be affixed before his departure. Cajetan writeth to Duke Frederic a sharp and a biting letter, in which he exhorteth the duke, that as he tendereth his own honour and safety, and regardeth the favour of the high bishop, he will send Luther up to Rome, or expel him out of his dominions.

To this letter of the cardinal the duke answereth, purging both Luther and himself; Luther, in that he, following his conscience, grounded upon the Word of God, would not revoke that for an error which could be proved no error. And himself he excuseth thus: that whereas it is required of him to banish him his country, or to send him up to Rome, it would be little honesty for him so to do, and less conscience, unless he knew just cause why he should so do; which if the cardinal would or could declare unto him, there should lack nothing in him which were the part of a Christian prince to do. And therefore he desired him to be a mean unto the Bishop of Rome, that innocency and truth be not oppressed before the crime or error be lawfully convicted.

This done, the duke sendeth the letter of the cardinal unto Martin Luther, who answered to the prince: 'I am not so much grieved for mine own cause, as that you should sustain for my matter any danger or peril. And therefore, seeing there is no place nor country which can keep me from the malice of mine adversaries, I am willing to depart hence, and to forsake my country, whithersoever it shall please the Lord to lead me.'

Here, no doubt, was the cause of Luther in great danger, being now brought to this strait, that both Luther was ready to fly the country, and the duke again was as much afraid to keep him, had not the marvellous providence of God, Who had this matter in guiding, provided a remedy where the power of man did fail, by stirring up the whole University of Wittenberg; who, seeing the cause of truth thus to decline, with a full and general consent addressed their letters unto the prince, in defence of Luther and of his cause; making their humble suit unto him, that he, of his princely honour, would not suffer innocency, and the simplicity of truth so clear as is the Scripture, to be foiled and oppressed by mere violence of certain malignant flatterers about the Pope.

By the occasion of these letters, the duke began more seriously to consider the cause of Luther, to read his works, and hearken to his sermons: whereby, through God's holy working, he grew to knowledge and strength; perceiving in Luther's quarrel more than he did before. This was about the beginning of December A.D. 1518.

Pope Leo, in the meantime, had sent forth new indulgences, with a new edict, wherein he declared this to be the catholic doctrine of the holy mother-church of Rome, prince of all other churches, that Bishops of Rome, who are successors of Peter, and vicars of Christ, have this power and authority given to release and dispense, also to grant indulgences, available both for the living and for the dead lying in the pains of purgatory: and this doctrine he charged to be received of all faithful Christian men, under pain of the great curse, and utter separation from all holy Church. This popish decree and indulgence, as a new merchandise or ale-stake to get money, being set up in all quarters of Christendom for the holy father's advantage, came also to be received in Germany about the month of December. Luther, hearing how they went about in Rome to pronounce against him, provided a certain appellation conceived in due form of law, wherein he appealeth from the Pope to the General Council.

When Pope Leo perceived, that neither his pardons would prosper to his mind, nor that Luther could be brought to Rome; to essay how to come to his purpose by crafty allurements, he sent his chamberlain, Carolus Miltitius (who was a German), into Saxony, to Duke Frederic, with a golden rose, after the usual ceremony accustomed every year, to be presented to him; with secret letters also to certain noblemen of the duke's council, to solicit the Pope's cause, and to remove the duke's mind, if it might be, from Luther. But before Miltitius approached into Germany, Maximilian the Emperor deceased in the month of January, A.D. 1519. At that time two there were who stood for the election; to wit, Francis the French King, and Charles, King of Spain, who was also Duke of Austria, and Duke of Burgundy. Through the means of Frederic prince-elector (who, having the offer of the preferment, refused the same), the election fell to Charles, called Charles V., surnamed Prudence: which was about the end of August.

In the month of June before, there was a public disputation ordained at Leipsic, which is a city under the dominion of George Duke of Saxony, uncle to Duke Frederic. This disputation began through the occasion of John Eckius, a friar, and Andreas Carolostadt, doctor of Wittenberg. This Eckius had impugned certain propositions of Martin Luther, which he had written the year before touching the Pope's pardons. Against him Carolostadt wrote in defence of Luther. Eckius again, to answer Carolostadt, set forth an apology, which apology Carolostadt confuted by writing. Upon this began the disputation, with safe-conduct granted by Duke George to all and singular persons that would resort to the same. To this disputation came Martin Luther, not thinking to dispute in any matter, but only to hear what there was said and done.

But, having free liberty granted by the duke, Luther was provoked, and forced against his will, to dispute with Eckius. The matter of their controversy was about the authority of the Bishop of Rome. Luther before had set forth in writing this doctrine: that they that do attribute the pre-eminency to the Church of Rome, have no foundation but out of the Pope's decrees, which decrees he affirmed to be contrary to the Holy Scriptures.

Against this assertion Eckius set up a contrary conclusion; saying, that they that succeeded in the see and faith of Peter, were always received for the successors of Peter, and vicars of Christ on earth. He contended that the supremacy of the Bishop of Rome was founded and grounded upon God's law.

Upon this question the disputation did continue the space of five days; during all which season, Eckius very unhonestly and uncourteously demeaned himself, studying by all means how to bring his adversary into the hatred of the auditors, and into danger of the Pope. The reasons of Eckius were these: 'Forasmuch as the Church, being a civil body, cannot be without a head, therefore, as it standeth with God's law that other civil regiments should not be destitute of their head, so is it by God's law requisite, that the Pope should be the head of the universal Church of Christ.'

To this Martin Luther answered, that he confesseth and granteth the Church not to be headless, so long as Christ is alive, Who is the only head of the Church; neither doth the Church require any other head beside Him, forasmuch as it is a spiritual kingdom, not earthly.

Then came Eckius to the place of St Matthew, 'Thou art Peter, and upon this Rock will I build My Church.' To this was answered, that this was a confession of faith, and that Peter there representeth the person of the whole universal Church. Also that Christ in that place meaneth Himself to be the Rock. Likewise they came to the place of St John, 'Feed My sheep;' which words Eckius alleged to be spoken, properly and peculiarly, to Peter alone. Martin answered, that after these words spoken, equal authority was given to all the apostles, where Christ saith unto them, 'Receive ye the Holy Ghost: whose sins soever ye remit, they are remitted.'

After this, Eckius came to the authority of the Council of Constance, alleging this amongst other articles: 'that it standeth upon necessity of our salvation, to believe the Bishop of Rome to be supreme head of the Church;' alleging moreover, that in the same Council it was debated and discussed, that the General Council could not err. Whereunto Martin Luther again did answer discreetly, saying, that of what authority that Council of Constance is to be esteemed, he left to other men's judgments. 'This is most certain,' said he, 'that no Council hath authority to make new articles of faith.'

The next year, which was 1520, the friars and doctors of Louvain, and also of Cologne, condemned the books of Luther as heretical; against whom Luther again effectually defended himself, and charged them with obstinate violence and malicious impiety. After this, within few days flashed out from Rome the thunderbolt of Pope Leo against the said Luther.

Another book also Luther wrote, addressed to the nobility of Germany, in which he impugneth and shaketh the three principal walls of the papists: I. No temporal or profane magistrate hath any power upon the spiritualty, but these have power over the other. II. Where any place of Scripture, being in controversy, is to be decided, no man may expound the Scripture, or be judge thereof, but only the Pope. III. When any Council is brought against them, they say, that no man hath authority to call a Council, but only the Pope. Moreover, in the aforesaid book divers other matters he handleth and discourseth: that the pride of the Pope is not to be suffered; what money goeth out of Germany yearly to the Pope, amounting to the sum of three millions of florins; that the emperor is not under the Pope; that priests may have wives; that liberty ought not to be restrained in meats: that wilful poverty and begging ought to be abolished: what misfortunes Sigismund the Emperor sustained, for not keeping faith and promise with John Huss and Jerome : that heretics should be convinced not by fire and faggot, but by evidence of Scripture, and God's Word : and that the first teaching of children ought to begin with the Gospel.

In this year moreover followed, not long after, the coronation of the new Emperor Charles V., which was in the month of October, at Aix-la-Chapelle. After which coronation, Pope Leo sent again to Duke Frederic two cardinals his legates, of whom one was Hierome Aleander, who, after a few words of high commendation first premised to the duke touching his noble progeny, and other his famous virtues, made two requests unto him in the Pope's name : first, that he would cause all books of Luther to be burned ; secondly, that he would either see the said Luther there to be executed, or else would make him sure, and send him up to Rome, unto the Pope's presence.

These two requests seemed very strange unto the duke ; who, answering the cardinals, said, that he, being long absent from thence about other public affairs, could not tell what there was done, neither did he communicate with the doings of Luther. As for himself, he was always ready to do his duty ; first, in sending Luther to Cajetan the cardinal at the city of Augsburg ; and afterwards, at the Pope's commandment, would have sent him away out of his dominion, had not Miltitius, the Pope's own chamberlain, given contrary counsel to retain him still in his own country, fearing lest he might do more harm in other countries, where he was less known. Forasmuch as the cause of Luther was not yet heard before the emperor, he desired the said legates to be a mean to the Pope's holiness, that certain learned persons of gravity and upright judgment might be assigned to have the hearing and determination of this matter, and that his error might first be known, before he were made a heretic, or his books burned: which being done, when he should see his error by manifest and sound testimonies of Scripture, Luther should find no favour at his hands.

Then the cardinals took the books of Luther, and openly burnt them. Luther, hearing this, in like manner called all the multitude of students and learned men in Wittenberg, and there, taking the Pope's decrees, and the bull lately sent down against him, openly and solemnly, accompanied with a great number of people following him, set them likewise on fire; which was the 10th of December A.D. 1520.

A little before these things thus passed between the Pope and Martin Luther, the emperor had commanded an assembly of the States of all the Empire to be holden at the city of Worms, the 6th day of January next ensuing; in which assembly, through the means of Duke Frederic, the emperor gave forth, that he would have the cause of Luther brought before him. Upon the 6th of March, the emperor, through the instigation of Duke Frederic, directed his letters unto Luther; signifying, that forasmuch as he had set abroad certain books, he, therefore, by the advice of his peers and princes about him, had ordained to have the cause brought before him in his own hearing; and therefore he granted him license to come, and return home again. And that he might safely and quietly so do, he promised unto him, by public faith and credit, in the name of the whole Empire, his passport and safe-conduct. Wherefore, he willed him eftsoons to make his repair unto him, and to be there present on the twenty-first day after the receipt thereof.

Martin Luther, after he had been first accursed at Rome upon Maunday Thursday by the Pope's censure, shortly after Easter speedeth his journey toward Worms, where the said Luther, appearing before the emperor and all the States of Germany, constantly stuck to the truth, defended himself, and answered his adversaries.

Luther was lodged, well entertained, and visited by many earls, barons, knights of the order, gentlemen, priests, and the commonalty, who frequented his lodging until night.

He came, contrary to the expectation of many, as well adversaries as others. His friends deliberated together, and many persuaded him not to adventure himself to such a present danger, considering how these beginnings answered not the faith of promise made. Who, when he had heard their whole persuasion and advice, answered in this wise: 'As touching me, since I am sent for, I am resolved and certainly determined to enter Worms, in the name of our Lord Jesus Christ; yea, although I knew there were as many devils to resist me, as there are tiles to cover the houses in Worms.'

The next day after his repair, a gentleman named Ulrick, of Pappenheim, lieutenant-general of the men-at-arms of the Empire, was commanded by the emperor before dinner to repair to Luther, and to enjoin him at four o'clock in the afternoon to appear before the Imperial Majesty, the princes electors, dukes, and other estates of the Empire, to understand the cause of his sending for: whereunto he willingly agreed, as his duty was. And after four o'clock, Ulrick of Pappenheim, and Caspar Sturm, the emperor's herald (who conducted Martin Luther from Wittenberg to Worms), came for Luther, and accompanied him through the garden of the knights-of-the-Rhodes' place, to the Earl Palatine's palace; and, lest the people that thronged in should molest him, he was led by secret stairs to the place where he was appointed to have audience. Yet many, who perceived the pretence, violently rushed in, and were resisted, albeit in vain: many ascended the galleries, because they desired to behold Luther.

Thus standing before the emperor, the electors, dukes, earls, and all the estates of the empire assembled there, he was first advertised by Ulrick of Pappenheim to keep silence, until such time as he was required to speak. Then John Eckius above mentioned, who then was the Bishop of Treves' general official, with a loud voice, said:

'Martin Luther! the sacred and invincible Imperial Majesty hath enjoined, by the consent of all the estates of the holy empire, that thou shouldest be appealed before the throne of his majesty, to the end I might demand of thee these two points.

'First, whether thou confessest these books here [for he showed a heap of Luther's books written in the Latin and German tongues], and which are in all places dispersed, entitled with thy name, be thine, and thou dost affirm them to be thine, or not?

'Secondly, whether thou wilt recant and revoke them, and all that is contained in them, or rather meanest to stand to what thou hast written?'

Luther answered: 'I humbly beseech the Imperial

Majesty to grant me liberty and leisure to deliberate; so that I may satisfy the interrogation made unto me, without prejudice of the Word of God, and peril of mine own soul.'

Whereupon the princes began to deliberate. This done, Eckius, the prolocutor, pronounced what was their resolution, saying, 'The Emperor's majesty, of his mere clemency, granteth thee one day to meditate for thine answer, so that to-morrow, at this instant hour, thou shalt repair to exhibit thine opinion, not in writing, but to pronounce the same with lively voice.'

This done, Luther was led to his lodging by the herald.

The next day, the herald brought him from his lodging to the emperor's court, where he abode till six o'clock, for that the princes were occupied in grave consultations; abiding there, and being environed with a great number of people, and almost smothered for the press that was there. Then after, when the princes were set, and Luther entered, Eckius, the official, spake in this manner: 'Answer now to the Emperor's demand. Wilt thou maintain all thy books which thou hast acknowledged, or revoke any part of them, and submit thyself?'

Martin Luther answered modestly and lowly, and yet not without some stoutness of stomach, and Christian constancy. 'Considering your sovereign majesty, and your honours, require a plain answer; this I say and profess as resolutely as I may, without doubting or sophistication, that if I be not convinced by testimonies of the Scriptures (for I believe not the Pope, neither his General Councils, which have erred many times, and have been contrary to themselves), my conscience is so bound and captived in these Scriptures and the Word of God, that I will not, nor may not revoke any manner of thing; considering it is not godly or lawful to do any thing against conscience. Hereupon I stand and rest: I have not what else to say. God have mercy upon me!'

The princes consulted together upon this answer given by Luther; and when they had diligently examined the same, the prolocutor began to repel him thus: 'The Emperor's majesty requireth of thee a simple answer, either negative or affirmative, whether thou mindest to defend all thy works as Christian, or no?'

Then Luther, turning to the emperor and the nobles, besought them not to force or compel him to yield against his conscience, confirmed with the Holy Scriptures, without manifest arguments alleged to the contrary by his adversaries. 'I am tied by the Scriptures.'

Night now approaching, the lords arose and departed. And after Luther had taken his leave of the emperor, divers Spaniards scorned and scoffed the good man in the way going toward his lodging, hallooing and whooping after him a long while.

Upon the Friday following, when the princes, electors, dukes, and other estates were assembled, the emperor sent to the whole body of the Council a certain letter, as followeth: 'Our predecessors, who truly were Christian princes, were obedient to the Romish Church, which Martin Luther impugneth. And therefore, inasmuch as he is not determined to call back his errors in any one point, we cannot, without great infamy and stain of honour, degenerate from the examples of our elders, but will maintain the ancient faith, and give aid to the see of Rome. And further, we be resolved to pursue Martin Luther and his adherents by excommunication, and by other means that may be devised, to extinguish his doctrine. Nevertheless we will not violate our faith, which we have promised him, but mean to give order for his safe return to the place whence he came.'

During this time, divers princes, earls, barons, knights of the order, gentlemen, priests, monks, with others of the laity and common sort, visited him. All these were present at all hours in the emperor's court, and could not be satisfied with the sight of him. Also there were bills set up, some against Luther, and some, as it seemed, with him. Notwithstanding many supposed, and especially such as well conceived the matter, that this was subtilely done by his enemies, that thereby occasion might be offered to infringe the safe-conduct given him; which the Roman ambassadors with all diligence endeavoured to bring to pass.

John Eckius, the archbishop's official, in the presence of the emperor's secretary, said unto Luther in his lodging, by the commandment of the emperor, that since he had been admonished by the Imperial Majesty, the electors, princes, and estates of the empire, and that notwithstanding, he would not return to unity and concord, it remained that the emperor, as advocate of the catholic faith, should proceed further: and it was the emperor's ordinance, that he should within twenty-one days return boldly under safe-conduct, and be safely guarded to the place whence he came; so that in the meanwhile he stirred no commotion among the people in his journey, either in conference, or by preaching.

Luther, hearing this, answered very modestly and Christianly, 'Even as it hath pleased God, so is it come to pass; the name of the Lord be blessed!' He thanked most humbly the emperor's majesty, and all the princes and estates of the empire, that they had given to him benign and gracious audience, and granted him safe-conduct to come and return. Finally he desired none other of them, than a reformation according to the sacred Word of God, and consonancy of Holy Scriptures, which effectually in his heart he desired: otherwise he was prest to suffer all chances for the Imperial Majesty, as life, and death, goods, fame, and reproach: reserving nothing to himself, but only the Word of God, which he would constantly confess to the latter end.

The morrow after, which was April the 26th, after he had taken his leave of such as supported him, and of the benevolent friends that oftentimes visited him, and had broken his fast, at ten o'clock he departed from Worms, accompanied with such as repaired thither with him.

It was not long after this, but the emperor to purchase favour with the Pope (because he was not yet confirmed in his Empire), directeth out a solemn writ of outlawry against Luther, and all them that took his part; commanding the said Luther, wheresoever he might be gotten, to be apprehended, and his books burned. In the meantime, Duke Frederic conveyed Luther a little out of sight secretly, by the help of certain noblemen whom he well knew to be faithful and trusty unto him in that behalf. There Luther, being close and out of company, wrote divers epistles, and certain books; among which he dedicated one to his company of Augustine friars, entitled, *De abroganda Missa*: which friars the same time being encouraged by him, began to lay down their private masses. Duke Frederic, fearing lest that would breed some great stir or tumult, caused the judgment of the University of Wittenberg to be asked in the matter.

It was showed to the duke, that he should do well to command the use of the mass to be abrogated through his dominion: and though it could not be done without tumult, yet that was no let why the course of true doctrine should be stayed, neither ought such disturbance to be imputed to the doctrine taught, but to the adversaries, who willingly and wickedly kick against the truth, whereof Christ also giveth us forewarning before. For fear of such tumults therefore, we ought not to surcease from that which we know is to be done, but constantly must go forward in defence of God's truth, howsoever the world doth esteem us, or rage against it.

It happened about the same time that King Henry VIII. wrote against Luther. In which book, first, he reproveth Luther's opinion about the Pope's pardons; secondly, he defendeth the supremacy of the Bishop of Rome; thirdly, he laboureth to refell all his doctrine of the sacraments of the Church.

This book, albeit it carried the King's name in the title, yet it was another that ministered the motion, another that framed the style. But whosoever had the labour of this book, the King had the thanks and the reward; for the Bishop of Rome gave to the said King Henry, and to his successors for ever, the style and title of *Defender of the Faith*.

Shortly after this, Pope Leo was stricken with sudden fever, and died shortly, being of the age of forty-seven years: albeit some suspect that he died of poison. Successor to him was Pope Adrian VI., schoolmaster some time to Charles the Emperor. This Adrian was a German born, brought up at Louvain, and as in learning he exceeded the common sort of Popes, so in moderation of life and manners he seemed not altogether so intemperate as some other Popes have been: and yet, like a right Pope, nothing degenerating from his see, he was a mortal enemy against Martin Luther and his partakers. In his time, shortly after the council of Worms was broken up, another assembly of the princes, nobles, and states of Germany was appointed by the emperor at Nuremberg, A.D. 1522.

Unto this assembly the said Adrian sent his letters, with an instruction unto his legate Cheregatus, to inform him what causes to allege against Luther.

Pope Adrian the Sixth, to the Renowned Princes of Germany, and to the Peers of the Roman Empire.

We hear that Martin Luther, a new raiser-up of old and damnable heresies, first after the fatherly advertisements of the see apostolic; then after the sentence also of condemnation awarded against him, and lastly, after the imperial decree of our well-beloved son Charles, elect Emperor of the Romans, and catholic King of Spain, being divulged through the whole nation of Germany; yet hath neither been by order restrained, nor of himself hath refrained from his madness begun, but daily more and more, ceaseth not to disturb and replenish the world with new books, fraught full of errors, heresies, contumelies and sedition, and to infect the country of Germany, and other regions about, with this pestilence; and endeavoureth still to corrupt simple souls and manners of men, with the poison of his pestiferous tongue. And (which is worst of all) hath for his fautors and supporters, not of the vulgar sort only, but also divers personages of the nobility; insomuch that they have begun also to invade the goods of priests contrary to the obedience which they owe to ecclesiastical and temporal persons, and now also at last have grown unto civil war and dissension among themselves.

Do you not consider, O princes and people of Germany! that these be but prefaces and preambles to those evils and mischiefs which Luther, with the sect of his Lutherans, do intend and purpose here-after? Do you not see plainly, and perceive with your eyes, that this defending of the verity of the Gospel, first begun by the Lutherans to be pretended, is now manifest to be but an invention to spoil your goods, which they have long intended? or do you think that these sons of iniquity do tend to any other thing, than under the name of liberty to supplant obedience, and so to open a general license to every man to do what him listeth? They who refuse to render due obedience to priests, to bishops, yea, to the high bishop of all, and who daily before your own faces make their booties of church-goods, and of things consecrated to God; think ye that they will refrain their sacrilegious hands from the spoil of laymen's goods? yea, that they will not pluck from you whatsoever they can rap or reave?

Nay, think you not contrary, but this miserable calamity will at length redound upon you, your goods, your houses, wives, children, dominions, possessions, and these your temples which you hallow and reverence; except you provide some speedy remedy against the same.

Wherefore we require you, in virtue of that obedience which all Christians owe to God, and blessed St Peter, and to his vicar here on earth, that you confer your helping hands every man to quench this public fire, and endeavour and study, the best way ye can, how to reduce the said Martin Luther, and all other fautors of these tumults and errors, to better conformity and trade both of life and faith. And if they who be infected shall refuse to hear your admonitions, yet provide that the other part, which yet remaineth sound, by the same contagion be not corrupted. When this pestiferous canker cannot with supple and gentle medicines be cured, more sharp salves must be proved, and fiery searings. The putrefied members must be cut off from the body, lest the sound parts also be infected. So God did cast down into hell the schismatical brethren Dathan and Abiram; and him that would not obey the authority of the priest, God commanded to be punished with death. So Peter, prince of the apostles, denounced sudden death to Ananias and Sapphira, who lied unto God. So the old and godly emperors commanded Jovinian and Priscillian, as heretics, to be beheaded. So St Jerome wished Vigilant, as a heretic, to be given to the destruction of the flesh, that the spirit might be saved in the day of the Lord. So also did our predecessors in the Council of Constance condemn to death John Huss and his fellow Jerome, who now appeareth to revive again in Luther. The worthy acts and examples of which forefathers, if you shall imitate, we do not doubt but God's merciful clemency shall eftsoons relieve his Church.

These instructions of the Pope himself against Luther, I thought, Christian reader! to set before thine eyes. They cry, 'Heresy, heresy!' but they prove no heresy. They inflame kings and princes against Luther, and yet they have no just cause wherefore. They charge Luther with disobedience, and none are so disobedient to magistrates and civil laws, as they. They lay to his charge oppression and spoiling of laymen's goods; and who spoileth the laymen's livings so much as the Pope?

Now let us see what the princes answer to these aforesaid suggestions and instructions of Pope Adrian.

The Answer of the Noble and Reverend Princes, and of the States of the sacred Roman Empire, exhibited to the Pope's Ambassador.

They understand that his holiness is afflicted with great sorrow for the prospering of Luther's sect, whereby innumerable souls committed to his charge are in danger of perdition. The lord lieutenant, and other princes and states do answer, that it is to them no less grief and sorrow than to his holiness. But why the sentence of the apostolic see, and the emperor's edict against Luther, hath not been put in execution hitherto, there hath been causes great and urgent; as first, that great evils and inconveniences would thereupon ensue. For the greatest part of the people of Germany have always had this persuasion, and now, by reading Luther's books, are more therein confirmed, that great grievances and inconveniences have come to this nation of Germany by the Court of Rome: and therefore, if they should have proceeded with any rigour in executing the Pope's sentence, and the emperor's edict, the multitude would conceive and suspect in their minds this to be done for subverting the verity of the Gospel, and for supporting and confirming the former abuses and grievances, whereupon great wars and tumults, no doubt, would have ensued. Unless such abuses and grievances shall be faithfully reformed, there is no true peace and concord between the ecclesiastical and secular estates, nor any true extirpation of this tumult and errors in Germany, that can be hoped.

Whereas the Pope's holiness desireth to be informed, what way were best to take in resisting these errors of the Lutherans, what more present or effectual remedy can be had than this, that the Pope's holiness, by the consent of the Emperor's majesty, do summon a free Christian Council in some convenient place of Germany, as at Strasburg, or at Mentz, or at Cologne, or at Metz? and that with as much speed as conveniently may be; in which Council it may be lawful for every person that there shall have interest, either temporal or ecclesiastical, freely to speak and consult, to the glory of God, and health of souls, and the public wealth of Christendom, without impeachment or restraint; whatsoever oath or other bond to the contrary notwithstanding: yea, and it shall be every good man's part there to speak, not only freely, but to speak that which is true, to the purpose, and to edifying, and not to pleasing or flattering, but simply and uprightly to declare his judgment, without all fraud or guile.

And as touching by what ways these errors and tumults of the German people may best be stayed and pacified in the meantime, the aforesaid lord lieutenant, with the other princes, thereupon have consulted and deliberated; that forasmuch as Luther, and certain of his fellows, be within the territory and dominion of the noble Duke Frederic, the said lord lieutenant and other states of the empire shall so labour the matter with the aforenamed prince, Duke of Saxony, that Luther and his followers, shall not write, set forth, or print any thing during the said mean space.

That the said lord lieutenant and princes shall labour so with the preachers of Germany, that they shall not in their sermons teach or blow into the people's ears such matters, whereby the multitude may be moved to rebellion or uproar, or be induced into error. Also, that they shall move no contention or disputation among the vulgar sort; but whatsoever hangeth in controversy, the same they shall reserve to the determination of the Council to come.

The archbishops, bishops, and other prelates within their dioceses shall assign godly and learned men, having good judgment in the Scripture, who shall diligently and faithfully attend upon such preachers: and if they shall perceive the said preachers either to have erred, or to have uttered any thing inconveniently, they shall godly, mildly, and modestly advertise and inform them thereof, in such sort that no man shall justly complain the truth of the Gospel to be impeached. But if the preachers, continuing still in their stubbornness, shall refuse to be admonished, and will not desist from their lewdness, then shall they be restrained and punished by the ordinaries of the place, with punishment for the same convenient.

Furthermore, the said princes and nobles shall provide and undertake, so much as shall be possible, that, from henceforth, no new book shall be printed, neither shall they privily or apertly be sold. Also order shall be taken amongst all potentates, that if any shall set out, sell, or print any new work, it shall first be seen and perused of certain godly, learned, and discreet men appointed for the same; so that if it be not admitted and approved by them, it shall not be permitted to be published.

Finally, as concerning priests who contract matrimony, and religious men leaving their cloisters, the aforesaid princes do consider, that forasmuch as in the civil law there is no penalty for them ordained, they shall be referred to the canonical constitutions, to be punished thereafter accordingly; that is, by the loss of their benefices and privileges, or other condign censures.

Let us return to the story of Luther, of whom ye heard before, how he was kept secret and solitary for a time, by the advice and conveyance of certain nobles in Saxony, because of the emperor's edict. In the meantime, while Luther had thus absented himself out of Wittenberg, Andreas Carolostadt, proceeding more roughly and eagerly in causes of religion, had stirred up the people to throw down images in the temples. Luther reproved the rashness of Carolostadt, declaring that their proceedings herein were not orderly, but that pictures and images ought first to be thrown out of the hearts and consciences of men; and that the people ought first to be taught that we are saved before God, and please him only by faith; and that images serve to no purpose: this done, and the people well instructed, there was no danger in images, but they would fall of their own accord. Not that he would maintain images to stand or to be suffered, but that this ought to be done by the magistrate; and not by force, upon every private man's head, without order and authority.

Albeit the Church of Christ (praised be the Lord) is not unprovided of sufficient plenty of worthy and learned writers, able to instruct in matters of doctrine; yet in the chief points of our consolation, where the glory of Christ, and the power of His passion, and strength of faith are to be opened to our conscience; and where the soul, wrestling for death and life, standeth in need of serious consolation, the same may be said of Martin Luther, among all this other variety of writers, what St Cyprian was wont to say of Tertullian, 'Da magistrum'; 'Give me my master.'

Those who write the lives of saints use to describe and extol their holy life and godly virtues, and also to set forth such miracles as be wrought in them by God; whereof there lacketh no plenty in Martin Luther. What a miracle might this seem to be, for one man, and a poor friar, creeping out of a blind cloister, to be set up against the Pope, the universal bishop, and God's mighty vicar on earth; to withstand all his cardinals, yea, and to sustain the malice and hatred of almost the whole world being set against him; and to work that against the said Pope, cardinals, and Church of Rome, which no king nor emperor could ever do, yea, durst ever attempt, nor all the learned men before him could ever compass: which miraculous work of God, I account nothing inferior to the miracle of David overthrowing the great Goliath.

Wherefore if miracles do make a saint (after the Pope's definition), what lacketh in Martin Luther, to make him a saint? who, standing openly against the Pope, cardinals, and prelates of the church, in number so many, in power so terrible, in practice so crafty, having emperors and all the kings of the earth against him; who, teaching and preaching Christ the space of nine and twenty years, could, without touch of all his enemies, so quietly in his own country where he was born, die and sleep in peace. In which Martin Luther, first to stand against the Pope, was a great miracle; to prevail against the Pope, a greater; so to die untouched, may seem greatest of all, especially having so many enemies as he had.

As he was mighty in his prayers, so in his sermons God gave him such a grace, that when he preached, they who heard him thought every one his own temptation severally to be noted and touched. Whereof, when his friends demanded how that could be; 'Mine own manifold temptations,' said he, ' and experiences are the cause thereof.' For this thou must understand, good reader! that Luther from his tender years was much beaten and exercised with spiritual conflicts. Hieronymus Wellerus, scholar and disciple of the said Martin Luther, recordeth, that he oftentimes heard Luther his master thus report of himself, that he had been assaulted and vexed with all kinds of temptations, saving only one, which was with covetousness; with this vice he was never, said he, in all his life troubled, nor once tempted.

Martin Luther, living to the year of his age sixty-three, continued writing and preaching about twenty-nine years. As touching the order of his death, the words of Melancthon be these, given to his auditory at Wittenberg, A.D. 1546:—

Wednesday last past, and the 17th of February, Dr Martin Luther sickened of his accustomed malady, to wit, of the oppression of humours in the orifice or opening of the stomach. This sickness took him after supper, with which he vehemently contending, required secess into a by-chamber, and there he rested on his bed two hours, all which time his pains increased; and as Dr Jonas was lying in his chamber, Luther awaked, and prayed him to rise, and to call up Ambrose his children's schoolmaster, to make a fire in another chamber; into which when he was newly entered, Albert, Earl of Mansfield, with his wife, and divers others at that instant came into his chamber. Finally, feeling his fatal hour to approach, before nine of the clock in the morning, on the 18th of February, he commended himself to God with this devout prayer: 'My heavenly Father, eternal and merciful God! Thou hast manifested unto me Thy dear Son, our Lord Jesus Christ. I have taught Him, I have known Him; I love Him as my life, my health, and my redemption; Whom the wicked have persecuted, maligned, and with injury afflicted. Draw my soul to Thee.'

After this he said as ensueth, thrice: 'I commend my spirit into Thy hands, Thou hast redeemed me, O God of Truth!' 'God so loved the world, that He gave His only Son, that all those that believe in Him should have life everlasting.' Having repeated oftentimes his prayers, he was called to God. So praying, his innocent ghost peaceably was separated from the earthly corpse.

Chapter Eight

JOHN HOOPER,
BISHOP OF WORCESTER

JOHN HOOPER, student and graduate in the University of Oxford, after the study of the sciences, wherein he had abundantly profited through God's secret vocation, was stirred with fervent desire to the love and knowledge of the Scriptures : in the reading and searching whereof, as there lacked in him no diligence, joined with earnest prayer, so neither wanted unto him the grace of the Holy Ghost to satisfy his desire, and to open unto him the light of true divinity.

Thus Master Hooper, growing more and more, by God's grace, in ripeness of spiritual understanding, and showing withal some sparkles of his fervent spirit, fell eftsoons into displeasure and hatred of certain rabbins in Oxford, who began to stir coals against him ; whereby, and especially by the procurement of Dr Smith, he was compelled to avoid the University; and removing from thence, was retained in the house of Sir Thomas Arundel, and there was his steward, till the time that Sir Thomas Arundel, having intelligence of his opinions and religion, which he in no case did favour, and yet exceedingly favouring the person of the man, found the means to send him in a message to the Bishop of Winchester, writing his letter privily to the bishop, by conference of learning to do some good upon him; but in any case requiring him to send home his servant to him again.

Winchester, after conference with Master Hooper four or five days together, when he perceived that neither he could do that good which he thought to him, nor that he would take any good at his hand, according to Master Arundel's request, sent home his servant again; right well commending his learning and wit, but yet bearing in his breast a grudging stomach against Master Hooper still.

It followed not long after this, as malice is always working mischief, that intelligence was given to Master Hooper to provide for himself, for danger that was working against him. Whereupon Master Hooper, leaving Master Arundel's house, and borrowing a horse of a certain friend (whose life he had saved a little before from the gallows), took his journey to the sea-side to go to France, sending back the horse again.

Master Hooper, being at Paris, tarried there not long, but in short time returned into England, and was retained of Master Sentlow, till the time that he was again molested; whereby he was compelled, under the pretence of being captain of a ship going to Ireland, to take the seas. And so escaped he (although not without extreme peril of drowning) through France, to the higher parts of Germany; where he, entering acquaintance with the learned men, was of them friendly and lovingly entertained, at Basil, and especially at Zurich, of Master Bullinger, being his singular friend. There also he married his wife who was a Burgonian, and applied very studiously to the Hebrew tongue.

When God saw good to give us King Edward to

reign over this realm, with some peace and rest unto his Gospel, amongst many other English exiles who repaired homeward, Master Hooper also, moved in conscience, thought not to absent himself; but, seeing such a time and occasion, offered to help forward the Lord's work, to the uttermost of his ability. And so, coming to Master Bullinger, and other of his acquaintance (as duty required), to give them thanks for their singular kindness and humanity toward him manifold ways declared, with like humanity purposed to take his leave of them. Unto whom Master Bullinger spake on this wise :—

'Master Hooper,' said he, 'although we are sorry to part with your company for our own cause, yet much greater causes we have to rejoice, both for your sake, and especially for the cause of Christ's true religion, that you shall now return, out of long banishment, into your native country again; where not only you may enjoy your own private liberty, but also the cause and state of Christ's Church, by you, may fare the better; as we doubt not but it shall.

'Another cause, moreover, why we rejoice with you and for you, is this: that you shall remove not only out of exile into liberty; but you shall leave here a barren, a sour and an unpleasant country, rude and savage; and shall go into a land flowing with milk and honey, replenished with all pleasure and fertility.

'Notwithstanding, with this our rejoicing one fear and care we have, lest you, being absent, and so far distant from us, or else coming to such abundance of wealth and felicity, in your new welfare and plenty of all things, and in your flourishing honours, where ye shall come, peradventure, to be a bishop, and where ye shall find so many new friends, you will forget us your old acquaintance and well-willers. Nevertheless, howsoever you shall forget and shake us off, yet this persuade yourself, that we will not forget our old friend and fellow Master Hooper. And if you will please not to forget us again, then I pray you let us hear from you.'

Whereunto Master Hooper answered again that neither the nature of country, nor pleasure of commodities, nor newness of friends, should ever induce him to the oblivion of such friends and benefactors, 'and therefore,' said he, 'from time to time I will write unto you, how it goeth with me. But the last news of all, I shall not be able to write : for there' said he (taking Master Bullinger by the hand), 'where I shall take most pains, there shall you hear of me to be burned to ashes.'

Master Hooper, coming to London, used continually to preach, most times twice, at least once, every day; and never failed. The people in great flocks daily came to hear his voice, as the most melodious sound and tune of Orpheus's harp, as the proverb saith ; insomuch that oftentimes when he was preaching, the church would be so full, that none could enter further than the doors thereof. In his doctrine he was earnest, in tongue eloquent, in the Scriptures perfect, in pains indefatigable.

Even as he began, so he continued unto his life's end. For neither could his labour and painstaking break him, neither promotion change him, neither dainty fare corrupt him. His life was so pure and good, that no kind of slander could fasten any fault upon him. He was of body strong, his health whole and sound, his wit very pregnant, his invincible patience able to sustain whatsoever sinister fortune and adversity could do. He was constant of judgment, a good justicer, spare of diet, sparer of words, and sparest of time: in house-keeping very liberal, and sometimes more free than his living would extend unto. He bare in countenance and talk always a certain severe grace, which might, peradventure, be wished sometimes to have been a little more popular in him: but he knew what he had to do best himself.

This, by the way, I thought to note, for that there was once an honest citizen, and to me not unknown, who, having in himself a certain grudge of conscience, came to Master Hooper's door for counsel: but, being abashed at his austere look, durst not come in, but departed, seeking remedy of his troubled mind at other men's hands. In my judgment, such as are made governors over the flock of Christ, to teach and instruct them, ought so to frame their life, manners, countenance, and external behaviour, as neither they show themselves too familiar and light, whereby to be brought into contempt, nor, on the other side, that they appear more lofty and austere, than appertaineth to the edifying of the simple flock of Christ.

At length, and that not without the great profit of many, Master Hooper was called to preach before the King's majesty, and soon after made Bishop of Gloucester. In that office he continued two years, and behaved himself so well, that his very enemies (except it were for his good doing, and sharp correcting of sin) could find no fault with him. After that, he was made Bishop of Worcester.

But I cannot tell what sinister and unlucky contention concerning the ordering and consecration of bishops, and of their apparel, with such other like trifles, began to disturb the good and lucky beginning of the godly bishop. For notwithstanding that godly reformation of religion then begun in the Church of England, besides other ceremonies more ambitious than profitable, or tending to edification, they used to wear such garments and apparel as the popish bishops were wont to do: first a chimere, and under that a white rochet: then, a mathematical cap with four angles, dividing the whole world into four parts. These trifles, tending more to superstition than otherwise, as he could never abide, so in no wise could he be persuaded to wear them. For this cause he made supplication to the King's majesty, most humbly desiring His Highness, either to discharge him of the bishopric, or else to dispense with him for such ceremonial orders; whose petition the King granted immediately.

Notwithstanding, the bishops still stood earnestly in the defence of the aforesaid ceremonies; saying it was but a small matter, and that the fault was in the abuse of the things, and not in the things themselves: adding moreover, that he ought not to be so stubborn in so light a matter; and that his wilfulness therein was not to be suffered.

Whilst both parties thus contended more than reason would, occasion was given to the true Christians to lament, to the adversaries to rejoice. This theological contention came to this end: that the bishops having the upper hand, Master Hooper was fain to agree to this condition—that sometimes he should in his sermon show himself apparelled as the other bishops were. Wherefore appointed to preach before the King, as a new player in a strange apparel, he cometh forth on the stage. His upper garment was a long scarlet chimere down to the foot, and under that a white linen rochet that covered all his shoulders. Upon his head he had a geometrical, that is, a four-squared cap, albeit that his head was round. What cause of shame the strangeness hereof was that day to that good preacher, every man may easily judge.

Master Hooper, entering into his diocese, was so careful in his cure, that he left neither pains untaken, nor ways unsought, how to train up the flock of Christ in the true word of salvation. No father in his household, no gardener in his garden, nor husbandman in his vineyard, was more or better occupied, than he in his diocese amongst his flock, going about his towns and villages in teaching and preaching to the people.

The time that he had to spare from preaching, he bestowed either in hearing public causes, or else in private study, prayer, and visiting of schools. With his continual doctrine he adjoined due and discreet correction, not so much severe to any, as to them which for abundance of riches, and wealthy state, thought they might do what they listed. He spared no kind of people, but was indifferent to all men, as well rich as poor. His life, in fine, was such, that to the Church and all churchmen, it might be a light and example; to the rest a perpetual lesson and sermon.

Though he bestowed the most part of his care upon the flock of Christ, for the which He spent His blood; yet, nevertheless, there lacked no provision in him to bring up his own children in learning and good manners; insomuch that ye could not discern whether he deserved more praise for his fatherly usage at home, or for his bishop-like doings abroad: for everywhere he kept one religion in one uniform doctrine and integrity. So that if you entered into the bishop's palace, you would suppose yourself to have entered into some church or temple. In every corner thereof there was some smell of virtue, good example, honest conversation, and reading of holy Scriptures. There was not to be seen in his house any courtly roisting or idleness; no pomp at all; no dishonest word, no swearing could there be heard.

As for the revenues of both his bishoprics, he pursed nothing, but bestowed it in hospitality. Twice I was, as I remember, in his house in Worcester, where, in his common hall, I saw a table spread with good store of meat, and beset full of beggars and poor folk: and I, asking his servants what this meant, they told me that every day their lord and master's manner was, to have to dinner a certain number of poor folk of the said city by course, who were served by four at a mess, with hot and wholesome meats; and, when they were served (being before examined by him or his deputies of the Lord's prayer, the articles of their faith, and the ten commandments), then he himself sat down to dinner, and not before.

King Edward being dead, and Mary being crowned Queen of England, this good bishop was one of the first that was sent for to be at London. And, although the said Master Hooper was not ignorant of the evils that should happen towards him (for he was admonished by certain of his friends to get him away, and shift for himself), yet he would not prevent them, but tarried still, saying: 'Once I did flee, and take me to my feet; but now, because I am called to this place and vocation, I am thoroughly persuaded to tarry, and to live and die with my sheep.'

And when at the day of his appearance, which was the first of September 1553, he was come to London, he was received very opprobriously. He freely and boldly told his tale, and purged himself. But, in fine, it came to this conclusion, that by them he was commanded to ward; it being declared unto him at his departure, that the cause of his imprisonment was only for certain sums of money, for which he was indebted to the Queen, and not for religion.

The next year, being 1554, the 19th of March, he was called again to appear before Winchester, and other the Queen's commissioners. The Lord Chancellor asked whether he was married. 'Yea, my lord,' replied Master Hooper, 'and will not be unmarried till death unmarry me.' The commissioners began to make such outcries, and laughed, and used such gesture, as was unseemly for the place. The Bishop of Chichester, Dr Day, called Master Hooper 'hypocrite,' with vehement words, and scornful countenance. Bishop Tonstal called him 'beast:' so did Smith, one of the clerks of the council, and divers others that stood by.

Tonstal, Bishop of Durham, asked Master Hooper, whether he believed the corporal presence in the sacrament. And Master Hooper said plainly, that there was none such, neither did he believe any such thing. Then asked Winchester what authority moved him not to believe the corporal presence? He said, the authority of God's Word. Whereupon they bade the notaries write that he was married; and said, that he would not go from his wife, and that he believed not the corporal presence in the sacrament: wherefore he was worthy to be deprived of his bishopric.

The true Report of Master Hooper's Entertainment in the Fleet; written with his own Hand, the 7th of January, 1555.

The 1st of September, 1553, I was committed unto the Fleet from Richmond, to have the liberty of the prison; and, within six days after, I paid for my liberty five pounds sterling to the warden, for fees: who, immediately upon the payment thereof, complained unto Stephen Gardiner, Bishop of Winchester; and so was I committed to close prison one quarter of a year in the Tower-chamber of the Fleet, and used very extremely.

Then by the means of a good gentlewoman, I had liberty to come down to dinner and supper, not suffered to speak with any of my friends; but, as soon as dinner and supper was done, to repair to my chamber again. Notwithstanding, while I came down thus to dinner and supper, the warden and his wife picked quarrels with me, and complained untruly of me to their great friend the Bishop of Winchester.

After one quarter of a year and somewhat more, Babington the warden, and his wife, fell out with me for the wicked mass; and thereupon the warden resorted to the Bishop of Winchester, and obtained to put me into the wards, where I have continued a long time; having nothing appointed to me for my bed, but a little pad of straw and a rotten covering, with a tick and a few feathers therein, the chamber being vile and stinking, until by God's means good people sent me bedding to lie in.

On the one side of which prison is the sink and filth of all the house, and on the other side the town-ditch, so that the stench of the house hath infected me with sundry diseases.—During which time I have been sick; and the doors, bars, hasps, and chains being all closed, and made fast upon me, I have mourned, called, and cried for help. But the warden, when he hath known me many times ready to die, and when the poor men of the wards have called to help me, hath commanded the doors to be kept fast, and charged that none of his men should come at me, saying, 'Let him alone; it were a good riddance of him.'

I paid always like a baron to the said warden, as well in fees, as for my board, which was twenty shillings a week, besides my man's table, until I was wrongfully deprived of my bishopric; and, since that time, I have paid him as the best gentleman doth in his house; yet hath he used me worse, and more vilely, than the veriest slave that ever came to the hall-commons.

The said warden hath also imprisoned my man William Downton, and stripped him out of his clothes to search for letters, and could find none, but only a little remembrance of good people's names, that gave me their alms to relieve me in prison; and to undo them also, the warden delivered the same bill unto the said Stephen Gardiner, God's enemy and mine.

I have suffered imprisonment almost eighteen months, my goods, living, friends, and comfort taken from me; the Queen owing me by just account four score pounds or more. She hath put me in prison, and giveth nothing to find me, neither is there suffered any to come at me whereby I might have relief. I am with a wicked man and woman, so that I see no remedy (saving God's help), but I shall be cast away in prison before I come to judgment. But I commit my cause to God, Whose will be done, whether it be by life or death.

The 22nd of January following, 1555, Babington, the warden of the Fleet, was commanded to bring Master Hooper before the Bishop of Winchester, with other bishops and commissioners, at the said Winchester's house, at St Mary Overy's. The Bishop of Winchester moved Master Hooper earnestly to forsake the evil and corrupt doctrine (as he termed it) preached in the days of King Edward the Sixth, and to return to the unity of the catholic Church, and to acknowledge the Pope's holiness to be head of the same Church, according to the determination of the whole parliament; promising, that as he himself, with other his brethren, had received the Pope's blessing, and the Queen's mercy; even so mercy was ready to be showed to him and others, if he would condescend to the Pope's holiness.

Master Hooper answered, that forasmuch as the Pope taught doctrine altogether contrary to the doctrine of Christ, he was not worthy to be head thereof; wherefore he would in no wise condescend to any such usurped jurisdiction. Neither esteemed he the Church, whereof they call him head, to be the catholic church of Christ: for the Church only heareth the voice of her spouse Christ, and flieth the strangers. 'Howbeit,' saith he, 'if in any point, to me unknown, I have offended the Queen's majesty, I shall most humbly submit myself to her mercy; if mercy may be had with safety of conscience and without the displeasure of God.' Answer was made that the Queen would show no mercy to the Pope's enemies. Whereupon Babington was commanded to bring him to the Fleet again.

The 28th of January, Winchester and the commissioners sat in judgment at St Mary Overy's, where Master Hooper appeared before them at afternoon again; and there, after much reasoning and disputation to and fro, he was commanded aside, till Master Rogers (who was then come) had been likewise examined. Examinations being ended, the two sheriffs of London were commanded, about four of the clock, to carry them to the Compter in Southwark, there to remain till the morrow at nine o'clock, to see whether they would relent and come home again to the catholic Church.

So Master Hooper went before with one of the sheriffs, and Master Rogers came after with the other, and being out of church door, Master Hooper looked back, and stayed a little till Master Rogers drew near, unto whom he said 'Come, brother Rogers! must we two take this matter first in hand, and begin to fry these faggots?'

'Yea, sir,' said Master Rogers, 'by God's grace.'

'Doubt not,' said Master Hooper, 'but God will give strength.'

So going forwards, there was such a press of people in the streets, who rejoiced at their constancy that they had much ado to pass.

Upon the next day, they were brought again by the sheriffs before the said Bishop and commissioners. After long and earnest talk, when they perceived that Master Hooper would by no means condescend unto them, they condemned him to be degraded, and read unto him his condemnation. That done, Master Rogers was brought before them, and in like manner entreated, and so they delivered both of them to the secular power, the two sheriffs of London, who were willed to carry them to the Clink, a prison not far from the Bishop of Winchester's house, and there to remain till night.

When it was dark, Master Hooper was led by one of the sheriffs, with many bills and weapons, first through the Bishop of Winchester's house, and so over London-bridge, through the city to Newgate. And by the way some of the sergeants were willed to go before, and put out the coster-mongers' candles, who used to sit with lights in the streets: either fearing, of likelihood, that the people would have made some attempt to have taken him away from them by force, if they had seen him go to that prison; or else, being burdened with an evil conscience, they thought darkness to be a most fit season for such a business.

But notwithstanding this device, the people having some foreknowledge of his coming, many of them came forth of their doors with lights, and saluted him; praising God for his constancy in the true doctrine which he had taught them, and desiring God to strengthen him in the same to the end. Master Hooper passed by, and required the people to make their earnest prayers to God for him : and so went through Cheapside to the place appointed, and was delivered as close prisoner to the keeper of Newgate, where he remained six days, nobody being permitted to come to him, or talk with him, saving his keepers, and such as should be appointed thereto.

During this time, Bonner, Bishop of London, and others at his appointment, resorted divers times unto him to assay if by any means they could persuade him to relent, and become a member of their antichristian church. All the ways they could devise, they attempted : for, besides the allegations of testimonies of the Scriptures, and of ancient writers wrested to a wrong sense, according to their accustomed manner, they also used all outward gentleness and significations of friendship, with many great proffers and promises of worldly commodities ; not omitting also most grievous threatenings, if with gentleness they could not prevail : but they found him always the same man, steadfast and immovable.

When they perceived that they could by no means reclaim him to their purpose with such persuasions and offers as they used for his conversion, then went they about, by false rumours and reports of recantations, to bring him and the doctrine of Christ which he professed, out of credit with the people. So the bruit being spread abroad, and believed of some of the weaker sort, by reason of the often resort of the Bishop of London and others, it at last came to Master Hooper's ears: wherewith he was not a little grieved, that the people should give credit unto false rumours. 'The report abroad (as I am credibly informed) is that I, John Hooper, a condemned man for the cause of Christ, should now, after sentence of death (being in Newgate, prisoner, and looking daily for execution) recant and abjure that which heretofore I have preached. And this talk ariseth of this, that the Bishop of London and his chaplains resort unto me. I have spoken and do speak with them when they come; for I fear not their arguments, neither is death terrible unto me; and I am more confirmed in the truth which I have preached heretofore, by their coming. I have left all things of the world, and suffered great pains and imprisonment, and, I thank God, I am as ready to suffer death, as a mortal man may be. I have taught the truth with my tongue, and with my pen heretofore; and hereafter shortly shall confirm the same by God's grace with my blood.'

Monday, the 4th of February, his keeper gave him an inkling that he should be sent to Gloucester to suffer death, whereat he rejoiced very much, lifting up his eyes and hands unto heaven, and praising God that He saw it good to send him amongst the people over whom he was pastor, there to confirm with his death the truth which he had before taught them; not doubting but the Lord would give him strength to perform the same to His glory. And immediately he sent to his servant's house for his boots, spurs, and cloak, that he might be in a readiness to ride when he should be called.

The next day following, about four o'clock in the

morning before day, the keeper with others came to him and searched him, and the bed wherein he lay, to see if he had written any thing; and then he was led by the sheriffs of London, and their officers, forth of Newgate to a place appointed, not far from St Dunstan's church in Fleet Street, where six of the Queen's guards were appointed to receive him, and to carry him to Gloucester, there to be delivered unto the sheriff, who, with the Lord Chandos, Master Wicks, and other commissioners, were appointed to see execution done.

The which guard brought him to the Angel, where he brake his fast with them, eating his meat at that time more liberally than he had used to do a good while before. About the break of the day he went to horse, and leaped cheerfully on horseback without help, having a hood upon his head under his hat, that he should not be known. And so he took his journey joyfully towards Gloucester, and always by the way the guard learned of him where he was accustomed to bait or lodge; and ever carried him to another inn.

On the Thursday following, he came to a town in his diocese called Cirencester, fifteen miles from Gloucester, about eleven o'clock, and there dined at a woman's house who had always hated the truth, and spoken all evil she could of Master Hooper. This woman, perceiving the cause of his coming, showed him all the friendship she could, and lamented his case with tears; confessing that she before had often reported, that if he were put to the trial, he would not stand to his doctrine.

After dinner he rode forwards, and came to Gloucester about five o'clock; and a mile without

the town was much people assembled, which cried
and lamented his estate, insomuch that one of the
guard rode post into the town, to require aid of the
mayor and sheriffs, fearing lest he should have been
taken from them. The officers and their retinue
repaired to the gate with weapons, and commanded
the people to keep their houses; but there was no
man that once gave any signification of any such
rescue or violence.

So was he lodged at one Ingram's house in
Gloucester; and that night (as he had done all
the way) he did eat his meat quietly, and slept his
first sleep soundly, as it was reported by them of
the guard, and others. After his first sleep he
continued all that night in prayer until the morning;
and then he desired that he might go into the next
chamber (for the guard were also in the chamber
where he lay), that there, being solitary, he might
pray and talk with God: so that all the day, saving
a little at meat, and when he talked at any time
with such as the guard licensed to speak with him,
he bestowed in prayer.

Amongst others that spake with him, Sir Anthony
Kingston, Knight, was one; who, seeming in time
past his very friend, was then appointed by the
Queen's letters to be one of the commissioners, to
see execution done upon him. Master Kingston,
being brought into the chamber, found him at his
prayer: and as soon as he saw Master Hooper, he
burst forth in tears. Master Hooper at the first
blush knew him not. Then said Master Kingston,
'Why, my lord, do you not know me, an old friend
of yours, Anthony Kingston?'

Hooper: 'Yes, Master Kingston, I do now know

you well, and am glad to see you in health, and do praise God for the same.'

Kingston: 'But I am sorry to see you in this case; for as I understand you be come hither to die. But, alas, consider that life is sweet, and death is bitter. Therefore, seeing life may be had, desire to live; for life hereafter may do good.'

Hooper: 'Indeed it is true, Master Kingston, I am come hither to end this life, and to suffer death here, because I will not gainsay the former truth that I have heretofore taught amongst you in this diocese, and elsewhere; and I thank you for your friendly counsel, although it be not so friendly as I could have wished it. True it is, Master Kingston, that death is bitter, and life is sweet: but, alas, consider that the death to come is more bitter, and the life to come is more sweet. Therefore, for the desire and love I have to the one, and the terror and fear of the other; I do not so much regard this death, nor esteem this life, but have settled myself, through the strength of God's holy Spirit, patiently to pass through the torments and extremities of the fire now prepared for me, rather than to deny the truth of His Word; desiring you, and others, in the meantime, to commend me to God's mercy in your prayers.'

Kingston: 'Well, my lord, then I perceive there is no remedy, and therefore I will take my leave of you: and I thank God that ever I knew you; for God did appoint you to call me, being a lost child.'

Hooper: I do highly praise God for it: and I pray God you may continually live in His fear.'

After these, and many other words, the one took leave of the other; Master Kingston, with bitter tears, Master Hooper with tears also trickling down his cheeks. At which departure Master Hooper told him that all the troubles he had sustained in prison had not caused him to utter so much sorrow.

The same day in the afternoon, a blind boy, after long intercession made to the guard, obtained license to be brought unto Master Hooper's speech. The same boy not long afore had suffered imprisonment at Gloucester for confessing of the truth. Master Hooper, after he had examined him of his faith, and the cause of his imprisonment, beheld him steadfastly, and (the water appearing in his eyes) said unto him, 'Ah, poor boy! God hath taken from thee thy outward sight, for what reason He best knoweth: but He hath given thee another sight much more precious, for He hath endued thy soul with the eye of knowledge and faith. God give thee grace continually to pray unto Him, that thou lose not that sight; for then shouldest thou be blind both in body and soul!'

The same night he was committed by the guard, their commission being then expired, unto the custody of the sheriffs of Gloucester, who, with the mayor and aldermen, repaired to Master Hooper's lodging, and took him by the hand.

Unto whom Hooper spake on this manner: 'Master mayor, I give most hearty thanks to you, and to the rest of your brethren, that you have vouchsafed to take me, a prisoner and a condemned man, by the hand; whereby to my rejoicing it is some deal apparent that your old love and friendship towards me is not altogether extinguished; and I trust also that all the things I have taught you in times past are not utterly forgotten, when I was

207

here, by the godly King that dead is, appointed to be your bishop and pastor. For the which most true and sincere doctrine, because I will not now account it falsehood and heresy, as many other men do, I am sent hither (as I am sure you know) by the Queen's commandment to die; and am come where I taught it, to confirm it with my blood. And now, master sheriffs, I understand by these good men, and my very friends' (meaning the guard), 'at whose hands I have found so much favour and gentleness, by the way hitherward, as a prisoner could reasonably require (for the which also I most heartily thank them), that I am committed to your custody, as unto them that must see me brought to-morrow to the place of execution. My request therefore to you shall be only, that there may be a quick fire, shortly to make an end; and in the meantime I will be as obedient unto you, as yourselves would wish. If you think I do amiss in any thing, hold up your finger, and I have done: for I am not come hither as one enforced or compelled to die (for it is well known, I might have had my life with worldly gain); but as one willing to offer and give my life for the truth, rather than consent to the wicked papistical religion of the Bishop of Rome, received and set forth by the magistrates in England, to God's high displeasure and dishonour; and I trust, by God's grace, to-morrow to die a faithful servant of God, and a true obedient subject to the Queen.'

These words used Master Hooper to the mayor, sheriffs, and aldermen, whereat many of them lamented. Notwithstanding the two sheriffs were determined to have lodged him in the common gaol of the town, called Northgate, if the guard had not made earnest intercession for him; who declared, how quietly, mildly, and patiently, he had behaved himself in the way; adding thereto, that any child might keep him well enough, and that they themselves would rather take pains to watch with him, than that he should be sent to the common prison.

So it was determined he should still remain in Robert Ingram's house; and the sheriffs and the sergeants, and other officers, did appoint to watch with him that night themselves. His desire was, that he might go to bed that night betimes, saying, that he had many things to remember: and so he did at five of the clock, and slept one sleep soundly, and bestowed the rest of the night in prayer. After he got up in the morning, he desired that no man should be suffered to come into the chamber, that he might be solitary till the hour of execution.

About eight o'clock came Sir John Bridges, Lord Chandos, with a great band of men, Sir Anthony Kingston, Sir Edmund Bridges, and other commissioners appointed to see execution done. At nine o'clock Master Hooper was willed to prepare himself to be in a readiness, for the time was at hand. Immediately he was brought down from his chamber by the sheriffs, who were accompanied with bills, glaves, and weapons. When he saw the multitude of weapons, he spake to the sheriffs on this wise: 'Master sheriffs,' said he, 'I am no traitor, neither needed you to have made such a business to bring me to the place where I must suffer: for if ye had willed me, I would have gone alone to the stake, and have troubled none of you all.' A multitude of people assembled to the number of seven thousand, for it was market-day, and many came to see his behaviour towards death.

So he went forward, led between the two sheriffs (as it were a lamb to the place of slaughter) in a gown of his host's, his hat upon his head, and a staff in his hand to stay himself withal: for the grief of the sciatica, which he had taken in prison, caused him somewhat to halt. He would look very cheerfully upon such as he knew: and he was never known, during the time of his being amongst them, to look with so cheerful and ruddish a countenance as he did at that present. When he came to the place appointed where he should die, smilingly he beheld the stake and preparation made for him, which was near unto the great elm-tree, over against the college of priests, where he was wont to preach. The place round about the houses, and the boughs of the tree, were replenished with people; and in the chamber over the college-gate stood the wolvish blood-suckers and turnelings, the priests of the college.

Then kneeled he down, forasmuch as he could not be suffered to speak unto the people. After he was somewhat entered into his prayer, a box was brought and laid before him upon a stool, with his pardon (or at least-wise it was feigned to be his pardon) from the Queen, if he would turn. At the sight whereof he cried, 'If you love my soul, away with it! if you love my soul, away with it!'

Prayer being done, he prepared himself to the stake, and put off his host's gown, and delivered it to the sheriffs, requiring them to see it restored unto the owner, and put off the rest of his gear, unto his doublet and hose, wherein he would have burned.

But the sheriffs would not permit that, such was their greediness; unto whose pleasures, good man, he very obediently submitted himself; and his doublet, hose, and petticoat were taken off. Then, being in his shirt, he took a point from his hose himself, and trussed his shirt between his legs, where he had a pound of gunpowder in a bladder, and under each arm the like quantity, delivered him by the guard.

So, desiring the people to say the Lord's prayer with him, and to pray for him (who performed it with tears, during the time of his pains), he went up to the stake. The hoop of iron prepared for his middle was brought, but when they offered to have bound his neck and legs with the other two hoops of iron, he utterly refused them.

Thus being ready, he looked upon all the people, of whom he might be well seen (for he was both tall, and stood also on a high stool), and in every corner there was nothing to be seen but weeping and sorrowful people. Then, lifting up his eyes and hands unto heaven, he prayed to himself. By and by, he that was appointed to make the fire, came to him, and did ask him forgiveness. Of whom he asked why he should forgive him, saying, that he knew never any offence he had committed against him. 'O sir!' said the man, 'I am appointed to make the fire.' 'Therein,' said Master Hooper, 'thou dost nothing offend me; God forgive thee thy sins, and do thine office, I pray thee.'

Then the reeds were cast up, and he received two bundles of them in his own hands, embraced them, kissed them, and put under either arm one of them, and showed with his hand how the rest should be bestowed, and pointed to the place where any did lack.

Anon commandment was given that the fire should be set to. But because there were put to no fewer green faggots than two horses could carry upon their backs, it kindled not by and by, and was a pretty while also before it took the reeds upon the faggots. At length it burned about him, but the wind having full strength in that place (it was a lowering and cold morning), it blew the flame from him, so that he was in a manner nothing but touched by the fire.

Within a space after, a few dry faggots were brought, and a new fire kindled with faggots (for there were no more reeds), and that burned at the nether parts, but had small power above, because of the wind, saving that it did burn his hair, and swell his skin a little. In the time of which fire even as at the first flame, he prayed, saying mildly and not very loud (but as one without pains), 'O Jesus, the Son of David, have mercy upon me, and receive my soul!' After the second was spent, he did wipe both his eyes with his hands, and beholding the people, he said with an indifferent loud voice, 'For God's love, good people, let me have more fire!' And all this while his nether parts did burn: for the faggots were so few, that the flame did not burn strongly at his upper parts.

The third fire was kindled within a while after, which was more extreme than the other two: and then the bladders of gunpowder brake, which did him small good, they were so placed, and the wind had such power. In the which fire he prayed with somewhat a loud voice, 'Lord Jesus, have mercy upon me; Lord Jesus, have mercy upon me: Lord Jesus receive my spirit.' And these were the last words he was heard to utter. But when he was black in the mouth, and his tongue swollen, that he could not speak, yet his lips went till they were shrunk to the gums: and he knocked his breast with his hands, until one of his arms fell off and then knocked still with the other, what time the fat, water, and blood, dropped out at his fingers' ends, until by renewing of the fire his strength was gone, and his hand did cleave fast, in knocking, to the iron upon his breast. So immediately, bowing forwards, he yielded up his spirit.

Thus was he three quarters of an hour or more in the fire. Even as a lamb, patiently he abode the extremity thereof, neither moving forwards, backwards, nor to any side: but he died as quietly as a child in his bed. And he now reigneth, I doubt not, as a blessed martyr in the joys of heaven, prepared for the faithful in Christ before the foundations of the world; for whose constancy all Christians are bound to praise God.

Chapter Nine

DR. ROWLAND TAYLOR,
PARISH CLERGYMAN

THE town of Hadley was one of the first that
received the Word of God in all England. The
Gospel of Christ had such gracious success, and took
such root there, that a great number of that parish
became exceeding well learned in the Holy Scriptures,
as well women as men, so that a man might have
found among them many, that had often read the
whole Bible through, and that could have said a
great sort of St Paul's Epistles by heart, and very
well and readily have given a godly learned sentence
in any matter of controversy. Their children and
servants were also brought up and trained so
diligently in the right knowledge of God's Word,
that the whole town seemed rather a University of
the learned, than a town of cloth-making or
labouring people; and (what most is to be commended) they were for the more part faithful
followers of God's Word in their living.

In this town was Dr Rowland Taylor, who, at his
first entering into his benefice, did not, as the
common sort of beneficed men do, let out his
benefice to a farmer, that shall gather up the profits,
and set in an ignorant unlearned priest to serve the
cure, and, so they have the fleece, little or nothing
care for feeding the flock: but, contrarily, he
forsook the Archbishop of Canterbury, Thomas

Cranmer, with whom he before was in household, and made his parsonal abode in Hadley, among the people committed to his charge; where he, as a good shepherd, dwelling among his sheep, gave himself wholly to the study of holy Scriptures. This love of Christ so wrought in him, that no Sunday nor holy-day passed, nor other time when he might get the people together, but he preached to them the Word of God, the doctrine of their salvation.

Not only was his word a preaching unto them, but all his life and conversation was an example of unfeigned Christian life and true holiness. He was void of all pride, humble and meek, as any child: so that none were so poor but they might boldly, as unto their father, resort unto him; neither was his lowliness childish or fearful, but, as occasion, time, and place required, he would be stout in rebuking the sinful and evil doers; so that none was so rich but he would tell them plainly his fault, with such earnest and grave rebukes as became a good curate and pastor. He was a man very mild, void of all rancour, grudge or evil will; ready to do good to all men; readily forgiving his enemies; and never sought to do evil to any.

To the poor that were blind, lame, sick, bedrid, or that had many children, he was a very father, a careful patron, and diligent provider; insomuch that he caused the parishioners to make a general provision for them: and he himself (beside the continual relief that they always found at his house) gave an honest portion yearly to the common alms-box. His wife also was an honest, discreet, and sober matron, and his children well

215

nurtured, brought up in the fear of God and good learning.

He was a good salt of the earth, savourly biting the corrupt manners of evil men; a light in God's house, set upon a candlestick for all good men to imitate and follow.

Thus continued this good shepherd among his flock, governing and leading them through the wilderness of this wicked world, all the days of the most innocent and holy King of blessed memory, Edward the Sixth. But after it pleased God to take King Edward from this vale of misery unto his most blessed rest, to live with Christ, and reign in everlasting joy and felicity, the papists violently overthrew the true doctrine of the Gospel, and persecuted with sword and fire all those that would not agree to receive again the Roman Bishop as supreme head of the universal Church, and allow all the errors, superstitions, and idolatries, that before by God's Word were disproved and justly condemned.

In the beginning of this rage of Antichrist, a certain petty gentleman, called Foster, conspired with one John Clerk, to bring in the Pope and his idol-worship again into Hadley Church. For as yet Dr Taylor had kept in his church the godly church service and reformation made by King Edward, and most faithfully and earnestly preached against the popish corruptions, which had infected the whole country round about.

Therefore the foresaid Foster and Clerk hired one John Averth, parson of Aldham, a popish idolater, to come to Hadley, and there to begin again the popish mass. To this purpose they builded up with all haste possible the altar, intending to bring in their mass again about Palm Monday. But this their device took none effect; for in the night the altar was beaten down: wherefore they built it up again the second time, and laid diligent watch, lest any should again break it down. On the day following came Foster and John Clerk, bringing with them their popish sacrificer, who brought with him all his implements and garments to play his popish pageant, whom they and their men guarded with swords and bucklers, lest any man should disturb him in his missal sacrifice.

When Dr Taylor, who, according to his custom, sat at his book studying the Word of God, heard the bells ringing, he arose and went into the church, supposing something had been there to be done, according to his pastoral office: and, coming to the church, he found the church doors shut and fast barred, saving the chancel door, which was only latched. Where he, entering in, and coming into the chancel, saw a popish sacrificer in his robes, with a broad new shaven crown, ready to begin his popish sacrifice, beset round about with drawn swords and bucklers, lest any man should approach to disturb him.

Then said Dr Taylor, 'Who made thee so bold to enter into this church of Christ to profane and defile it with this abominable idolatry?' With that started up Foster, and with an ireful and furious countenance said to Dr Taylor, 'Thou traitor! what dost thou here, to let and perturb the Queen's proceedings?' Dr Taylor answered, 'I am no traitor, but I am the shepherd that God, my Lord Christ, hath appointed to feed this flock: wherefore I have good authority to be here; and I command thee, in the name of God, to avoid hence, and not to presume here to poison Christ's flock.'

Then said Foster, 'Wilt thou, traitorly heretic, make a commotion, and resist violently the Queen's proceedings?'

Dr Taylor answered, 'I make no commotion; but it is you papists, that make commotions and tumults. I resist only with God's Word against your popish idolatries, which are against God's Word, the Queen's honour, and tend to the utter subversion of this realm of England.'

Then Foster, with his armed men, took Dr Taylor, and led him with strong hand out of the church; and the popish prelate proceeded in his Romish idolatry. Dr Taylor's wife, who followed her husband into the church, when she saw him thus violently thrust out of his church, kneeled down and held up her hands, and with a loud voice said, 'I beseech God, the righteous Judge, to avenge this injury, that this popish idolater doth to the blood of Christ.' Then they thrust her out of the church also, and shut the doors; for they feared that the people would have rent their sacrificer in pieces.

Thus you see how, without consent of the people, the popish mass was again set up with battle array, with swords and bucklers, with violence and tyranny.

Within a day or two after, with all haste possible, this Foster and Clerk made a complaint of Dr Taylor, by a letter written to Stephen Gardiner, Bishop of Winchester, and Lord Chancellor.

When the bishop heard this, he sent a letter to Dr Taylor, commanding him within certain days to come and appear before him.

When Dr Taylor's friends heard of this, they were exceeding sorry and grieved in mind; which then foreseeing to what end the matter would come, came to him and earnestly counselled him to flee.

Then said Dr Taylor, 'Dear friends, I most heartily thank you, for that you have so tender a care over me. And although I know that there is neither justice nor truth to be looked for at my adversaries's hand, but rather imprisonment and cruel death: yet know I my cause to be so good and righteous, and the truth so strong upon my side, that I will, by God's grace, go and appear before them, and to their beards resist their false doings.'

Then said his friends, 'Master doctor, we think it not best so to do. You have sufficiently done your duty, and testified the truth both by your godly sermons, and also in resisting the parson of Aldham, with others that came hither to bring again the popish mass. And forasmuch as our Saviour Christ willeth and biddeth us, that when they persecute us in one city, we should flee into another: we think, in flying at this time ye should do best, keeping yourself against another time, when the church shall have great need of such diligent teachers, and godly pastors.'

'Oh,' quoth Dr Taylor, 'what will ye have me to do? I am now old, and have already lived too long, to see these terrible and most wicked days. Fly you, and do as your conscience leadeth you; I am fully determined (with God's grace) to go to the bishop, and to his beard to tell him that he doth naught. God shall hereafter raise up teachers of His people, which shall, with much more diligence and fruit, teach them, than I have done. For God will not forsake His church, though now for a time He trieth and correcteth us. As for me, I believe before God, I shall never be able to do God so good service, as I may do now; nor shall I ever have so glorious a calling as I now have, nor so great mercy of God proffered me, as is now at this present. Wherefore I beseech you, and all other my friends, to pray for me; and I doubt not but God will give me strength and His holy Spirit.'

When his friends saw him so constant, and fully determined to go, they, with weeping eyes, commended him unto God.

Dr Taylor, being accompanied with a servant of his own, named John Hull, took his journey towards London. By the way, this John Hull laboured to counsel and persuade him very earnestly to fly, and not come to the Bishop; and proffered himself to go with him to serve him, and in all perils to venture his life for him, and with him. But in no wise would Dr Taylor consent thereunto; but said, 'O John! shall I give place to this thy counsel and worldly persuasion, and leave my flock in this danger. Remember the good shepherd Christ, Which not alone fed His flock, but also died for His flock. Him must I follow, and with God's grace, will do.'

Shortly after Dr Taylor presented himself to the Bishop of Winchester, Stephen Gardiner, then Lord Chancellor of England. Now, when Gardiner saw Dr Taylor, he, according to his custom, reviled him, calling him knave, traitor, heretic, with many other villainous reproaches; all which Dr Taylor heard patiently, and at the last said unto him: 'My lord,' quoth he, 'I am neither traitor nor heretic, but a true subject, and a faithful Christian man; and am come, according to your commandment, to know what is the cause that your lordship hath sent for me.'

Then said the bishop, 'Art thou come, thou villain? How darest thou look me in the face for shame? Knowest thou not who I am?'

'Yes,' quoth Dr Taylor, 'I know who you are. You are Dr Stephen Gardiner, Bishop of Winchester, and Lord Chancellor; and yet but a mortal man, I trow. But if I should be afraid of your lordly looks, why fear you not God, the Lord of us all? How dare ye for shame look any Christian man in the face, seeing ye have forsaken the truth, denied our Saviour Christ and His word, and done contrary to your own oath and writing? With what countenance will ye appear before the judgment-seat of Christ and answer to your oath made first unto King Henry the Eighth of famous memory, and afterward unto King Edward the Sixth his son?'

The bishop answered, 'Tush, tush, that was Herod's oath, unlawful; and therefore worthy to be broken: I have done well in breaking it; and, I thank God, I am come home again to our mother the catholic Church of Rome; and so I would thou shouldest do.'

Dr Tayor answered, 'Should I forsake the Church of Christ, which is founded upon the true foundation of the apostles and prophets, to approve those lies, errors, superstitions, and idolatries, that the Popes and their company at this day so blasphemously do approve? Nay, God forbid. Let the Pope and his return to our Saviour Christ and His Word, and thrust out of the Church such abominable idolatries as he maintaineth, and then will Christian men turn unto him. You wrote truly against him, and were sworn against him.'

'I tell thee,' quoth the Bishop of Winchester, 'it was Herod's oath, unlawful; and therefore ought to be broken, and not kept: and our holy father, the Pope, hath discharged me of it.'

Then said Dr Taylor, 'But you shall not so be discharged before Christ, Who doubtless will require it at your hands, from Whose obedience no man can assoil you, neither the Pope nor any of his.'

'I see,' quoth the Bishop, 'thou art an arrogant knave, and a very fool.'

'My lord,' quoth Dr Taylor, " leave your railing at me, which is not seemly for such a one in authority as you are. For I am a Christian man, and you know, that 'he that saith to his brother, Raca, is in danger of a council; and he that saith, Thou fool, is in danger of hell fire.'

Then said the bishop, 'Thou hast resisted the Queen's proceedings, and wouldest not suffer the parson of Aldham (a very virtuous and devout priest) to say mass in Hadley.'

Dr Taylor answered, 'My lord, I am parson of Hadley; and it is against all right, conscience, and laws, that any man should come into my charge, and presume to infect the flock committed unto me, with venom of the popish idolatrous mass.'

With that the bishop waxed very angry, and said, 'Thou art a blasphemous heretic indeed, that blasphemest the blessed sacrament: and speakest against the holy mass, which is made a sacrifice for the quick and the dead.'

Dr Taylor answered, 'Nay, I blaspheme not the blessed sacrament which Christ instituted, but I reverence it as a true Christian man ought to do; and confess, that Christ ordained the holy communion in the remembrance of His death and passion. Christ gave Himself to die for our redemption upon the cross, Whose body there offered was the propitiatory sacrifice, full, perfect, and sufficient unto salvation, for all them that believe in Him. And this sacrifice did our Saviour Christ offer in His own person Himself once for all, neither can any priest any more offer Him, nor need we any more propitiatory sacrifice.'

Then called the bishop his men, and said, 'Have this fellow hence, and carry him to the King's Bench, and charge the keeper he be straitly kept.'

Then kneeled Dr Taylor down, and held up both his hands, and said, 'Good Lord, I thank thee; and from the tyranny of the Bishop of Rome, and all his detestable errors, idolatries, and abominations, good Lord deliver us: and God be praised for good King Edward.'

Dr Taylor lay prisoner almost two years. He spent all his time in prayer, reading the holy Scriptures, writing, preaching, and exhorting the prisoners, and such as resorted to him, to repentance and amendment of life.

On the 22nd of January 1555, Dr Taylor, and Master Bradford and Master Saunders, were again called to appear before the Bishop of Winchester, the Bishops of Norwich, London, Salisbury, and Durham; and there were charged again with heresy and schism: and therefore a determinate answer was required; whether they would submit themselves to the Roman Bishop, and abjure their errors; or else they would, according to the laws, proceed to their condemnation.

When Dr Taylor and his fellows heard this, they answered stoutly and boldly, that they would not depart from the truth which they had preached in King Edward's days, neither would they submit themselves to the Romish Antichrist; but they thanked God for so great mercy, that he would call them to be worthy to suffer for His Word and truth.

When the bishops saw them so boldly, constantly, and unmovably fixed in the truth, they read the sentence of death upon them.

Dr Taylor was committed to the Clink, and when the keeper brought him toward the prison, the people flocked about to gaze upon him: unto whom he said, 'God be praised, good people, I am come away from them undefiled, and will confirm the truth with my blood.' So was he bestowed in the Clink till it was toward night; and then he was removed to the Compter by the Poultry.

When Dr Taylor had lain in the said Compter a seven-night or thereabouts prisoner, the 4th of February, A.D. 1555, Edmund Bonner, Bishop of London, with others, came to degrade him, bringing with them such ornaments as do appertain to their massing-mummery. He called for Dr Taylor to be brought unto him; and at his coming, the bishop said, 'Master doctor, I would you would remember yourself, and turn to your mother, holy church; so may you do well enough, and I will sue for your pardon.'

Whereunto Master Taylor answered, 'I would you and your fellows would turn to Christ. As for me, I will not turn to Antichrist.'

'Well,' quoth the bishop, 'I am come to degrade you: wherefore put on these vestures.'

'No,' quoth Dr Taylor, 'I will not.'

'Wilt thou not?' said the bishop. 'I shall make thee ere I go.'

Quoth Dr Taylor, 'You shall not, by the grace of God.'

Then he charged him upon his obedience to do it: but he would not do it for him; so he willed another to put them upon his back. And when he was thoroughly furnished therewith, he set his hands to his side, walking up and down, and said, 'How say you, my lord? am not I a goodly fool? How say you, my masters? If I were in Cheap, should I not have boys enough to laugh at these apish toys, and toying trumpery?'

So the bishop scraped his fingers, thumbs, and the crown of his head.

At the last, when he should have given Dr Taylor a stroke on the breast with his crosier-staff, the bishop's chaplain said: 'My lord! strike him not, for he will sure strike again.' 'Yea, by St Peter will I,' quoth Dr Taylor. 'The cause is Christ's, and I were no good Christian, if I would not fight in my Master's quarrel.' So the bishop laid his curse upon him, but struck him not. Then Dr Taylor said, 'Though you do curse me, yet God doth bless me. I have the witness of my conscience, that ye have done me wrong and violence: and yet I pray God, if it be his will, to forgive you. But from the tyranny of the Bishop of Rome, and his detestable enormities, good Lord deliver us!' And when he came up to his chamber he told Master Bradford (for they both lay in one chamber), that he had made the Bishop of London afraid : 'for,' saith he laughingly, 'his chaplain gave him counsel not to strike me with his crosier-staff, for that I would strike again ; and, by my troth,' said he, rubbing his hands, 'I made him believe I would do so indeed.'

The night after that he was degraded, his wife and his son Thomas and John Hull, his servant, resorted unto him, and were, by the gentleness of the keepers, permitted to sup with him. At their coming-in, they kneeled down and prayed, saying the litany. After supper walking up and down, he gave God thanks for His grace, that had given him strength to abide by His holy word. With tears they prayed together, and kissed one the other. Unto his son Thomas he gave a Latin book, containing the notable sayings of the old martyrs, and in the end of that he wrote his testament :

'I say to my wife, and to my children, The Lord gave you unto me, and the Lord hath taken me from you, and you from me : blessed be the name of the Lord ! I believe that they are blessed which die in the Lord. God careth for sparrows, and for the hairs of our heads. I have ever found Him more faithful and favourable, than is any father or husband. Trust ye therefore in Him by the means of our dear Saviour Christ's merits : believe, love, fear and obey Him : pray to Him, for He hath promised to help. Count me not dead, for I shall certainly live, and never die. I go before, and you shall follow after, to our long home.

I say to my dear friends of Hadley, and to all others which have heard me preach ; that I depart hence with a quiet conscience, as touching my doctrine, for the which I pray you thank God with me. For I have, after my little talent, declared to others those lessons that I gathered out of God's book, the blessed Bible. Therefore if I, or an angel from heaven, should preach to you any other Gospel than that ye have received, God's great curse upon that preacher!

Departing hence in sure hope, without all doubting of eternal salvation, I thank God my heavenly Father, through Jesus Christ my certain Saviour.'

On the morrow the sheriff of London with his officers came to the Compter by two o'clock in the morning, and brought forth Dr Taylor; and without any light led him to the Woolsack, an inn without Aldgate. Dr Taylor's wife, suspecting that her husband should that night be carried away, watched all night in St Botolph's church-porch beside Aldgate, having her two children, the one named Elizabeth, of thirteen years of age (whom, being left without father or mother, Dr Taylor had brought up of alms from three years old), the other named Mary, Dr Taylor's own daughter.

Now, when the sheriff and his company came against St Botolph's church, Elizabeth cried, saying, 'O my dear father! mother, mother, here is my father led away.' Then cried his wife, 'Rowland, Rowland, where art thou?'—for it was a very dark morning, that the one could not well see the other. Dr Taylor answered, 'Dear wife, I am here;' and staid. The sheriff's men would have led him forth; but the sheriff said, 'Stay a little, masters, I pray you; and let him speak to his wife:' and so they staid.

Then came she to him, and he took his daughter Mary in his arms: and he, his wife, and Elizabeth kneeled down and said the Lord's prayer. At which sight the sheriff wept apace, and so did divers others of the company. After they had prayed, he rose up and kissed his wife, and shook her by the hand, and said, 'Farewell, my dear wife; be of good comfort, for I am quiet in my conscience. God shall stir up a father for my children.' And then he kissed his daughter Mary, and said, 'God bless thee, and make thee His servant:' and kissing Elizabeth, he said, 'God bless thee; I pray you all stand strong and steadfast unto Christ and His Word.' Then said his wife, 'God be with thee, dear Rowland; I will, with God's grace, meet thee at Hadley.'

And so was he led forth to the Woolsack, and his wife followed him. As soon as they came to the Woolsack, he was put into a chamber, wherein he was kept with four yeomen of the guard, and the sheriff's men. Dr Taylor, as soon as he was come into the chamber, fell down on his knees and gave himself wholly to prayer. The sheriff then, seeing Dr Taylor's wife there, would in no case grant her to speak any more with her husband, but gently desired her to go to his house, and take it as her own, and promised her she should lack nothing, and sent two officers to conduct her thither. Notwithstanding she desired to go to her mother's, whither the officers led her, and charged her mother to keep her there till they came again.

Thus remained Dr Taylor in the Woolsack, kept by the sheriff and his company, till eleven o'clock; at which time the sheriff of Essex was ready to receive: and so they set him on horseback within the inn, the gates being shut.

At the coming out of the gates, John Hull, before spoken of, stood at the rails with Thomas, Dr Taylor's son. When Dr Taylor saw them, he called them, saying, 'Come hither, my son Thomas.' And John Hull lifted the child up, and set him on the horse before his father: and Dr Taylor put off his hat, and said to the people that stood there looking on him, 'Good people, this is mine own son.' Then lifted he up his eyes towards heaven, and prayed for his son; laid his hat upon the child's head and blessed him; and so delivered the child to John Hull, whom he took by the hand and said, 'Farewell, John Hull, the faithfullest servant that ever man had.' And so they rode forth, the sheriff of Essex, with four yeomen of the guard, and the sheriff's men leading him.

And so they came to Brentwood, where they caused to be made for Dr Taylor a close hood, with two holes for his eyes to look out at, and a slit for his mouth to breathe at. This they did, that no man should know him, nor he speak to any man: which practice they used also with others. They feared lest, if the people should have heard them speak, or have seen them, they might have been much more strengthened by their godly exhortations, to stand steadfast in God's Word, and to fly the superstitions and idolatries of the papacy.

All the way Dr Taylor was joyful and merry, as one that accounted himself going to a most pleasant banquet or bridal. He spake many notable things to the sheriff and yeomen of the guard that conducted him, and often moved them to weep, through his much earnest calling upon them to repent, and to amend their evil and wicked living. Oftentimes also he caused them to wonder and rejoice, to see him so constant and steadfast, void of all fear, joyful in heart, and glad to die.

At Chelmsford met them the sheriff of Suffolk, there to receive him, and to carry him forth into Suffolk. And being at supper, the sheriff of Essex very earnestly laboured him to return to the popish religion, thinking with fair words to persuade him; and said, 'Good master doctor! we are right sorry for you. God hath given you great learning and wisdom; wherefore ye have been in great favour and reputation in times past with the council and highest of this realm. Besides this, ye are a man of goodly personage, in your best strength, and by nature like to live many years. Ye are well beloved of all men, as well for your virtues as for your learning: and me thinketh it were great pity you should cast away yourself willingly, and so come to such a painful and shameful death. Ye should do much better to revoke your opinions. I and all these your friends will be suitors for your pardon; which, no doubt, ye shall obtain.'

Dr Taylor staid a little, as one studying what answer he might give. At the last thus he said, 'Master sheriff, and my masters all, I heartily thank you for your good-will: I have hearkened to your words, and marked well your counsels. And to be plain with you, I do perceive that I have been deceived myself, and am like to deceive a great many of Hadley of their expectation.'

With that word they all rejoiced. 'Yea, good master doctor,' quoth the sheriff, 'God's blessing on your heart! hold you there still. It is the comfortablest word that we heard you speak yet. What!

should ye cast away yourself in vain? Play a wise man's part, and I dare warrant it, ye shall find favour.' Thus they rejoiced very much at the word, and were very merry. At the last, 'Good master doctor,' quoth the sheriff, 'what meant ye by this, that ye say ye think ye have been deceived yourself, and think ye shall deceive many a one in Hadley?'

'Would ye know my meaning plainly?' quoth he.

'Yea,' quoth the sheriff, 'good master doctor, tell it us plainly.'

Then said Dr Taylor, 'I will tell you how I have been deceived, and, as I think, I shall deceive a great many. I am, as you see, a man that hath a very great carcase, which I thought should have been buried in Hadley churchyard, if I had died in my bed, as I well hoped I should have done; but herein I see I was deceived: and there are a great number of worms in Hadley churchyard, which should have had jolly feeding upon this carrion, which they have looked for many a day. But now I know we be deceived, both I and they; for this carcase must be burnt to ashes: and so shall they lose their bait and feeding, that they looked to have had of it.'

When the sheriff and his company heard him say so, they were amazed, and looked one on another, marvelling at the man's constant mind, that thus, without all fear, made but a jest at the cruel torment and death now at hand prepared for him. Thus was their expectation clean disappointed.

At Lavenham, there came to him a great number of gentlemen and justices upon great horses, which all were appointed to aid the sheriff. These gentlemen laboured Dr Taylor very sore to reduce him to the Romish religion, promising him his pardon, 'which,' said they, 'we have here for you.' They promised him great promotions, yea, a bishopric, if he would take it: but all their labour and flattering words were in vain.

Coming within two miles of Hadley, Dr Taylor desired to light off his horse: which done, he leaped, and fet a frisk or twain, as men commonly do in dancing. 'Why, master doctor,' quoth the sheriff, 'how do you now?' He answered: 'Well, God be praised, good master sheriff, never better: for now I know I am almost at home. I lack not past two stiles to go over, and I am even at my Father's house.—But, master sheriff,' said he, 'shall we not go through Hadley?' 'Yes,' said the sheriff, 'you shall go through Hadley.' Then said he, 'O Lord! I thank Thee, I shall yet once or I die see my flock, whom Thou, Lord, knowest I have most heartily loved and truly taught. Lord! bless them, and keep them steadfast in Thy Word and truth.'

When they were now come to Hadley, and came riding over the bridge, at the bridge-foot waited a poor man with five small children; who, when he saw Dr Taylor, he and his children fell down upon their knees, and held up their hands, and cried with a loud voice, and said, 'O dear Father and good shepherd, Dr Taylor? God help and succour thee, as thou hast many a time succoured me and my poor children.'

The streets of Hadley were beset on both sides the way with men and women who waited to see him; whom when they beheld so led to death, with weeping eyes and lamentable voices they cried, saying one to another, 'Ah, Lord! there goeth our good shepherd from us, that so faithfully hath taught us, so fatherly hath cared for us, and so godly hath governed us. O merciful God! what shall we poor scattered lambs do? What shall come of this most wicked world? Lord strengthen him, and comfort him.'

And Dr Taylor evermore said to the people, 'I have preached to you God's Word and truth, and am come this day to seal it with my blood.'

Coming against the almshouses, which he well knew, he cast to the poor people money which remained of that which had been given him in time of his imprisonment. As for his living, they took it from him at his first going to prison, so that he was sustained all the time of his imprisonment by the charitable alms of good people that visited him. Therefore, the money that now remained he put in a glove and gave it to the poor almsmen standing at their doors to see him. And, coming to the last of the almshouses, and not seeing the poor that there dwelt, ready at their doors, as the other were, he asked: 'Is the blind man and blind woman, that dwelt here, alive?' It was answered, 'Yea, they are there within.' Then threw he glove and all in at the window.

Thus this good father and provider for the poor now took his leave of those, for whom all his life he had a singular care and study.

At the last, coming to Aldham-common, the place assigned where he should suffer, and seeing a great multitude of people gathered thither, he asked, 'What place is this, and what meaneth it that so much people are gathered hither?' It was answered, 'It is Aldham-common, the place where you must

suffer: and the people are come to look upon you.'
Then said he, 'Thanked be God, I am even at
home;' and so alighted from his horse, and with
both his hands rent the hood from his head.

When the people saw his reverend face, with a
long white beard, they burst out with weeping tears,
and cried, saying 'God save thee, good Dr Taylor!
Jesus Christ strengthen thee and help thee; the
Holy Ghost comfort thee.' Then would he have
spoken to the people, but the yeomen of the guard
were so busy about him, that as soon as he opened
his mouth, one or other thrust a tipstaff into his
mouth, and would in nowise permit him.

Dr Taylor thereupon sat down, and seeing one
named Soyce, called him and said, 'Soyce, I pray
thee come and pull off my boots, and take them for
thy labour. Thou hast long looked for them, now
take them.' Then rose he up, and put off his
clothes unto his shirt, and gave them away: which
done, he said with a loud voice, 'Good people! I
have taught you nothing but God's holy Word, and
those lessons that I have taken out of God's blessed
book, the holy Bible: and I am come hither this
day to seal it with my blood.' With that word,
Homes, yeoman of the guard, who had used Dr
Taylor very cruelly all the way, gave him a great
stroke upon the head. Then he kneeled down and
prayed, and a poor woman that was among the
people, stepped in and prayed with him: but her
they thrust away, and threatened to tread her down
with horses: notwithstanding she would not remove,
but abode and prayed with him. He went to the
stake, and kissed it, and set himself into a pitchbarrel, which they had set for him and so stood

with his back upright against the stake, with his hands folded together, and his eyes toward heaven, and so he continually prayed.

Then they bound him with chains, and the sheriff called one Richard Donningham, a butcher, and commanded him to set up faggots: but he refused to do it, and said, 'I am lame, sir; and not able to lift a faggot.' The sheriff threatened to send him to prison; notwithstanding he would not do it.

Then appointed he Mulleine, Soyce, Warwick, and Robert King, to set up the faggots, and to make the fire, which they most diligently did. Warwick cruelly cast a faggot at him, which lit upon his head, and brake his face, that the blood ran down his visage. Then said Dr Taylor, 'O friend, I have harm enough; what needed that?'

Furthermore, Sir John Shelton there standing by, as Dr Taylor was saying the psalm 'Miserere,' in English, struck him on the lips: 'Ye knave,' said he, 'speak Latin: I will make thee.'

At the last they set to fire; and Dr Taylor, holding up both his hands, called upon God, and said, 'Merciful Father of heaven, for Jesus Christ my Saviour's sake, receive my soul into Thy hands.' So stood he still without either crying or moving, with his hands folded together, till Soyce with a halbert struck him on the head that the brains fell out, and the corpse fell into the fire.

Chapter Ten

THE MARTYRS OF SCOTLAND

LIKE as there was no place, either of Germany, Italy, or France, wherein there were not some branches sprung out of that most fruitful root of Luther; so likewise was not this isle of Britain without his fruit and branches. Amongst whom was Patrick Hamilton, a Scotsman born of high and noble stock, and of the king's blood, of excellent towardness, twenty-three years of age, called abbot of Ferne. Coming out of his country with three companions to seek godly learning, he went to the University of Marburg in Germany, which University was then newly erected by Philip, Landgrave of Hesse. Using conference with learned men, especially with Frances Lambert, he so profited in knowledge and judgment that, through the incitation of the said Lambert, he was the first in all that University who publicly did set up conclusions there to be disputed of, concerning faith and works. Which young man, if he had chosen to lead his life after the manner of other courtiers, in all kind of licentious riotousness, should peradventure have found praise without peril or punishment; but, forsomuch as he joined godliness with his stock, and virtue with his age, he could by no means escape the hands of the wicked. For there is nothing safe or sure in this world but wickedness and sin.

Whoever saw the cardinals or bishops rage with their cruel inquisitions against riot, ambition, unlawful gaming, drunkenness, and rapines? But if any man were truly addict to the desire and study of godliness, confessing Christ to be his only patron and advocate, excluding the merits of saints, acknowledging free justification by faith in Christ, denying purgatory (for these articles Hamilton was burned), they spare neither age nor kindred, neither is there any so great power in the world, that may withstand their majesty or authority.

How great an ornament might so noble, learned, and excellent a young man have been unto that realm, being endued with so great godliness, and such a singular wit and disposition, if the Scots had not envied their own commodity!

This learned Patrick, increasing daily more and more in knowledge, and inflamed with godliness, at length began to revolve with himself touching his return into his country, being desirous to impart unto his countrymen some fruit of understanding which he had received abroad. Whereupon, persisting in his godly purpose, he took one of the three whom he brought out of Scotland, and so returned home without any longer delay. Not sustaining the miserable ignorance and blindness of that people, he valiantly taught and preached the truth, was accused of heresy, and, stoutly sustaining the quarrel of God's Gospel against the high priest and Archbishop of St Andrew's, named James Beaton, was cited to appear before him and his college of priests on the 1st of March, A.D. 1527. Being not only forward in knowledge, but also ardent in spirit, not tarrying for the hour appointed, he came very early in the morning before he was looked for; and there mightily disputing against them, when he could not by the Scriptures be convicted, by force he was oppressed. And so the sentence of condemnation being given against him, the same day after dinner, in all hot haste, he was had away to the fire, and there burned.

And thus was this noble Hamilton, the blessed servant of God, without all just cause, made away by cruel adversaries, yet not without great fruit to the Church of Christ; for the grave testimony of his blood left the truth of God more fixed and confirmed in the hearts of many than ever could after be plucked away: insomuch that divers afterwards, standing in his quarrel, sustained the like martyrdom.

Within a few years after the martyrdom of Master Patrick Hamilton, one Henry Forest, a young man born in Linlithgow, who, a little before, had received the orders of Benet and Collet (as they term them), affirmed that Master Patrick Hamilton died a martyr. For this he was apprehended, and put in prison by James Beaton, Archbishop of St Andrew's, who, shortly after, caused a certain friar, named Walter Laing, to hear his confession. When Henry Forest had declared his conscience, how he thought Master Patrick to be a good man and not heretical, and wrongfully to be put to death, the friar came and uttered to the bishop the confession that he had heard, which before was not thoroughly known. Hereupon it followed that, his confession being brought as sufficient probation against him, Henry Forest was concluded to be a heretic, equal in iniquity with Master Patrick Hamilton, and given to the secular judges, to suffer death.

When the day came for his death, and that he should first be degraded, he was brought before the clergy in a green place, being between the castle of St Andrew and another place called Monymaill. As soon as he entered in at the door, and saw the faces of the clergy, perceiving whereunto they tended, he cried with a loud voice, saying, 'Fie on falsehood! Fie on false friars, revealers of confession! After this day let no man ever trust any false friars, contemners of God's Word, and deceivers of men!' After his degradation, he suffered death for his faithful testimony of the truth of Christ and of His Gospel, at the north church-stile of the abbey church of St Andrew, to the intent that all the people of Forfar might see the fire, and so might be the more feared from falling into the doctrine which they term heresy.

Within a year after the martyrdom of Henry Forest, or thereabout, James Hamilton, of Linlithgow; his sister Katherine Hamilton, the spouse of the captain of Dunbar; also another honest woman of Leith; David Straton, of the house of Lauriston; and Master Norman Gurley were called to the abbey church of Holyrood House in Edinburgh, by James Hay, Bishop of Ross, commissioner to James Beaton, Archbishop, in presence of King James the Fifth, who was altogether clad in red apparel. James Hamilton was accused as one that maintained the opinion of Master Patrick his brother; to whom the King gave counsel to depart, and not to appear: for in case he appeared, he could not help him; because the bishops had persuaded the King, that the cause of heresy did in no wise appertain unto *him*. And so Hamilton fled, and was condemned as a heretic, and all his goods and lands confiscated.

Katherine Hamilton, his sister, appeared upon the

scaffold, and being accused of a horrible heresy, to wit, that her own works could not save her, she granted the same; and after a long reasoning between her and Master John Spens, the lawyer, she concluded in this manner, 'Work here, work there; what kind of working is all this? I know perfectly, that no kind of works can save me, but only the works of Christ my Lord and Saviour.' The King, hearing these words, turned him about and laughed, called her unto him, and caused her to recant, because she was his aunt.

Master Norman Gurley was accused for that he said there was no such thing as purgatory, and that the Pope was not a bishop but Antichrist, and had no jurisdiction in Scotland. Also David Straton, for that he said, there was no purgatory, but the passion of Christ, and the tribulations of this world. And because, when Master Robert Lawson, vicar of Eglesgrig, asked his tithe-fish of him, he did cast them to him out of the boat, so that some of them fell into the sea; therefore he accused him, as one that should have said, that no tithes should be paid. These two, because, after great solicitation made by the King, they refused to abjure and recant, were condemned by the Bishop of Ross as heretics, and were burned upon the green side, between Leith and Edinburgh, to the intent that the inhabitants of Fife, seeing the fire, might be struck with terror and fear, not to fall into the like.

Not long after the burning of David Straton and Master Gurley, a canon of St Colm's Inche, and vicar of Dolor, called Dean Thomas Forret, preached every Sunday to his parishioners out of the Epistle or Gospel as it fell for the time; which then was a great novelty in Scotland, to see any man preach, except a black friar or a grey friar: and therefore the friars envied him, and accused him to the Bishop of Dunkeld (in whose diocese he remained) as a heretic, and one that showed the mysteries of the Scriptures to the vulgar people in English, to make the clergy detestable in the sight of the people. The Bishop of Dunkeld, moved by the friars' instigation, called the said Dean Thomas, and said to him, 'My joy, Dean Thomas, I love you well, and therefore I must give you my counsel, how you shall rule and guide yourself.' To whom Thomas said, 'I thank your lordship heartily.' Then the Bishop began his counsel after this manner:

Bishop: 'My joy, Dean Thomas! I am informed that you preach the Epistle or Gospel every Sunday to your parishioners, and that you take not the cow nor the uppermost cloth from your parishioners, which thing is very prejudicial to the churchmen; and therefore, my joy, Dean Thomas, I would you took your cow, and your uppermost cloth, as other churchmen do; or else it is too much to preach every Sunday: for in so doing you may make the people think that we should preach likewise. But it is enough for you, when you find any good Epistle, or any good Gospel, that setteth forth the liberty of the holy Church, to preach that, and let the rest be.'

The Martyr: 'My lord, I think that none of my parishioners will complain that I take not the cow, nor the uppermost cloth, but will gladly give me the same, together with any other thing that they have; and I will give and communicate with them any thing that I have; and so, my lord, we agree right well, and there is no discord among us. And whereas your lordship saith, It is too much to preach every Sunday, indeed I think it is too little, and also would wish that your lordship did the like.'

Bishop: 'Nay, nay, Dean Thomas, let that be, for we are not ordained to preach.'

Martyr: 'Whereas your lordship biddeth me preach when I find any good epistle, or a good Gospel, truly, my lord, I have read the New Testament and the Old, and all the epistles and the Gospels, and among them all I could never find an evil epistle, or an evil Gospel: but, if your lordship will show me the good epistle, and the good Gospel, and the evil epistle and the evil Gospel, then I shall preach the good, and omit the evil.'

Bishop: Then spake my lord stoutly and said, 'I thank God that I never knew what the Old and New Testament was; therefore, Dean Thomas, I will know nothing but my portuese and my pontifical. Go your way, and let be all these fantasies; for if you persevere in these erroneous opinions, you will repent it, when you may not mend it.'

Martyr: 'I trust my cause be just in the presence of God, and therefore I pass not much what do follow thereupon.'

And so my lord and he departed at that time. And soon after a summons was directed from the Cardinal of St Andrews and the Bishop of Dunkeld, upon the said Dean Thomas Forret, and others; who, at the day of their appearance, were condemned to the death without any place for recantation, because (as was alleged) they were heresiarchs, or chief heretics and teachers of heresies; and, especially, because many of them were at the marriage of a priest, who was vicar of Tulibothy beside Stirling, and did eat flesh in Lent at the said bridal. And so they were all together burned upon the Castle Hill at Edinburgh.

There was a certain Act of Parliament made in the government of the Lord Hamilton, Earl of Arran, giving privilege to all men of the realm of Scotland, to read the Scriptures in their mother tongue; secluding nevertheless all reasoning, conference, convocation of people to hear the Scriptures read or expounded. Which liberty of private reading lacked not its own fruit, so that in sundry parts of Scotland were opened the eyes of the elect of God to see the truth, and abhor the papistical abominations; amongst whom were certain persons in St John's-town.

At this time there was a sermon made by friar Spence, in St John's-town, otherwise called Perth, affirming prayer made to saints to be so necessary, that without it there could be no hope of salvation to man. This blasphemous doctrine a burgess of the said town, called Robert Lamb, could not abide, but accused him, in open audience, of erroneous doctrine, and adjured him, in God's name, to utter the truth. This the friar, being stricken with fear, promised to do; but the trouble, tumult, and stir of the people increased so, that the friar could have no audience.

At this time, A.D. 1543, the enemies of the truth procured John Charterhouse, who favoured the truth, and was provost of the said city and town of Perth, to be deposed from his office by the said governor's authority, and a papist, called Master Alexander Marbeck, to be chosen in his room, that they might bring the more easily their wicked and ungodly enterprise to an end.

On St Paul's day came to St John's-town, the Governor, the cardinal, the Earl of Argyle, with certain other of the nobility. And although there were many accused for the crime of heresy (as they term it), yet these persons only were apprehended: Robert Lamb, William Anderson, James Hunter, James Raveleson, James Finlason, and Helen Stirke his wife, and were cast that night in the Spay Tower.

Upon the morrow, when they were brought forth to judgment, were laid to their charge, the violating of the Act of Parliament before expressed, and their conference and assemblies in hearing and expounding of Scripture against the tenor of the said Act. Robert Lamb was accused, in special, for interrupting the friar in the pulpit; which he not only confessed, but also affirmed constantly, that it was the duty of no man, who understood and knew the truth, to hear the same impugned without contradiction; and therefore sundry who were there present in judgment, who hid the knowledge of the truth, should bear the burden in God's presence, for consenting to the same.

The said Robert also, with William Anderson and James Raveleson, were accused for hanging up the image of St Francis in a cord, nailing of rams' horns to his head, and a cow's rump to his tail, and for eating of a goose on Allhallow-even.

James Hunter, being a simple man and without learning, and a flesher by occupation, so that he could be charged with no great knowledge in doctrine, yet, because he often used that suspected company of the rest, was accused.

The woman Helen Stirke was accused, for that in her childbed she was not accustomed to call upon the name of the Virgin Mary, being exhorted thereto by her neighbours, but only upon God for Jesus Christ's sake; and because she said that if she herself had been in the time of the Virgin Mary, God might have looked to her humility and base estate, as He did to the Virgin's, in making her the mother of Christ: thereby meaning, that there were no merits in the Virgin, which procured her that honour, to be made the mother of Christ, and to be preferred before other women, but that only God's free mercy exalted her to that estate: which words were counted most execrable in the face of the clergy, and of the whole multitude.

James Raveleson aforesaid, building a house, set upon the round of his fourth stair the three-crowned diadem of Peter carved of tree, which the cardinal took as done in mockage of his cardinal's hat. After sentence given, their hands were bound, and the men cruelly treated: which thing the woman beholding, desired likewise to be bound by the sergeants with her husband for Christ's sake.

There was great intercession made by the town for the life of these persons to the Governor, who of himself was willing that they might have been delivered: but he was so subject to the appetite of the cruel priests, that he could not do that which he would. Yea, they menaced to assist his enemies and to depose him, except he assisted their cruelty.

The martyrs were carried by a great band of

armed men (for they feared rebellion in the town except they had their men of war) to the place of execution, which was common to all thieves, and that to make their cause appear more odious to the people. Every one comforting another, and assuring themselves that they should sup together in the Kingdom of Heaven that night, they commended themselves to God, and died constantly in the Lord.

The woman desired earnestly to die with her husband, but she was not suffered; yet, following him to the place of execution, she gave him comfort, exhorting him to perseverance and patience for Christ's sake, and, parting from him with a kiss, said, 'Husband, rejoice, for we have lived together many joyful days; but this day, in which we must die, ought to be most joyful unto us both, because we must have joy for ever; therefore I will not bid you good night, for we shall suddenly meet with joy in the Kingdom of Heaven.' The woman, after that, was taken to a place to be drowned, and albeit she had a child sucking on her breast, yet this moved nothing the unmerciful hearts of the enemies. So, after she had commended her children to the neighbours of the town for God's sake, and the sucking bairn was given to the nurse, she sealed up the truth by her death.

With most tender affection consider, gentle reader, the uncharitable manner of the accusation of Master George Wishart, made by the bloody enemies of Christ's faith. Ponder the furious rage and tragical cruelness of the malignant Church, in persecuting this blessed man of God; and, on the contrary, his humble, patient, and most godly answers made to them without all fear, not having respect to their boastful menacings and boisterous threats, but charitably and without stop of tongue answering, not changing his visage.

I thought it not impertinent somewhat to touch concerning the life and conversation of this godly man, according as of late it came to my hands, certified in writing by a certain scholar of his, named Emery Tylney, whose words here follow:

About the year of our Lord 1543, there was, in the University of Cambridge, one Master George Wishart, commonly called Master George of Benet's College, a man of tall stature, polled-headed, and on the same a round French cap of the best; judged to be of melancholy complexion by his physiognomy, black haired, long bearded, comely of personage, well spoken after his country of Scotland, courteous, lowly, lovely, glad to teach, desirous to learn, and well travelled; having on him for his clothing a frieze gown to the shoes, a black millian fustian doublet, and plain black hosen, coarse new canvass for his shirts, and white falling bands and cuffs at his hands.

He was a man modest, temperate, fearing God, hating covetousness; for his charity had never end, night, noon, nor day; he forbare one meal in three, one day in four for the most part, except something to comfort nature. He lay hard upon a puff of straw and coarse new canvass sheets, which, when he changed, he gave away. He had commonly by his bed-side a tub of water, in the which (his people being in bed, the candle put out and all quiet) he used to bathe himself. He loved me tenderly, and

I him. He taught with great modesty and gravity, so that some of his people thought him severe, and would have slain him; but the Lord was his defence. And he, after due correction for their malice, by good exhortation amended them and went his way. Oh that the Lord had left him to me, his poor boy, that he might have finished that he had begun! for he went into Scotland with divers of the nobility, that came for a treaty to King Henry.

If I should declare his love to me and all men; his charity to the poor, in giving, relieving, caring, helping, providing, yea, infinitely studying how to do good unto all, and hurt to none, I should sooner want words, than just cause to commend him.

To the said Master George, being in captivity in the Castle of St Andrews, the Dean of the same town was sent by the commandment of the cardinal and by his wicked counsel, and there summoned the said Master George, that he should, upon the morning following, appear before the judge, then and there to give account of his seditious and heretical doctrine.

Upon the next morning, the lord cardinal caused his servants to address themselves in their most warlike array, with jack, knapskal, splent, spear, and axe, more seeming for the war, than for the preaching of the true Word of God. And when these armed champions, marching in warlike order, had conveyed the bishops into the Abbey Church, incontinently they sent for Master George, who was conveyed unto the said church by the captain of the Castle, accompanied with a hundred men, addressed in manner aforesaid. Like a lamb led they him to sacrifice. As he entered in at the Abbey Church door, there was a poor man lying, vexed with great infirmities, asking of his alms, to whom he flung his purse. And when he came before the lord cardinal, the sub-prior of the Abbey, called Dane John Winryme, stood up in the pulpit, and made a sermon to all the congregation there assembled.

And when he ended his sermon, they caused Master George to ascend into the pulpit, there to hear his accusation. And right against him stood up one of the fed flock, a monster, John Lander, laden full of cursings written in paper: the which he took out—a roll, long and full of threats, maledictions, and words of devilish spite and malice, saying to the innocent Master George so many cruel and abominable words, and hitting him so spitefully with the Pope's thunder, that the ignorant people dreaded lest the earth would have swallowed him up quick. Notwithstanding Master George stood still with great patience, hearing their sayings, not once moving or changing his countenance.

When that this fed sow had read all his lying menacings, his face running down with sweat, and frothing at the mouth like a boar, he spit at Master George's face, saying, 'What answerest thou to these sayings, thou runnagate! traitor! thief! which we have duly proved by sufficient witness against thee?' Master George, hearing this, kneeled down upon his knees in the pulpit. When he had ended his prayer, sweetly and Christianly he answered to them all in this manner:

'It is just and reasonable, that your discretions should know what my words and doctrine are, and what I have ever taught, that I perish not unjustly, to the great peril of your souls. Wherefore, both for the glory and honour of God, your own health, and safeguard of my life, I beseech your discretions to hear me; and, in the mean time, I shall recite my doctrine without any colour.'

Suddenly with a high voice cried the accuser, the fed sow, 'Thou heretic, runnagate, traitor, and thief! it was not lawful for thee to preach. Thou hast taken the power at thine own hand, without any authority of the Church.'

Then all the congregation of the prelates, with their complices, said: 'If we give him license to preach, he is so crafty, and in the holy Scripture so exercised, that he will persuade the people to his opinion, and raise them against us.'

Master George, seeing their malicious intent, appealed from the lord cardinal to the Lord Governor, as to an indifferent and equal judge. To whom the accuser, John Lander, with hoggish voice answered, 'Is not my lord cardinal the second person within this realm, Chancellor of Scotland, Archbishop of St Andrews, Bishop of Mirepois, Commendator of Aberbroshok, *legatus natus, legatus à latere?*' And so, reciting as many titles of his unworthy honours as would have loden a ship, much sooner an ass, 'Is not he,' quoth John Lander, 'an equal judge apparently unto thee? Whom other desirest thou to be thy judge?'

To whom this humble man answered, saying: 'I refuse not my lord cardinal, but I desire the

Word of God to be my judge, and the temporal estate, with some of your lordships mine auditors, because I am here my Lord Governor's prisoner.'

Hereupon the prideful and scornful people mocked him. And without all delay, they would have given sentence upon Master George, had not certain men counselled the cardinal to read again the articles, and to hear his answers thereupon, that the people might not complain of his wrongful condemnation.

They caused the common people to void away, whose desire was always to hear that innocent man to speak. Then the sons of darkness pronounced their sentence definitive, not having respect to the judgment of God. And when all this was done and said, the cardinal caused his tormentors to pass again with the meek lamb into the Castle, until such time as the fire was made ready. When he was come unto the Castle, there came friar Scot and his mate, saying, 'Sir, ye must make you confession unto us.' He answered and said; I will make no confession unto you.'

When the fire was made ready, and the gallows, the lord cardinal dreading that Master George should have been taken away by his friends, commanded to bend all the ordnance of the Castle against that part, and commanded all his gunners to stand beside their guns, unto such time as he were burned. All this being done, they bound Master George's hands behind his back, and led him forth with their soldiers to the place of their wicked execution. As he came forth of the Castle gate, there met him certain beggars, asking of his alms for God's sake. To whom he answered, 'I want my hands, wherewith I should give you alms; but the merciful Lord, of His benignity and abundance of grace, that feedeth all men, vouchsafe to give you necessaries, both unto your bodies and souls.' Then afterwards met him two friars, saying, 'Master George, pray to our Lady, that she may be mediatrix for you to her Son.' To whom he answered meekly, 'Cease, tempt me not, my brethren!' After this he was led to the fire with a rope about his neck, and a chain of iron about his middle.

When he came to the fire, he sat down upon his knees, and rose again, and thrice he said these words, 'O thou Saviour of the world! have mercy on me. Father of heaven! I commend my spirit into Thy holy hands.' When he had made this prayer, he turned to the people, and said: 'For the Word's sake and true evangel, which was given to me by the grace of God, I suffer this day by men, not sorrowfully, but with a glad heart and mind. For this cause I was sent, that I should suffer this fire, for Christ's sake. Consider and behold my visage, ye shall not see me change my colour. This grim fire I fear not. I know surely that my soul shall sup with my Saviour Christ this night.'

The hangman, that was his tormentor, sat down upon his knees, and said, 'Sir, I pray you forgive me, for I am not guilty of your death.' To whom he answered, 'Come hither to me.' When that he was come to him, he kissed his cheek, and said, 'Lo! here is a token that I forgive thee. My heart, do thine office.' And then he was put upon the gibbet and hanged, and burned to powder. When that the people beheld the great tormenting, they might not withhold from piteous mourning and complaining of this innocent lamb's slaughter.

It was not long after the martyrdom of this blessed man of God, Master George Wishart, who was put to death by David Beaton, the bloody Archbishop and Cardinal of Scotland, A.D. 1546, the first day of March, that the said David Beaton, by the just revenge of God's mighty judgment, was slain within his own Castle of St Andrews, by the hands of one Leslie and other gentlemen, who, by the Lord stirred up, brake in suddenly upon him, and in his bed murdered him the said year, the last day of May, crying out, 'Alas! alas! slay me not! I am a priest!' And so, like a butcher he lived, and like a butcher he died, and lay seven months and more unburied, and at last like a carrion was buried in a dunghill.

After this David Beaton succeeded John Hamilton, Archbishop of St Andrews, who, to the intent that he might in no ways appear inferior to his predecessor, in augmenting the number of the holy martyrs of God, called a certain poor man to judgment, whose name was Adam Wallace. The order and manner of whose story here followeth.

There was set, upon a scaffold made hard to the chancelary wall of the Black-friars' Church in Edinburgh, on seats made thereupon, the Lord Governor. Behind the seats stood the whole senate. In the pulpit was placed Master John Lander, parson of Marbotle, accuser, clad in a surplice and red hood.

Was brought in Adam Wallace, a simple poor

man in appearance, conveyed by John of Cumnock, servant to the Bishop of St Andrews, and set in the midst of the scaffold. He was commanded to look to the accuser, who asked him what was his name. He answered, 'Adam Wallace.' Then asked he where he was born? 'Within two miles of Fayle,' said he, 'in Kyle.' Then said the accuser, 'I repent that ever such a poor man as you should put these noble lords to so great incumbrance this day by your vain speaking.' 'And I must speak,' said he, 'as God giveth me grace, and I believe I have said no evil to hurt any body.' 'Would God,' said the accuser, 'ye had never spoken; for you are brought forth for such horrible crimes of heresy, as never were imagined in this country before.'

Wallace answered that he said nothing but agreeing to the Holy Word as he understood; and thereby would he abide unto the time he were better instructed by Scripture, even to the death. 'If you condemn me for holding by God's Word, my innocent blood shall be required at your hands, when ye shall be brought before the judgment-seat of Christ.'

Then they condemned him and delivered him to the Provost of Edinburgh to be burned on the Castle Hill, who made him to be put in the uppermost house in the town, with irons about his legs and neck, and gave charge to Hugh Terry, an ignorant minister of Satan and of the bishops, to keep the key of the said house. The said Terry sent to the poor man two grey friars to instruct him, with whom he would enter into no communing. Soon after that were sent in two black friars, an English friar, and another subtle sophister, called Arbuthnot, with the which English friar he would have reasoned and declared his faith by the Scriptures; who answered, he had no commission to enter into disputation with him: and so left him.

Then was sent to him a worldly wise man, and not ungodly in the understanding of the truth, the Dean of Restalrig, who gave him Christian consolation, and exhorted him to believe the reality of the sacrament after the consecration. But Wallace would consent to nothing that had not evidence in the holy Scripture, and so passed that night in singing, and lauding God, to the ears of divers hearers, having learned the Psalter of David without book, to his consolation: for they had before spoiled him of his Bible, which always, till after he was condemned, was with him wherever he went.

After Hugh Terry knew that he had certain books to read and comfort his spirit, he came in a rage, and took the same from him, endeavouring to pervert him from the patience and hope he had in Christ his Saviour: but God suffered him not to be moved therewith.

All the next morning abode this poor man in irons, and provision was commanded to be made for his burning against the next day; which day came the Dean of Restalrig to him again, and reasoned with him; who answered as before, that he would say nothing concerning his faith, but as the Scripture testifieth, yea, though an angel came from heaven to persuade him to the same. Then after came in Hugh Terry again, and examined him after his old manner, and said he would gar devils to come forth of him ere even. To whom he answered, 'You should rather be a godly man to give me consolation in my case. When I knew you were come, I prayed God I might resist your temptations; which, I thank Him, He hath made me able to do: therefore I pray you, let me alone in peace.' Then he asked of one of the officers that stood by, 'Is your fire making ready?' who told him, it was. He answered, 'As it pleaseth God; I am ready soon or late, as it shall please Him.'

At his forthcoming, the Provost, with great menacing words, forbade him to speak to any man, or any to him. Coming from the town to the Castle Hill, the common people said, 'God have mercy upon him.' 'And on you too,' said he. Being beside the fire, he lifted up his eyes to heaven twice or thrice, and said to the people, 'Let it not offend you that I suffer death this day for the truth's sake; for the disciple is not greater than his Master.' The cord being about his neck, the fire was lighted, and so departed he to God constantly, and with good countenance.

Among the rest of the martyrs of Scotland, the marvellous constancy of Walter Mill is not to be passed over with silence; out of whose ashes sprang thousands, who chose rather to die, than to be any longer overtrodden by the tyranny of the cruel, ignorant, and brutal bishops, abbots, monks, and friars.

In the year of our Lord, 1558, this Walter Mill (who in his youth had been a papist), after he had been in Almain, and had heard the doctrine of the Gospel, returned into Scotland; and, setting aside all papistry, married a wife; which thing made him unto the bishops of Scotland to be suspected of heresy: and, after long watching, he was taken by two popish priests, and brought to St Andrews and imprisoned in the castle thereof. The papists threatened him with death and corporal torments, to the intent they might cause him to forsake the truth. But seeing they could profit nothing thereby, and that he remained firm and constant, they laboured to persuade him by fair promises, and offered unto him a monk's portion, for all the days of his life, in the Abbey of Dunfermline, so that he would deny the things he had taught, and grant that they were heresy; but he, continuing in the truth even unto the end, despised their threatenings and fair promises.

The said Walter Mill was brought to the metropolitan church of St Andrews, where he was put in a pulpit before the bishops to be accused. Seeing him so weak and feeble of person, partly by age and travail, and partly by evil entreatment, that without help he could not climb up, they were out of hope to have heard him, for weakness of voice. But when he began to speak, he made the church to ring again with so great courage and stoutness, that the Christians who were present were no less rejoiced, than the adversaries were confounded and ashamed. Being in the pulpit, and on his knees at prayer, Andrew Oliphant, one of the archbishop's priests, commanded him to arise, saying on this manner, 'sir Walter Mill, arise, and answer to the articles; for you hold my lord here over-long.' To whom Walter, after he had finished his prayer, answered, saying, 'Ye call me sir Walter, call me Walter, and not *sir* Walter; I have been over-long one of the Pope's knights. Now say what thou hast to say.'

Oliphant: 'Thou sayest there be not seven sacraments.'

Mill: 'Give me the Lord's supper and baptism, and take you the rest, and part them among you.'

Oliphant: 'Thou art against the blessed sacrament of the altar, and sayest, that the mass is wrong, and is idolatry.'

Mill: 'A lord or a king sendeth and calleth many to a dinner; and when the dinner is in readiness, he causeth to ring the bell, and the men come to the hall, and sit down to be partakers of the dinner; but the Lord, turning his back unto them, eateth all himself, and mocketh them:—so do ye.'

Oliphant: 'Thou deniest the sacrament of the altar to be the very body of Christ really in flesh and blood.'

Mill: 'As for the mass, it is wrong, for Christ was once offered on the cross for man's trespass, and will never be offered again, for then He ended all sacrifice.'

Oliphant: 'Thou preachedst secretly and privately in houses, and openly in the fields.'

Mill: 'Yea man, and on the sea also, sailing in a ship.'

Oliphant: 'Wilt thou not recant thy erroneous opinions?'

Mill: 'I will not recant the truth, for I am corn, I am no chaff: I will not be blown away with the wind, nor burst with the flail; but I will abide both.'

Then Oliphant pronounced sentence against him, that he should be delivered to the temporal judge, and punished as a heretic; which was, to be burned. Notwithstanding, his boldness and constancy moved so the hearts of many, that the provost of the town, called Patrick Lermond, refused to be his temporal judge; to whom it appertained, if the cause had been just: also the bishop's chamberlain, being therewith charged, would in no wise take upon him so ungodly an office. Yea, the whole town was so offended with his unjust condemnation, that the bishop's servants could not get for their money so much as one cord to tie him to the stake, or a tar-barrel to burn him; but were constrained to cut the cords of their master's own pavilion, to serve their turn.

Nevertheless, one servant of the bishop's more ignorant and cruel than the rest, called Alexander Somervaile, enterprising the office of a temporal judge in that part, conveyed him to the fire, where, against all natural reason of man, his boldness and hardiness did more and more increase, so that the Spirit of God working miraculously in him, made it manifest to the people, that his cause was just, and he innocently put down.

When all things were ready for his death, and he conveyed with armed men to the fire, Oliphant bade him pass to the stake. And he said, 'Nay! wilt thou put me up with thy hand, and take part of my death, thou shalt see me pass up gladly: for by the law of God I am forbidden to put hands upon myself.' Then Oliphant put him up with his hand, and he ascended gladly, saying, 'I will go to the altar of God;' and desired that he might have space to speak to the people, which Oliphant and other of the burners denied, saying, that he had spoken over much; for the bishops were altogether offended that the matter was so long continued. Then some of the young men committed both the burners, and the bishops their masters, to the devil, saying, that they should lament that day; and desired the said Walter to speak what he pleased.

And so after he made his humble supplication to God on his knees, he arose, and standing upon the coals, said on this wise:

'Dear friends! the cause why I suffer this day is not for any crime laid to my charge (albeit I be a miserable sinner before God), but only for the defence of the faith of Jesus Christ, set forth in the New and Old Testament unto us: for which as the faithful martyrs have offered themselves gladly before, being assured, after the death of their bodies, of eternal felicity, so this day I praise God, that He hath called me of His mercy, among the rest of His servants, to seal up His truth with my life: which, as I have received it of Him, so willingly I offer it to His glory. Therefore, as you will escape the eternal death, be no more seduced with the lies of priests, monks, friars, priors, abbots, bishops, and the rest of the sect of Antichrist; but depend only upon Jesus Christ and His mercy, that ye may be delivered from condemnation.'

All that while there was great mourning and lamentation of the multitude; for they, perceiving his patience, stoutness and boldness, constancy and hardiness, were not only moved and stirred up, but their hearts also were inflamed. After his prayer, he was hoisted up upon the stake, and being in the fire, he said, 'Lord, have mercy on me! Pray, people, while there is time!' and so he departed.

After this, by the just judgment of God, in the same place where Walter Mill was burnt, the images of the great church of the abbey, which surpassed both in number and costliness, were burned in the time of reformation.

Chapter Eleven

HUGH LATIMER,
PREACHER OF THE GOSPEL

THIS old practised soldier of Christ, Master Hugh Latimer, was the son of one Hugh Latimer, of Thurkesson in the county of Leicester, a husbandman, of a good and wealthy estimation; where also he was born and brought up until he was the age of four years, or thereabout: at which time his parents, having him as then left for their only son, with six daughters, seeing his ready, prompt, and sharp wit, purposed to train him up in erudition, and knowledge of good literature; wherein he so profited in his youth at the common schools of his own country, that at the age of fourteen years, he was sent to the University of Cambridge; where, after some continuance of exercises in other things, he gave himself to the study of such divinity, as the ignorance of that age did suffer.

Zealous he was then in the popish religion, and therewith so scrupulous, as himself confesseth, that being a priest, and using to say mass, he was so servile an observer of the Romish decrees, that he had thought he had never sufficiently mingled his massing wine with water; he thought that he should never be damned, if he were once a professed friar; with divers such superstitious fantasies. In this blind zeal he was a very enemy

262

to the professors of Christ's Gospel; as his oration made, when he proceeded Bachelor of Divinity, against Philip Melancthon and his works, did plainly declare.

Notwithstanding, such was the goodness and merciful purpose of God, that where he thought by that his oration to have utterly defaced the professors of the Gospel and true Church of Christ, he was himself by a member of the same prettily catched in the blessed net of God's Word. For Master Thomas Bilney, being at that time a trier out of Satan's subtleties, and a secret overthrower of Antichrist's kingdom, and seeing Master Latimer to have a zeal in his ways, although without knowledge, was stricken with a brotherly pity towards him, and bethought by what means he might best win this zealous, yet ignorant brother to the true knowledge of Christ. He came to Master Latimer's study, and desired him to hear him make his confession; which thing he willingly granted; with the hearing whereof he was, by the good Spirit of God, so touched, that he forsook his former studying of the school-doctors and other such fooleries, and became a true scholar of the true divinity. So that whereas before he was an enemy, and almost a persecutor of Christ, he was now an earnest seeker after Him, changing his old manner of calumnying into a diligent kind of conferring, both with Master Bilney and others.

After his winning to Christ, he was not satisfied with his own conversion only, but, like a true disciple of the blessed Samaritan, pitied the misery of others, and became a public preacher, and a private instructor, to the rest of his brethren within the University, by the space of three years, spending his time partly in the Latin tongue among the learned, and partly amongst the simple people in his natural and vulgar language. Howbeit, as Satan never sleepeth when he seeth his kingdom begin to decay, so likewise now, seeing that this worthy member of Christ would be a shrewd shaker thereof, he raised up his children to molest and trouble him.

Amongst these there was an Augustine friar, who took occasion, upon certain sermons that Master Latimer made about Christenmas 1529, to envy against him, for that Master Latimer in the said sermons, alluding to the common usage of the season, gave the people certain cards out of the fifth, sixth, and seventh chapters of St Matthew, whereupon they might, not only then, but always occupy their time. For the chief, as their triumphing card, he limited the heart, as the principal thing that they should serve God withal, whereby he quite overthrew all external ceremonies, not tending to the necessary beautifying of God's holy Word and sacraments. For the better attaining hereof, he wished the Scriptures to be in English, that the common people might thereby learn their duties, as well to God as to their neighbours.

The handling of this matter was so apt for the time, and so pleasantly applied of Latimer, that not only it declared a singular towardness of wit in him that preached, but also wrought in the hearers much fruit, to the overthrow of popish superstition, and setting up of perfect religion.

On the Sunday before Christenmas day coming to the church, and causing the bell to be tolled, he entereth into the pulpit, exhorting and inviting all men to serve the Lord with inward heart and true affection, and not with outward ceremonies: meaning thereby how the Lord would be worshipped and served in simplicity of the heart and verity, wherein consisteth true Christian religion, and not in the outward deeds of the letter only, or in the glistering show of man's traditions, of pardons, pilgrimages, ceremonies, vows, devotions, voluntary works, works of supererogation, foundations, oblations, the Pope's supremacy; so that all these either be needless, where the other is present, or else be of small estimation, in comparison.

It would ask a long discourse to declare what a stir there was in Cambridge, upon this preaching of Master Latimer. Belike Satan began to feel himself and his kingdom to be touched too near, and therefore thought it time to look about him, and to make out his men at arms.

First came out the prior of the Black Friars, called Buckenham, declaring that it was not expedient the Scripture to be in English, lest the ignorant might haply be brought in danger to leave their vocation, or else to run into some inconvenience: as for example, the ploughmam, when he heareth this in the Gospel, 'No man that layeth his hand on the plough and looketh back, is meet for the kingdom of God,' might peradventure, hearing this, cease from his plough. Likewise the baker, when he heareth that a little leaven corrupteth a whole lump of dough, may percase leave our bread unleavened, and so our bodies shall be unseasoned. Also the simple man, when he heareth in the Gospel, 'If thine eye offend thee, pluck it out, and cast it from thee,' may make himself blind, and so fill the world full of beggars.

Master Latimer, hearing this friarly sermon of Dr Buckenham, cometh again to the church, to answer the friar, where resorted to him a great multitude, as well of the University as of the town, both doctors and other graduates, with great expectation to hear what he could say: among whom also, directly in the face of Latimer, underneath the pulpit, sat Buckenham with his black-friar's cowl about his shoulders.

Then Master Latimer so refuted the friar; so answered to his objections; so dallied with his bald reasons of the ploughman looking back, and of the baker leaving his bread unleavened, that the vanity of the friar might to all men appear, well proving and declaring to the people, how there was no such fear nor danger for the Scriptures to be in English, as the friar pretended; at least this requiring, that the Scripture might be so long in the English tongue, till Englishmen were so mad, that neither the ploughman durst look back, nor the baker should leave his bread unleavened. 'Every speech,' saith he, 'hath its metaphors and like figurative significations, so common to all men, that the very painters do paint them on walls, and in houses.' As for example (saith he, looking toward the friar), when they paint a fox preaching out of a friar's cowl, none is so mad to take this to be a fox that preacheth, but know well enough the meaning of the matter, which is to paint out unto us, what hypocrisy, craft, and subtle dissimulation, lieth hid many times in these friars' cowls, willing us thereby to beware of them.

In fine, friar Buckenham with this sermon was so dashed, that never after he durst peep out of the pulpit against Master Latimer.

Besides this Buckenham, there was also another railing friar, not of the same coat, but of the same note and faction, a grey friar and a doctor, an outlandishman called Dr Venetus, who likewise, in his brawling sermons, railed and raged against Master Latimer, calling him a mad and brainless man, and willing the people not to believe him. To whom Master Latimer answering again, taketh for his ground the words of our Saviour Christ, 'Thou shalt not kill,' etc. 'But I say unto you, whosoever is angry with his neighbour shall be in danger of judgment: and whosoever shall say unto his neighbour, Raca (or any other like words of rebuking, as *brainless*), shall be in danger of council: and whosoever shall say to his neighbour, Fool, shall be in danger of hell fire.' He declared to the audience, that the true servants and preachers of God in this world commonly are scorned and reviled of the proud enemies of God's Word, which count them here as madmen, fools, brainless, and drunken: so did they, said he, in the Scripture call them which most purely preached and set forth the glory of God's Word. He so confounded the poor friar, that he drove him not only out of countenance, but also clean out of the University.

Whole swarms of friars and doctors flocked against him on every side, almost through the whole University, preaching and barking against him. Then came at last Dr West, Bishop of Ely, who preaching against Master Latimer at Barnwell Abbey, forbade him, within the churches of that

University, to preach any more. Notwithstanding that—so the Lord provided—Dr Barnes, prior of the Augustine friars, did license Master Latimer to preach in his church of the Augustines.

Thus Master Latimer, notwithstanding the malice of the adversaries, continued yet in Cambridge, preaching the space of three years together with such favour and applause of the godly, also with such admiration of his enemies that heard him, that the Bishop himself, coming in and hearing his gift, wished himself to have the like, and was compelled to commend him. Master Latimer, with Master Bilney, used much to company together, insomuch that the place where they most used to walk in the fields, was called long after, the Heretics'-hill. The society of these two, as it was much noted of many in that University, so it was full of many good examples, to all such as would follow their doings, both in visiting the prisoners, in relieving the needy, in feeding the hungry.

Master Latimer maketh mention of a certain history which happened about this time in Cambridge between them two and a certain woman then prisoner in the Castle or Tower of Cambridge. It so chanced, that after Master Latimer had been acquainted with Master Bilney, he went with him to visit the prisoners in the tower in Cambridge, and among other prisoners there was a woman which was accused that she had killed her own child, which act she plainly and steadfastly denied. Whereby it gave them occasion to search for the matter, and at length they found that her husband loved her not, and therefore sought all means he could to make her away. The matter was thus:

268

a child of hers had been sick a whole year, and at length died in harvest time, as it were in a consumption; which when it was gone, she went to have her neighbours to help her to the burial: but all were in harvest abroad, whereby she was enforced, with heaviness of heart, alone to prepare the child to the burial. Her husband coming home, and not loving her, accused her of murdering the child. This was the cause of her trouble, and Master Latimer, by earnest inquisition of conscience, thought the woman not guilty. Then, immediately after, was he called to preach before King Henry the Eighth at Windsor, where, after his sermon, the King's majesty sent for him, and talked with him familiarly. At which time Master Latimer, finding opportunity, kneeled down, opened his whole matter to the King, and begged her pardon; which the King most graciously granted, and gave it him at his return homeward.

By the means of Dr Buts, the King's physician, a singular good man, and a special favourer of good proceedings, Master Latimer was in the number of them which laboured in the cause of the King's supremacy. Then went he to the court, where he remained a certain time in the said Dr Buts' chamber, preaching then in London very often. At last, being weary of the court, having a benefice offered by the King at the suit of the Lord Cromwell and Dr Buts, he was glad thereof, and, contrary to the mind of Dr Buts, he would needs depart, and be resident at the same.

This benefice was in Wiltshire, under the diocese of Sarum, the name of which town was called West-Kington, where this good preacher did exercise himself to instruct his flock, and not only to them his diligence extended, but also to all the country about. In fine, his diligence was so great, his preaching so mighty, the manner of his teaching so zealous, that there, in like sort, he could not escape without enemies. He was cited to appear before William Warham, Archbishop of Canterbury, and John Stokesley, Bishop of London, Jan. 29, A.D. 1531. He was greatly molested, and detained a long space from his cure at home, being called thrice every week before the said bishops, to make answer for his preaching. At length, much grieved with their troublesome unquietness, which neither would preach themselves, nor yet suffer him to preach and do his duty, he writeth to the archbishop, excusing his infirmity, whereby he could not appear at their commandment, expostulating with them for detaining him from his duty-doing, and that for no just cause, but only for preaching the truth against the certain vain abuses crept into religion.

The story he showeth forth himself in a certain sermon preached at Stamford, Oct. 9, A.D. 1550: 'I was once,' saith he, 'in examination before five or six bishops, where I had much turmoiling. Every week thrice I came to examinations, and many snares and traps were laid to get something. Now God knoweth I was ignorant of the law, but God gave me answer and wisdom what I should speak. It was God indeed: for else I had never escaped them. At the last I was brought forth to be examined into a chamber hanged with arras, where I was wont to be examined: but now, at this time, the chamber was somewhat altered. For whereas before there was wont ever to be a fire in the chimney, now the fire was taken away, and an arras hanged over the chimney, and the table stood near the chimney's end.

'There was amongst the bishops that examined me one with whom I had been very familiar, and took him for my great friend, an aged man, and he sat next the table's end. Then, amongst all other questions he put forth one, a very subtle and crafty one, and such a one indeed, as I could not think so great danger in. And when I should made answer, "I pray you, Master Latimer," said one, "speak out; I am very thick of hearing, and here be many that sit far off." I marvelled at this, that I was bidden speak out, and began to misdeem, and gave an ear to the chimney; and, sir, there I heard a pen walking in the chimney behind the cloth. They had appointed one there to write all mine answers, for they made sure that I should not start from them: there was no starting from them. God was my good Lord, and gave me answer; I could never else have escaped it.'

The question to him there and then objected was this: 'Whether he thought in his conscience that he hath been suspected of heresy.' This was a captious question. There was no holding of peace would serve; for that was to grant himself faulty. To answer it was every way full of danger; but God, which alway giveth in need what to answer, helped him. Albeit what was his answer, he doth not express.

King Henry the Eighth with much favour embraced Master Latimer, and with his power delivered him out of the crooked claws of his enemies. Moreover, through the procurement partly of Dr Buts, partly of good Cromwell, he advanced him to the dignity of Bishop of Worcester, who so continued a few years, instructing his diocese, according to the duty of a diligent and vigilant pastor, with wholesome doctrine and example of perfect conversation duly agreeing to the same.

It were a long matter to stand particularly upon such things as might here be brought to the commendation of his pains; as study, readiness, and continual carefulness in teaching, preaching, exhorting, visiting, correcting, and reforming, either as his ability could serve, or else the time would bear. But the days then were so dangerous and variable, that he could not in all things do that he would. Yet what he might do, that he performed to the uttermost of his strength, so that although he could not utterly extinguish all the sparkling relics of old superstition, yet he so wrought, that though they could not be taken away, yet they should be used with as little hurt, and with as much profit, as might be. As for example, when it could not be avoided but holy water and holy bread must needs be received, he so instructed them of his diocese that in receiving thereof superstition should be excluded, charging the ministers in delivering the holy water and the holy bread, to say these words following:

Words spoken to the People in giving them Holy Water.

> Remember your promise in baptism;
> Christ His mercy and blood-shedding:
> By Whose most holy sprinkling,
> Of all your sins you have free pardoning.

What to say in giving Holy Bread.

Of Christ's body this is a token,
Which on the cross for your sins was broken.
Wherefore of your sins you must be forsakers,
If of Christ's death ye will be partakers.

It is to be thought that he would have brought more things else to pass, if the time then had answered to his desire; for he was not ignorant how the institution of holy water and holy bread not only had no ground in Scripture, but also how full of profane exorcisms and conjurations they were, contrary to the rule and learning of the Gospel.

As before, both in the University and at his benefice, he was tost and turmoiled by wicked and evil-disposed persons, so in his bishopric also, he was not clear and void of some that sought his trouble. One especially there was, and that no small person, which accused him to the King for his sermons. The story, because he himself showeth in a sermon of his before King Edward, I thought therefore to use his own words, which be these:

'In the King's days that dead is, many of us were called together before him, to say our minds in certain matters. One accuseth me that I had preached seditious doctrine. The King turned to me, and said, "What say you to that, sir?"

'Then I kneeled down, and turned me first to my accuser, and required him. "Sir, what form of preaching would you appoint me to preach before a King? Would you have me for to preach nothing as concerning a King in the King's sermon? have you any commission to appoint me, what I shall preach?" Besides this, I asked him divers other questions, and he would make no answer to none of them all: he had nothing to say.

'Then I turned me to the King, and submitted myself to his grace, and said, "I never thought myself worthy, nor I never sued, to be a preacher before your grace; but I was called to it, and would be willing (if you mislike me) to give place to my betters: for I grant there be a great many more worthy of the room than I am. And if it be your grace's pleasure so to allow them for preachers, I could be content to bear their books after them. But, if your grace allow me for a preacher, I would desire your grace to give me leave to discharge my conscience."

'And I thank Almighty God (Which hath always been my remedy), that my sayings were well accepted of the King. Certain of my friends came to me with tears in their eyes, and told me they looked I should have been in the Tower the same night.'

Thus he continued in this laborious function of a bishop the space of certain years, till the coming in of the Six Articles. Then, being distressed through the straitness of time, so that either he must lose the quiet of a good conscience, or else forsake his bishopric, he did of his own free accord resign his pastorship. At what time he first put off his rochet in his chamber among his friends, suddenly he gave a skip on the floor for joy, feeling his shoulder so light. Howbeit, troubles and labours followed him wheresoever he went. For a little after he had renounced his bishopric, he was sore bruised and almost slain with the fall of a tree. Then, coming up to London for remedy, he was molested of the bishops, whereby he was again in no little danger; and at length was cast into the Tower, where he remained prisoner, till the time that blessed King Edward entered his crown, by means whereof the golden mouth of this preacher, long shut up before, was now opened again.

Beginning afresh to set forth his plough he laboured in the Lord's harvest most fruitfully, discharging his talent as well in divers places of this realm, as before the King at the court. In the same place of the inward garden, which was before applied to lascivious and courtly pastimes, there he dispensed the fruitful Word of the glorious Gospel of Jesus Christ, preaching there before the King and his whole court, to the edification of many. In this his painful travail he occupied himself all King Edward's days, preaching for the most part every Sunday twice. Though a sore bruised man by the fall of a tree, and above sixty-seven years of age, he took little ease and care of sparing himself. Every morning, winter and summer, about two of the clock, he was at his book most diligently.

Master Latimer ever affirmed that the preaching of the Gospel would cost him his life, to the which he cheerfully prepared himself. After the death of King Edward, not long after Queen Mary was proclaimed, a pursuivant was sent down into the country, to call him up, of whose coming, although Master Latimer lacked no forewarning, yet so far off was it that he thought to escape, that he prepared himself towards his journey before the said pursuivant came to his house. When the pursuivant marvelled, he said unto him—'My friend, you be a welcome messenger to me. And be it known unto you, and to all the world, that I go as willingly to

London at this present, called to render a reckoning of my doctrine, as ever I was at any place in the world. I doubt not but that God, as He hath made me worthy to preach His Word before two excellent princes, so will He able me to witness the same unto the third, either to her comfort, or discomfort eternally.'

When the pursuivant had delivered his letters he departed, affirming that he had commandment not to tarry for him; by whose sudden departure it was manifest that they would not have him appear, but rather to have fled out of the realm. They knew that his constancy should deface them in their popery, and confirm the godly in the truth.

Thus Master Latimer coming up to London, through Smithfield (where merrily he said that Smithfield had long groaned for him), was brought before the council, where he patiently bore all the mocks and taunts given him by the scornful papists. He was cast into the Tower, where he, being assisted with the heavenly grace of Christ, sustained imprisonment a long time, notwithstanding the cruel and unmerciful handling of the lordly papists, which thought then their kingdom would never fall; he showed himself not only patient, but also cheerful in and above all that which they could or would work against him. Yea, such a valiant spirit the Lord gave him, that he was able not only to despise the terribleness of prisons and torments, but also to laugh to scorn the doings of his enemies.

When the lieutenant's man upon a time came to him, the aged father, kept without fire in the frosty winter, and well nigh starved with cold, merrily bade the man tell his master, that if he did not look the better to him, perchance he would deceive him. The lieutenant of the Tower, hearing this, bethought himself of these words, and fearing lest that indeed he thought to make some escape, began to look more straitly to his prisoner, and so coming to him, chargeth him with his words. 'Yea, master lieutenant, so I said,' quoth he, 'for you look, I think, that I should burn; but except you let me have some fire, I am like to deceive your expectation, for I am like here to starve for cold.'

Many such like answers and reasons, merry, but savoury, coming not from a vain mind, but from a con tant and quiet reason, proceeded from that man, declaring a firm and stable heart, little passing of all this great blustering of their terrible threats, but rather deriding the same.

Thus Master Latimer, passing a long time in the Tower, from thence was transported to Oxford, with Dr Cranmer, Archbishop of Canterbury, and Master Ridley, Bishop of London, there to dispute upon articles sent down from Gardiner, Bishop of Winchester. The said Latimer, with his fellow-prisoners, was condemned, and committed again to prison, and there they continued from the month of April, to the month of October; where they were most godly occupied, either with brotherly conference, or with fervent prayer, or with fruitful writing. Albeit Master Latimer, by reason of the feebleness of his age, wrote least of them all; yet oftentimes so long he continued kneeling in prayer that he was not able to rise without help. These were three principal matters he prayed for.

First, that as God had appointed him to be a preacher of His Word, so also He would give him grace to stand to his doctrine until his death, that he might give his heart blood for the same.

Secondly, that God of His mercy would restore His Gospel to England once again; and these words 'once again, once again,' he did so beat into the ears of the Lord God, as though he had seen God before him, and spoken to Him face to face.

The third matter was, to pray for the preservation of the Queen's Majesty that now is, at that time the Princess Elizabeth, whom even with tears he desired God to make a comfort to His comfortless realm of England.

The Lord most graciously did grant all those his requests.

First, concerning his constancy, even in the most extremity the Lord graciously assisted him. For when he stood at the stake without Bocardo-gate at Oxford, and the tormentors about to set the fire to him, and to the learned and godly Bishop, Master Ridley, he lifted up his eyes towards heaven with an amiable and comfortable countenance, saying these words, 'God is faithful, Which doth not suffer us to be tempted above our strength.'

How mercifully the Lord heard his second request in restoring His Gospel once again unto this realm these present days can bear record. And what, then shall England say now for her defence, which being so mercifully visited and refreshed with the Word of God, so slenderly and unthankfully considereth either her own misery past, or the great benefit of God now present? The Lord be merciful unto us.

Again, concerning his third request, it seemeth likewise most effectuously granted, to the great praise of God, the furtherance of His Gospel, and to the unspeakable comfort of this realm. When all was so desperate that the enemies mightily flourished and triumphed; when God's Word was banished, Spaniards received, and no place left for Christ's servants to cover their heads, suddenly the Lord called to remembrance His mercy, and, forgetting our former iniquity, made an end of all these miseries. Queen Elizabeth was appointed and anointed, for whom this grey-headed father so earnestly prayed in his imprisonment: through whose true, natural and imperial crown, the brightness of God's Word was set up again to confound the dark and false-vizored kingdom of Antichrist, the true temple of Christ re-edified, and the captivity of sorrowful Christians released.

(A detailed account of the trial, condemnation, and martyrdom of Bishop Latimer and Bishop Ridley, begins on page 295.)

Chapter Twelve

THE STORY OF BISHOP RIDLEY

AMONG many other worthy histories and notable acts of such as have been martyred for the true Gospel of Christ, the tragical story of Dr Ridley I thought good to chronicle, and leave to perpetual memory ; beseeching thee (gentle reader) with care and study well to peruse, diligently to consider, and deeply to print the same in thy breast, seeing him to be a man beautified with such excellent qualities, so ghostly inspired and godly learned, and now written doubtless in the Book of Life, with the blessed saints of the Almighty, crowned and throned amongst the glorious company of martyrs.

Descending of a stock right worshipful, he was born in Northumberlandshire; he learned his grammar with great dexterity in Newcastle, and was removed from thence to the University of Cambridge, where he in short time became so famous, that for his singular aptness he was called to be head of Pembroke-hall, and there made doctor of Divinity. Departing from thence, he travelled to Paris; at his return was made chaplain to King Henry the Eighth and promoted afterwards by him to the Bishopric of Rochester and so from thence translated to the see and Bishopric of London, in King Edward's days.

He so occupied himself by preaching and teaching the true and wholesome doctrine of Christ, that never good child was more singularly loved of his dear parents, that he of his flock and diocese. Every holiday and Sunday he preached in some place or other, except he were letted by weighty affairs. To his sermons the people resorted, swarming about him like bees, coveting the sweet flowers and wholesome juice of the fruitful doctrine, which he did not only preach, but showed the same by his life, as a glittering lanthorn to the eyes and senses of the blind, in such pure order that his very enemies could not reprove him in any one jot.

He was well learned, his memory was great, and he of such reading withal, that of right he deserved to be comparable to the best of this our age, as can testify his notable works, pithy sermons, and disputations in both the Universities, as also his very adversaries, all which will say no less themselves.

Wise he was of counsel, deep of wit, and very politic in all his doings. In fine, he was such a prelate, and in all points so good, godly, and ghostly a man, that England may justly rue the loss of so worthy a treasure.

He was a man right comely and well proportioned, both in complexion and lineaments of the body. He took all things in good part, bearing no malice nor rancour in his heart, but straightways forgetting all injuries and offences done against him. He was very kind to his kinsfolk, and yet not bearing with them any thing otherwise than right would require, giving them always for a general rule, yea to his own brother and sister, that they, doing evil, should seek or look for nothing at his hand, but should be as strangers and aliens unto him; and they to be his brother and sister, which used honesty, and a godly trade of life.

He, using all kinds of ways to mortify himself, was given to much prayer and contemplation; for duly every morning, so soon as his apparel was done upon him, he went forthwith to his bed-chamber, and there, upon his knees, prayed the space of half an hour; which being done, immediately he went to his study, if there came no other business to interrupt him, where he continued till ten of the clock, and then came to the common prayer, daily used in his house. The prayers being done, he went to dinner, where he used little talk, except occasion by some had been ministered, and was it sober, discreet, and wise, and some times merry, as cause required.

The dinner done, which was not very long, he used to sit an hour or thereabouts, talking, or playing at the chess: that done, he returned to his study, and there would continue, except suitors or business abroad were occasion of the contrary, until five of the clock at night, and then would come to common prayer, as in the forenoon: which being finished, he went to supper, behaving himself there as at his dinner before. After supper recreating himself in playing at chess the space of an hour, he would return again to his study; continuing there till eleven of the clock at night, which was his common hour to go to bed, then saying his prayers upon his knees, as in the morning when he rose.

Being at his manor of Fulham, as divers times he used to be, he read daily a lecture to his family at the common prayer, beginning at the Acts of the Apostles, and so going through all the Epistles of St Paul, giving to every man that could read a New Testament, hiring them besides with money to learn by heart certain principal chapters but especially Acts xiii., reading also unto his household oftentimes Psalm ci., being marvellous careful over his family, that they might be a spectacle of all virtue and honesty to others. To be short, as he was godly and virtuous himself, so nothing but virtue and godliness reigned in his house, feeding them with the food of our Saviour Jesus Christ.

Remaineth a word or two to be declared of his gentle nature and kindly pity in the usage of an old woman called Mrs Bonner, mother to Dr Bonner, sometime Bishop of London. Bishop Ridley, being at his manor of Fulham, always sent for this said Mrs Bonner, dwelling in a house adjoining to his house, to dinner and supper, saying, 'Go for my mother Bonner'; who, coming, was ever placed in the chair at the table's end, being so gently entreated, as though he had been born of her own body, being never displaced of her seat, although the King's council had been present; saying, when any of them were there, as divers times they were, 'By your lordship's favour, this place of right and custom is for my mother Bonner.'

But how well he was recompensed for this his singular gentleness and pitiful piety after, at the hands of the said Dr Bonner, almost the least child that goeth by the ground can declare. For who afterward was more enemy to Ridley than Bonner? Who more went about to seek his destruction than he? recompensing this his gentleness with extreme cruelty; as well appeared by the strait handling of Ridley's own sister, and George Shipside her husband. Whereas the gentleness of Ridley did suffer Bonner's mother, sister, and other of his kindred, not only quietly to enjoy all that which they had of Bonner, but also entertained them in his house, showing much courtesy and friendship daily unto them, on the other side, Bishop Bonner, being restored again, currishly, without all order of law or honesty, by extort power wrested from the brother and sister of Bishop Ridley all the livings they had. And being not therewith satisfied, he sought to work the death of the foresaid Shipside, which had been brought to pass indeed, at what time he was prisoner at Oxford, had not God otherwise wrought his deliverance by means of Dr Heath, the Bishop of Worcester.

About the eighth of September, 1552, Dr Ridley, then Bishop of London, lying at his house at Hadham in Hertfordshire, went to visit the Lady Mary,[1] then lying at Hunsdon, two miles off; and was gently entertained of Sir Thomas Wharton, and other her officers, till it was almost eleven of the clock; about which time the said Lady Mary came forth into her chamber of presence, and then the said bishop there saluted her grace, and said, that he was come to do this duty to her grace. Then she thanked him for his pains, and, for a quarter of an hour, talked with him very pleasantly; said that she knew him in the court when he was chaplain to her father: and so dismissed him to dine with her officers.

After dinner was done, the bishop being called for by the said Lady Mary, resorted again to her grace, between whom this communication was. First the bishop beginneth in manner as followeth: 'Madam, I came not only to do my duty, to see your grace, but also to offer myself to preach before you on Sunday, if it will please you to hear me.'

[1] Afterwards Queen Mary.

At this her countenance changed, and, after silence for a space, she answered thus:

Mary: 'My lord, as for this last matter I pray you make the answer to it yourself.'

Bishop: 'Madam, considering mine office and calling, I am bound in duty to make to your grace this offer, to preach before you.'

Mary: 'Well, I pray you make the answer (as I have said) to this matter yourself; for you know the answer well enough. But if there be no remedy but I must make you answer, this shall be your answer; the door of the parish-church adjoining shall be open for you if you come, and ye may preach if you list; but neither I, nor any of mine, shall hear you.'

Bishop: 'Madam, I trust you will not refuse God's Word.'

Mary: 'I cannot tell what ye call God's Word: that is not God's Word now, that was God's Word in my father's days.'

Bishop: 'God's Word is all one in all times; but hath been better understood and practised in some ages than in others.'

Mary: 'You durst not, for your ears, have avouched that for God's Word in my father's days that now you do. And as for your new books, I thank God I never read any of them: I never did, nor ever will do.'

And after many bitter words against the form of religion then established, and against the government of the realm and the laws made in the young years of her brother (which, she said, she was not bound to obey till her brother came to perfect age, and then, she affirmed, she would obey them), she asked the bishop whether he were one of the council. He answered, 'No.' 'You might well enough,' said she, 'as the council goeth now-a-days.'

And so she concluded with these words: 'My lord, for your gentleness to come and see me, I thank you; but for your offering to preach before me, I thank you never a whit.'

Then the said bishop was brought by Sir Thomas Wharton to the place where they dined, and was desired to drink. And after he had drunk, he paused awhile, looking very sadly; and suddenly brake out into these words: 'Surely I have done amiss.' 'Why so?' quoth Sir Thomas Wharton. 'For I have drunk,' said he, 'in that place where God's Word offered hath been refused: whereas, if I had remembered my duty, I ought to have departed immediately, and to have shaken off the dust of my shoes for a testimony against this house.' These words were by the said bishop spoken with such a vehemency, that some of the hearers afterwards confessed their hair to stand upright on their heads.

What time King Edward, by long sickness, began to appear more feeble and weak, a marriage was concluded between the Lord Guilford, son to the Duke of Northumberland, and the Lady Jane, the Duke of Suffolk's daughter; whose mother, being then alive, was daughter to Mary, King Henry's second sister, who first was married to the French King, and afterward to Charles, Duke of Suffolk. The King, waxing every day more sick than other, whereas indeed there seemed in him no hope of recovery, it was brought to pass by the consent not only of the nobility, but also of the chief lawyers of the realm, that the King, by his testament, did appoint the aforesaid Lady Jane to be inheritrix unto the crown of England, passing over his two sisters, Mary and Elizabeth. The causes laid against Lady Mary were that it was feared she would marry with a stranger, and thereby entangle the crown: also that she would clean alter religion, bring in the Pope, to the utter destruction of the realm.

King Edward, not long after this, departed by the vehemency of his sickness, when he was sixteen years of age; with whom decayed in a manner the whole flourishing estate and honour of the English nation.

This Jane was forthwith published Queen at London, and in other cities where was any great resort. Between this young damsel and King Edward there was little difference in age, though in learning and knowledge of the tongues she was superior unto him. If her fortune had been as good as was her bringing up, joined with fineness of wit, undoubtedly she might have seemed comparable not only to your Aspasias, and Sempronias (to wit, the mother of the Gracchi), yea, to any other women beside, that deserved high praise for their singular learning; but also to the University-men, which have taken many degrees of the schools.

In the meantime, while these things were a-working at London, Mary, who had knowledge of her brother's death, writeth to the lords of the council a letter wherein she claimeth the crown. 'My lords, we require you, that of your allegiance which you owe to God and us, and to none other, forthwith, upon receipt hereof, do cause our right and title to the crown and government of this realm to be proclaimed in our city of London and other places.'

To this letter of the Lady Mary, the lords of the council made answer: 'This is to advertise you, that forasmuch as our Sovereign Lady Queen Jane is invested and possessed with the just and right title in the imperial crown of this realm, not only by good order of old ancient laws of this realm, but also by our late Sovereign Lord's letters patent, signed with his own hand, and sealed with the great seal of England: we must, therefore, as of most bounden duty and allegiance, assent unto her said grace, and to none other.'

This answer received, and the minds of the lords perceived, Lady Mary speedeth herself secretly away far off from the city, hoping chiefly upon the good will of the commons, and yet perchance not destitute altogether of the secret advertisements of some of the nobles. When the council heard of her sudden departure, and perceived her stoutness, and that all came not to pass as they supposed, they gathered speedily a power of men together, appointing an army, and first assigned that the Duke of Suffolk should take that enterprise in hand, and so have the leading of the band. But afterward, altering their minds, they thought it best to send forth the Duke of Northumberland, with certain other lords and gentlemen; and that the Duke of Suffolk should keep the Tower, where the Lord Guilford and the Lady Jane the same time were lodged.

Mary, in the meanwhile, tossed with much travail up and down, to work the surest way for her best advantage, withdrew herself into Norfolk and Suffolk, where she understood the Duke's name to be had in much hatred for the service that had been done there of late under King Edward in subduing the rebels; and there, gathering to her such aid of the commons on every side as she might, kept herself close for a space within Framlingham Castle. To whom first of all resorted the Suffolk men; who, being always forward in promoting the proceedings of the Gospel, promised her their aid so that she would not attempt the alteration of the religion, which her brother King Edward had before established by laws and orders publicly enacted, and received by the consent of the whole realm. Unto this condition she eftsoons agreed. Thus Mary, being guarded with the power of the gospellers, did vanquish the duke, and all those that came against her.

In the mean time, God turned the hearts of the people to her, and against the council. Which after the council perceived, and that certain noblemen began to go the other way, they turned their song, and proclaimed for Queen the Lady Mary.

And so the Duke of Northumberland was left destitute, and forsaken at Cambridge with some of his sons, and a few others, who were arrested and brought to the Tower of London, as traitors to the crown.

Mary, when she saw all in quiet by means that her enemies were conquered, followed up the 3rd day of August to London, with the great rejoicing of many men, but with a greater fear of more, and yet with flattery peradventure most great of feigned hearts. Her first lodging she took at the Tower, where the aforesaid Lady Jane, with her husband the Lord Guilford were imprisoned; where they remained waiting her pleasure almost five months. Lady

Jane Grey was executed on the 12th February, 1554. But the Duke, within a month after his coming to the Tower, being adjudged to death, was brought forth to the scaffold, and there beheaded.

Mary, besides hearing mass herself in the Tower, every day more and more discomforted the people, declaring herself to bear no good will to the present state of religion. Such whose consciences were joined to truth perceived already coals to be kindled, which after should be the destruction of many a true Christian man.

Divers bishops were removed, and others placed in their rooms; amongst whom was Dr Ridley. In the time of Queen Jane, he had made a sermon at Paul's Cross, so commanded by the council; declaring there his mind to the people as touching the Lady Mary, alleging the inconveniences which might rise by receiving her to be their Queen; prophesying—as it were before, that which after came to pass—that she would bring in foreign power to reign over them, besides subverting all Christian religion: showing that there was no other hope of her to be conceived, but to disturb and overturn all that, which, with so great labours, had been confirmed and planted by her brother. Shortly after this sermon, Queen Mary was proclaimed; whereupon he, speedily repairing to Framlingham to salute the Queen, had such cold welcome there, that, being despoiled of all his dignities, he was sent back upon a lame halting horse to the Tower.

About the 10th of March, Cranmer, Archbishop of Canterbury, Ridley, Bishop of London, and Hugh Latimer, Bishop also some time of Worcester, were conveyed as prisoners from the Tower to Windsor;

and from thence to the University of Oxford, there to dispute with the divines and learned men of both the Universities, Oxford and Cambridge, about the presence, substance, and sacrifice of the sacrament. The articles whereupon they should dispute were these:

> First, Whether the natural body of Christ be really in the sacrament after the words spoken by the priest, or no?
>
> Secondly, Whether in the sacrament, after the words of consecration, any other substance do remain, than the substance of the body and blood of Christ?
>
> Thirdly, Whether in the mass be a sacrifice propitiatory for the sins of the quick and the dead?

Dr Ridley answered without any delay, saying they were all false; and that they sprang out of a bitter and sour root. His answers were sharp, witty, and very learned. He was asked, whether he would dispute or no? He answered that as long as God gave him life, he should not only have his heart, but also his mouth and pen to defend His truth: but he required time and books. They said that he should dispute on Thursday, and till that time he should have books. Then gave they him the articles, and bade him write his mind of them that night.

The Report and Narration of Master Ridley, concerning the misordered Disputation had against him and his Fellow-Prisoners at Oxford.

I never yet, since I was born, saw anything handled more vainly or tumultuously, than the disputation which was with me in the schools at Oxford. Yea, verily, I could never have thought that it had been possible to have found amongst men recounted to be of knowledge and learning in this realm, any so brazen-faced and shameless, so disorderly and vainly to behave themselves, more like to stage-players in interludes to set forth a pageant, than to grave divines in schools to dispute. And no great marvel, seeing they which should have been moderators and overseers of others, and which should have given good examples in words and gravity, gave worst example, above all others, and did, as it were, blow the trump to the rest, to rave, roar, rage, and cry out. By reason whereof (good Christian reader) manifestly it may appear, that they never sought for any truth of verity, but only for the glory of the world, and their own bragging victory.

A great part of the time appointed for the disputations was vainly consumed in opprobrious checks and reviling taunts (with hissing and clapping of hands), to procure the people's favour withal. All which things, when I with great grief of heart did behold, protesting openly, that such excessive and outrageous disorder was unseemly for those schools, and men of learning and gravity, and that they which were the doers and stirrers of such things, did nothing else but betray the slenderness of their cause, and their own vanities: I was so far off, by this my humble complaint, from doing any good at all, that I was enforced to hear such rebukes, checks, and taunts for my labour, as no person of any honesty, without blushing, could abide to hear the like spoken of a most vile varlet, against a most wretched ruffian.

At the first beginning of the disputation, when I should have confirmed mine answer to the first proposition in few words, afore I could make an end of my first probation, even the doctors themselves cried out, 'He speaketh blasphemies! he speaketh blasphemies!' And when I on my knees besought them, and that heartily, that they would vouchsafe to hear me to the end (whereat the prolocutor, being moved, cried out on high, 'Let him read it! let him read it!'): yet, when I began to read again, there followed immediately such shouting, such a noise and tumult, such confusion of voices, crying, 'Blasphemies! blasphemies!' as I, to my remembrance, never heard or read the like; except it be that one, which was in the Acts of the Apostles, stirred up of Demetrius the silversmith, and others of his occupation, crying out against Paul, 'Great is Diana of the Ephesians! great is Diana of the Ephesians!'

The which cries and tumults of them against me so prevailed, that I was enforced to leave off the reading of my probations, although they were short.

After the disputation, the Friday following, which was the 20th of April, the commissioners sat in St Mary's Church, and Dr Weston used particular dissuasions with every one of them, and would not suffer them to answer in any wise, but directly and peremptorily, as his words were, to say whether they would subscribe, or no. And first to the Archbishop of Canterbury, he said he was overcome in disputations. To whom the archbishop answered, that he was not suffered to oppose as he would, nor could answer as he was required, unless he would have brawled with them; so thick their reasons came one after another. Ever four or five did interrupt him, that he could not speak. Master Ridley and Master Latimer were asked what they would do: they replied, that they would stand to that they had said. Then were they all called together, and sentence read over them, that they were no members of the church: and therefore they, their fautors and patrons, were condemned as heretics.

After which, they answered again every one in his turn:

The Archbishop of Canterbury: 'From this your judgment and sentence, I appeal to the just judgment of God Almighty; trusting to be present with Him in heaven, for Whose presence in the altar I am thus condemned.'

Dr Ridley: 'Although I be not of your company, yet doubt I not but my name is written in another place, whither this sentence will send us sooner than we should by the course of nature have come.'

Master Latimer: 'I thank God most heartily, that he hath prolonged my life to this end, that I may in this case glorify God by that kind of death.'

After the sentence pronounced, they were separated one from another; the archbishop was returned to Bocardo, Dr Ridley was carried to the sheriff's house, Master Latimer to the bailiffs.

(A detailed account of the martyrdom of Bishop Ridley will be found in the next chapter.)

Chapter Thirteen

THE MARTYRDOM OF RIDLEY
AND LATIMER

AND thus hast thou, gentle reader, the whole life, both of Master Ridley and of Master Latimer, severally set forth. Now we couple them together, as they were together joined in one martyrdom.

Upon the 28th of September (1555), was sent down to Oxford a commission from Cardinal Pole to John White, Bishop of Lincoln, to Dr Brooks, Bishop of Gloucester, and to Dr Holyman, Bishop of Bristol, that they, or two of them, should have full power to judge Master Hugh Latimer, and Master Dr Ridley, for divers erroneous opinions, which they did maintain in open disputations had in Oxford. The which opinions if the named persons would recant, then they, the deputed judges, should have power to receive the said penitent persons, and forthwith minister unto them the reconciliation of the holy father the Pope. But if the said Hugh Latimer and Nicholas Ridley would maintain their erroneous opinions, then the said lords should pronounce them heretics, cut them clean off from the Church, and yield them to receive punishment.

Wherefore, the last of September, the said lords were placed and set in the divinity school at Oxford; and first appeared Master Dr Ridley. After his coming into the school, the cardinal's commission was read. But Dr Ridley, standing bareheaded, humbly expecting the cause of that his appearance, eftsoons as he had heard the cardinal named, and the Pope's holiness, put on his cap. 'The usurped supremacy, and abused authority of the Bishop of Rome, I utterly refuse and renounce. I may in no wise give any obeisance or honour unto him, lest my so doing might be a derogation to the verity of God's Word.'

The Bishop of Lincoln, after the third admonition, commanded one of the beadles to pluck Master Ridley's cap from his head. Master Ridley, bowing his head to the officer, gently permitted him to take away his cap. After this the bishop in a long oration exhorted Master Ridley to recant, and acknowledge the supremacy of the Pope.

Then Master Ridley said in this manner: 'As touching the saying of Christ, from whence your lordship gathereth the foundation of the Church upon Peter, truly the place is not so to be understood as you take it. For after that Christ had asked His disciples whom men judged Him to be, and they had answered, that some had said He was a prophet, some Elias, some one thing, some another, then He said, "Whom say ye that I am?" Then Peter said, "I say that Thou art Christ, the Son of God." To whom Christ answered, "I say, thou art Peter, and upon this stone I will build My Church;" that is to say, upon this stone—not meaning Peter himself, as though He would have constituted a mortal man, so frail and brickle a foundation of His stable and infallible Church; but upon this rock-stone—that is, this confession of thine, that I am the Son of God, I will build My Church. For this is the foundation and beginning of all Christianity, with word, heart, and mind, to confess that Christ is the Son of God.'

But the bishop, not attending to this answer, proceeded: 'We came not to reason with you, but must proceed, proposing certain articles, unto the which we require your answer directly, either affirmatively or negatively to every of them, either denying them or granting them, without further disputations or reasoning; the which articles you shall hear now; and to-morrow, at eight of the clock in St Mary's Church, we will require and take your answers.'

ARTICLES, JOINTLY AND SEVERALLY MINISTERED TO DR RIDLEY AND MASTER LATIMER, BY THE POPE'S DEPUTY

1. We do object to thee, Nicholas Ridley and to thee Hugh Latimer, jointly and severally; that thou hast affirmed, and openly defended and maintained, that the true and natural body of Christ, after the consecration of the priest, is not really present in the sacrament of the altar.

2. That thou hast publicly affirmed and defended, that in the sacrament of the altar remaineth still the substance of bread and wine.

3. That thou hast openly affirmed, and obstinately maintained, that in the mass is no propitiatory sacrifice for the quick and the dead.

After Master Ridley was committed to the mayor, the bishop commanded the bailiffs to bring in the other prisoner. Then Master Latimer bowed his knee down to the ground, holding his hat in his hand, having a kerchief on his head, and upon it a night-cap or two, and a great cap (such as townsmen use, with two broad flaps to button under the chin), wearing an old thread-bare Bristol frieze-gown girded to his body with a penny leather girdle, at the which hanged by a long string of leather his Testament, and his spectacles without case, depending about his neck upon his breast. After this the bishop began on this manner: 'What should stay you to confess that which all the realm confesseth, to forsake that which the King and Queen have renounced, and all the realm recanted. It was a common error, and it is now of all confessed: it shall be no more shame to you, than it was to us all. Therefore, Master Latimer, for God's love, remember you are an old man; spare your body, accelerate not your death, and specially remember your soul's health. If you should die in this state, you shall be a stinking sacrifice to God; for it is the cause that maketh the martyr, and not the death: consider that if you die in this state, you die without grace, for without the Church can be no salvation.' The bishop said that they came not to dispute with Master Latimer, but to take his determinate answers to their articles; and so began to propose the same articles which were proposed to Master Ridley.

The next day following (which was the first day of October), somewhat after eight of the clock, the said lords repaired to St Mary's Church, and after they were set in a high throne well trimmed with cloth of tissue and silk, appeared Master Ridley.

Then spake the Bishop of Lincoln: 'We came to take your determinate answers to our articles. If you have brought your answer in writing, we will receive it: but if you have written any other matter, we will not receive it.'

Then Master Ridley took a sheet of paper out of his bosom, and began to read that which he had written : but the Bishop of Lincoln commanded the beadle to take it from him. But Master Ridley desired license to read it, saying that it was nothing but his answer, but the bishop would in no wise suffer him.

Ridley : 'Why, my lord, will you require my answer, and not suffer me to publish it?'

Lincoln : 'Master Ridley, we will first see what you have written, and then, if we shall think it good to be read, you shall have it published; but, except you will deliver it first, we will take none at all of you.'

With that Master Ridley, seeing no remedy, delivered it to an officer, who delivered it to the bishop. After he had secretly communicated it to the other two bishops, he would not read it as it was written, saying, that it contained words of blasphemy; therefore he would not fill the ears of the audience therewithal, and so abuse their patience.

The Bishop of Gloucester and likewise the Bishop of Lincoln, with many words, desired Master Ridley to turn. But he made an absolute answer, that he was fully persuaded the religion which he defended to be grounded upon God's Word ; and, therefore, without great offence towards God, great peril and damage of his soul, he could not forsake his Master and Lord God, but desired the bishop to perform his grant, in that his lordship said the day before, that he should have license to show his cause why he could not with a safe conscience admit the authority of the Pope. The bishop bade him take his license: but he should speak but forty words, and he would tell them upon his fingers. And eftsoons Master Ridley began to speak: but before he had ended half a sentence, the doctors sitting by cried that his number was out; and with that he was put to silence.

And forthwith the Bishop of Lincoln did read the sentence of condemnation, degrading Master Ridley from the degree of a bishop, from priesthood, and all ecclesiastical order; declaring him to be no member of the church: and committing him to the secular powers, of them to receive due punishment. Then Master Ridley was committed as a prisoner to the mayor.

Immediately Master Latimer was sent for, whom the Bishop of Lincoln desired to recant, revoke his errors, and turn to the catholic church.

'No, my lord,' interrupted Master Latimer, 'I confess there is a catholic church, but not the church which you call catholic, which sooner might be termed diabolic. It is one thing to say Romish church, and another thing to say catholic church: I must use here the counsel of Cyprian, who at what time he was ascited before certain bishops demanded of them sitting in judgment, which was most like to be of the Church of Christ, whether he who was persecuted, or they who did persecute? "Christ," said he, "hath foreshowed, that he that doth follow Him, must take up His cross. Christ gave knowledge that the disciples should have persecution and trouble. How think you then, my lords, is it most like that the see of Rome, which hath been a continual persecutor, is rather the Church, or that flock which hath continually been persecuted of it, even to death?"'

After Master Latimer had answered that he neither could nor would deny his Master Christ, and His verity, the Bishop of Lincoln desired Master Latimer to hearken to him: and then Master Latimer, hearkening for some new matter, the bishop read his condemnation; after which, the said three bishops brake up their sessions, and dismissed the audience. But Master Latimer required the bishop to perform his promise in saying the day before, that he should have license briefly to declare why he refused the Pope's authority. But the Bishop said that now he could not hear him, neither ought to talk with him. Then he committed Master Latimer to the mayor, saying, 'Now he is your prisoner, master mayor.'

And so continued Bishop Ridley and Master Latimer, in durance till the 16th day of October A.D. 1555.

Upon the 15th day in the morning, Dr Brooks, the Bishop of Gloucester, and the vice-chancellor of Oxford, Dr Marshal, with divers other of the heads of the University, came unto Master Irish's house, then Mayor of Oxford, where Dr Ridley was close prisoner. The Bishop of Gloucester told him for what purpose their coming, saying that yet once again the Queen's majesty did offer unto him her gracious mercy, if that he would come home to the faith which he was baptized in. If he would not recant they must needs proceed according to the law.

'My lord,' quoth Dr Ridley, 'as for the doctrine which I have taught, my conscience assureth me that it was sound, and according to God's Word;

the which doctrine, the Lord God being my helper, I will maintain so long as my tongue shall wag, and breath is within my body, and in confirmation thereof seal the same with my blood.'

'Seeing,' saith the Bishop of Gloucester, 'that you will not receive the Queen's mercy, we must proceed according to our commission to disgrading, taking from you the dignity of priesthood. So, committing you to the secular power, you know what doth follow.'

Ridley: 'Do with me as it shall please God to suffer you, I am well content to abide the same with all my heart.'

Gloucester: 'Put off your cap, Master Ridley, and put upon you this surplice.'

Ridley: 'Not I, truly.'

Gloucester: 'But you must.'

Ridley: 'I will not.'

Gloucester: 'You must: therefore make no more ado, but put this surplice upon you.'

Ridley: 'Truly, if it come upon me, it shall be against my will.'

Gloucester: 'Will you not do it upon you?'

Ridley: 'No, that I will not.'

Gloucester: 'It shall be put upon you by one or other.'

Ridley: 'Do therein as it shall please you; I am well contented with that, and more than that; " the servant is not above his Master." If they dealt so cruelly with our Saviour Christ, as the Scripture maketh mention, and He suffered the same patiently, how much more doth it become us His servants.'

They put upon Dr Ridley all the trinkets appertaining to the mass; and the same did vehemently inveigh against the Romish Bishop, and all that foolish apparel, insomuch that Bishop Brooks was exceeding angry with him, and bade him hold his peace. Dr Ridley answered that so long as his tongue and breath would suffer him, he would speak against their abominable doings, whatsoever happened unto him for so doing.

At which words one Edridge, the reader then of the Greek lecture, standing by, said to Dr Brooks; 'Sir, the law is, he should be gagged; therefore let him be gagged.' At which words Dr Ridley, looking earnestly upon him that so said, wagged his head at him, and with a sigh said, 'Oh well, well, well!' So they proceeded in their doings, yet nevertheless Dr Ridley was ever talking things not pleasant to their ears, although one or other bade him hold his peace, lest he should be caused against his will.

When they came to that place where Dr Ridley should hold the chalice and the wafer-cake, called the singing-bread, they bade him hold the same in his hands. And Dr Ridley said, 'they shall not come in my hands; for, if they do, they shall fall to the ground for all me.' Then there was one appointed to hold them in his hand, while Bishop Brooks read a certain thing in Latin law, the effect whereof was: 'We do take from you the office of preaching the Gospel.' At which words Dr Ridley gave a great sigh, looking up towards heaven, saying, 'O Lord God, forgive them this their wickedness!'

When all this their abominable and ridiculous degradation was ended very solemnly, Dr Ridley said unto Dr Brooks, 'If you have done, give me leave to talk with you a little concerning these matters.' Brooks answered and said, 'Master Ridley, we may not talk with you; you be out of the Church, and our law is, that we may not talk with any that be out of the Church.' Then Master Ridley said, 'Seeing that you will not suffer me to talk, neither will vouchsafe to hear me, what remedy but patience? I refer the cause to my heavenly Father, Who will reform things that be amiss, when it shall please Him.'

Then Master Ridley said, 'I pray you, my lord, be a mean to the Queen's majesty, in the behalf of a great many of poor men, and especially for my poor sister and her husband which standeth there. They had a poor living granted unto them by me, whiles I was in the see of London, and the same is taken away from them, by him that now occupieth the same room, without all law or conscience. Here I have a supplication to the Queen's majesty in their behalfs. You shall hear the same read, so shall you perceive the matter the better.' When he came to the place that touched his sister by name, he wept, so that for a little space he could not speak. After that he had left off weeping, he said, 'This is nature that moveth me: but I have now done.' Whereunto Brooks said, 'Indeed, Master Ridley, your request is very lawful and honest: therefore I must needs in conscience speak to the Queen's majesty for them.'

All things being finished, Dr Brooks called the bailiffs, delivering to them Master Ridley with this charge, to keep him safely from any man speaking with him, and that he should be brought to the place of execution when they were commanded.

The night before he suffered, as he sat at supper at Master Irish's (who was his keeper), he bade his hostess, and the rest at the board, to his marriage; 'for,' said he, 'to-morrow I must be married:' and so showed himself to be as merry as ever he was at any time before. And wishing his sister at his marriage, he asked his brother sitting at the table, whether she could find in her heart to be there or no. And he answered, 'Yea, I dare say, with all her heart:' at which word he said he was glad. At this talk Mistress Irish wept.

But Master Ridley comforted her, and said, 'O Mrs Irish, you love me not now, I see well enough; for in that you weep, it doth appear you will not be at my marriage, neither are content therewith. Indeed you be not so much my friend, as I thought you had been. But quiet yourself: though my breakfast shall be somewhat sharp and painful, yet I am sure my supper shall be more pleasant and sweet.'

When they arose from the table, his brother offered to watch all night with him. But he said, 'No, no, that you shall not. For I mind (God willing) to go to bed, and to sleep as quietly to-night, as ever I did in my life.'

Upon the north-side of the town, in the ditch over against Balliol-college, the place of execution was appointed: and for fear of any tumult that might arise, to let the burning of them, the Lord Williams was commanded, by the Queen's letters, to be there assistant, sufficiently appointed. And when every thing was in a readiness, the prisoners were brought forth.

Master Ridley had a fair black gown furred, and faced with foins, such as he was wont to wear being bishop, and a tippet of velvet furred likewise about his neck, a velvet night-cap upon his head, and a corner cap upon the same, going in a pair of slippers to the stake, between the mayor and an alderman.

After him came Master Latimer in a poor Bristol frieze frock all worn, with his buttoned cap, and a kerchief on his head, a new long shroud hanging over his hose, down to the feet.

The sight stirred men's hearts to rue, beholding the honour they sometime had, and the calamity whereunto they were fallen.

Master Doctor Ridley, as he passed toward Bocardo, looked up where Master Cranmer did lie, hoping belike to have seen him at the glass-window, and to have spoken unto him. But then Master Cranmer was busy with friar Soto and his fellows, disputing together, so that he could not see him. Master Ridley, looking back, espied Master Latimer coming after, unto whom he said, 'Oh, be ye there!' 'Yea,' said Master Latimer, 'have after as fast as I can follow.' So at length they both came to the stake. Dr Ridley, marvellous earnestly holding up both his hands, looked towards heaven. Then espying Master Latimer, with a wondrous cheerful look he ran to him, embraced, and kissed him; and comforted him, saying, 'Be of good heart, brother, for God will either assuage the fury of the flame, or else strengthen us to abide it.' With that went he to the stake, kneeled down by it, kissed it, and most effectuously prayed, and behind him Master Latimer kneeled, as earnestly calling upon God as he.

Then Dr Smith began his sermon to them upon this text of St Paul, 'If I yield my body to the fire to be burnt, and have not charity, I shall gain nothing thereby.' Wherein he alleged that the goodness of the cause, and not the order of death, maketh the holiness of the person; which he confirmed by the examples of Judas, and of a woman in Oxford that of late hanged herself. He ended with a very short exhortation to them to recant, and come home again to the church, and save their lives and souls.

Dr Ridley said to Master Latimer, 'Will you begin to answer the sermon, or shall I?' Master Latimer said, 'Begin you first, I pray you.' 'I will,' said Master Ridley.

Then, the wicked sermon being ended, Dr Ridley and Master Latimer kneeled down upon their knees towards my Lord Williams of Thame, unto whom Master Ridley said, 'I beseech you, my lord, even for Christ's sake, that I may speak but two or three words.' And whilst my lord bent his head to the mayor and vice-chancellor, to know whether he might give him leave to speak, the bailiffs and Dr Marshal, vice-chancellor, ran hastily unto him, and with their hands stopped his mouth, and said, 'Master Ridley, if you will revoke your erroneous opinions, and recant the same, you shall not only have liberty so to do, but also the benefit of a subject: that is, have your life.'

'Not otherwise?' said Master Ridley.

'No,' quoth Dr Marshal.

'Well,' quoth Master Ridley, 'so long as the breath is in my body, I will never deny my Lord Christ, and His known truth: God's will be done in me!'

Incontinently they were commanded to make them ready, which they with all meekness obeyed. Master Ridley took his gown and his tippet, and gave it to his brother-in-law, Master Shipside. Some other of his apparel that was little worth, he gave away; other the bailiffs took. He gave away besides, divers other small things to gentlemen standing by, pitifully weeping, as to Sir Henry Lea a new groat; and to divers of my Lord Williams's gentlemen some napkins, some nutmegs, and rases of ginger; his dial, and such other things as he had about him, to every one that stood next him. Some plucked the points off his hose. Happy was he that might get any rag of him.

Master Latimer very quietly suffered his keeper to pull off his hose, and his other array, which was very simple: being stripped into his shroud, he seemed as comely a person to them that were there present, as one should see; and whereas in his clothes he appeared a withered and crooked old man, he now stood bolt upright, as comely a father as one might lightly behold.

Master Ridley held up his hand and said, 'O heavenly Father, I give unto Thee most hearty thanks, for that Thou hast called me to be a professor of Thee, even unto death. I beseech Thee, Lord God, take mercy upon this realm of England, and deliver the same from all her enemies.'

Then the smith took a chain of iron, and brought

the same about both Dr Ridley's, and Master Latimer's middles: and, as he was knocking in a staple, Dr Ridley took the chain in his hand, and shaked the same, and looking aside to the smith, said, 'Good fellow, knock it in hard, for the flesh will have his course.' Then his brother did bring him gunpowder in a bag, and would have tied the same about his neck. Master Ridley asked, what it was. His brother said, 'Gunpowder.' 'Then,' said he, 'I take it to be sent of God; therefore I will receive it as sent of Him. And have you any,' said he, 'for my brother'; meaning Master Latimer. 'Yea sir, that I have,' quoth his brother. 'Then give it unto him,' said he, 'betime; lest ye come too late.' So his brother went, and carried off the same gunpowder unto Master Latimer.

Then they brought a faggot, kindled with fire, and laid the same down at Dr Ridley's feet. To whom Master Latimer spake in this manner: 'Be of good comfort, Master Ridley, and play the man. We shall this day light such a candle, by God's grace, in England, as I trust shall never be put out.'

When Dr Ridley saw the fire flaming up towards him, he cried with a wonderful loud voice, 'Lord, Lord, receive my spirit.' Master Latimer, crying as vehemently on the other side, 'O Father of heaven, receive my soul!' received the flame as it were embracing of it. After that he had stroked his face with his hands, and as it were bathed them a little in the fire, he soon died (as it appeareth) with very little pain or none.

By reason of the evil making of the fire unto Master Ridley, because the wooden faggots were laid about the gorse, and over-high built, the fire burned first beneath, being kept down by the wood; which when Master Ridley felt, he desired them for Christ's sake to let the fire come unto him. Which when his brother-in-law heard, but not well understood, intending to rid him out of his pain (for the which cause he gave attendance), as one in such sorrow not well advised what he did, he heaped faggots upon him, so that he clean covered him, which made the fire more vehement beneath, that it burned clean all his nether parts, before it once touched the upper; and that made him often desire them to let the fire come unto him, saying, 'I cannot burn.' Which indeed appeared well; for, after his legs were consumed he showed that side towards us clean, shirt and all untouched with flame. Yet in all this torment he forgot not to call unto God, having in his mouth, 'Lord have mercy upon me,' intermingling his cry, 'Let the fire come unto me, I cannot burn.'

In which pangs he laboured till one of the standers by with his bill pulled off the faggots above, and where he saw the fire flame up Master Ridley wrested himself unto that side. And when the flame touched the gunpowder, he was seen to stir no more.

It moved hundreds to tears, in beholding the horrible sight; for I think there was none that had not clean exiled all humanity and mercy, which would not have lamented to behold the fury of the fire so to rage upon their bodies. Signs there were of sorrow on every side. Some took it grievously to see their deaths, whose lives they held full dear: some pitied their persons, that

thought their souls had no need thereof. Well!
dead they are, and the reward of this world they
have already. What reward remaineth for them in
heaven, the day of the Lord's glory, when he
cometh with His saints, shall declare.

Chapter Fourteen

THE FIRES OF SMITHFIELD

An Account of some of the Martyrs that
with their Lives sealed their Testimony
there for the Protestant Faith

About the third year of King Henry I. the hospital
of St Bartholomew in Smithfield was founded, by
means of a minstrel belonging unto the King, named
Rayer, and it was afterwards finished by Richard
Whittington, alderman and mayor of London. This
place of Smithfield was at that day the place where
the felons and other transgressors of the King's
laws were put to execution.

John Badby, Artificer

In the year of our Lord 1410, on Saturday, being
the first day of March, the examination of one John
Badby, tailor, was made in a certain house or hall
within the precinct of the preaching friars of London,
before Thomas Arundel, Archbishop of Canterbury.
Which John Badby did answer, that it was impossible
that any priest should make the body of Christ, by
words sacramentally spoken.

The archbishop considering that he would in no
wise be altered, and seeing, moreover, his countenance
stout, and heart confirmed, so that he began to
persuade others as it appeared, pronounced the said

John Badby an open and public heretic and delivered him to the secular powers.

These things concluded by the bishops in the forenoon, in the afternoon the King's writ was not far behind. John Badby was brought into Smithfield, and there, being put in an empty barrel, was bound with iron chains fastened to a stake, having dry wood put about him. And as he was thus standing it happened that the Prince, the King's eldest son, was there present, who, showing some part of the good Samaritan, began to essay how to save his life.

In the mean season the prior of St Bartholomew's in Smithfield brought, with all solemnity, the sacrament of God's body, with twelve torches borne before, and so showed the sacrament to the poor man being at the stake. And then they demanding of him how he believed in it, he answered, that he knew well it was hallowed bread, and not God's body. And then was the fire put unto him. When the innocent soul felt the fire, he cried 'Mercy!' calling belike upon the Lord; with which horrible cry the Prince being moved, commanded them to quench the fire. This commandment being done, he asked him if he would forsake heresy, which thing, if he would do, he should have goods enough; promising also unto him a yearly stipend out of the King's treasury, so much as should suffice for his sustentation.

But this valiant champion of Christ, neglecting the Prince's fair words, as also contemning all men's devices, being fully determined rather to suffer any kind of torment, were it never so grievous, than so great idolatry and wickedness, refused the offer. Wherefore the Prince commanded him straight to be put again into the fire. Even so was he nothing at all abashed at their torments, but persevered invincibly to the end.

William Sweeting and John Brewster

William Sweeting, and John Brewster were both burned together, the 18th day of October, A.D. 1511. The chief case alleged against them was their faith concerning the sacrament of Christ's body and blood. There were other things besides objected, as the reading of certain forbidden books, and accompanying with such persons as were suspected of heresy. But one great and heinous offence counted amongst the rest, was their leaving off the painted faggots, which they were at their first abjuring enjoined to wear as badges during their lives, or so long as it should please their ordinary to appoint.

John Stilman

John Stilman was charged for speaking against the worshipping, praying, and offering unto images; as also for denying the carnal and corporal presence in the sacrament of Christ's memorial: and further, for that he had highly commended and praised John Wickliff, affirming that he was a saint in heaven.

He was delivered unto the sheriffs of London, to be openly burned, 1518.

Thomas Man

Thomas Man was apprehended for the profession of Christ's Gospel. He had spoken against auricular confession, and denied the corporal presence of Christ's body in the sacrament of the altar; he believed that images ought not to be worshipped, and neither believed in the crucifix, nor yet would worship it. For such like matters was he a long time imprisoned, and, at last, through fear of death, was content to abjure and yield himself unto the judgment of the Romish church. Thereupon he was enjoined, not only to make open recantation, but from thenceforth to remain as prisoner within the monastery of Osney beside Oxford, and to bear a faggot before the first cross, at the next general procession within the University. Howbeit not long after, the bishop having need of the poor man's help in his household business, took him out of the monastery, and placed him within his own house. All which notwithstanding, he fled, seeking abroad in other counties for work, thereby to sustain his poor life; he most commonly abode, sometimes in Essex, sometimes in Suffolk; where also he joined himself unto such godly professors of Christ's Gospel, as he there could hear of. But within few years after, he was accused of relapse, apprehended and brought before the Bishop of London. But because he would seem to do all things by order of justice, and nothing against law, he therefore appointed unto the said Thomas Man certain doctors and advocates of the Arches, as his counsellors to plead in his behalf. He was condemned as a heretic, and delivered to the sheriff of London sitting on horseback in Paternoster-row, before the bishop's door (A.D. 1518). The sheriff immediately carried him to Smithfield, and there, the same day in the forenoon, caused him to be 'put into God's angel,' 1518.

John Frith, a young man, had so profited in all kind of learning and knowledge, that there was scarcely his equal amongst his companions. He had such a godliness of life joined with his doctrine, that it was hard to judge in which of them he was more commendable. At last he fell into knowledge and acquaintance with William Tyndale, through whose instructions he first received into his heart the seed of the Gospel and sincere godliness.

At that time Thomas Wolsey, Cardinal of York, prepared to build a college in Oxford, marvellously sumptuous, which had the name and title of Frideswide, but is now named Christ's-church. This ambitious Cardinal gathered together into that college whatsoever excellent thing there were in the whole realm, either vestments, vessels, or other ornaments, beside provision of all kind of precious things. He also appointed unto that company all such men as were found to excel in any kind of learning and knowledge; among the which was John Frith.

These most picked young men, of grave judgment and sharp wits, conferring together upon the abuses of religion, were therefore accused of heresy, and cast into a prison, within a deep cave under the ground of the same college, where their salt fish was laid; so that, through the filthy stench thereof, they were all infected, and certain of them, being taken out of the prison into their chambers, deceased.

John Frith with others, by the cardinal's letter,

who sent word that he would not have them so straitly handled, were dismissed out of prison, upon condition not to pass above ten miles out of Oxford. Albeit this, his safety continued not long, through the great hatred and deadly pursuit of Sir Thomas More, who, at that time being Chancellor of England, persecuted him both by land and sea, besetting all the ways and havens, yea, and promising great rewards, if any man could bring him any news or tidings of him.

Thus Frith, being on every part beset with troubles, not knowing which way to turn him, seeketh for some place to hide him in. Thus fleeting from one place to another, and often changing both his garments and place, yet could he be in safety in no place; no not long amongst his friends; so that at last he was taken.

When no reason would prevail against the force and cruelty of these furious foes, he was brought before the Bishops of London, Winchester, and Lincoln, who, sitting in St Paul's, ministered certain interrogatories upon the sacrament of the supper and purgatory. When Frith by no means could be persuaded to recant, he was condemned by the Bishop of London to be burned. When the faggots were put unto him, he embraced the same; thereby declaring with what uprightness of mind he suffered his death for Christ's sake, 1533.

Andrew Hewet burned with John Frith

Andrew Hewet, born in Feversham, a young man of the age of four and twenty years, went upon a holy-day into Fleet-street, towards St Dunstan's.

He met with one William Holt, who was foreman with the King's tailor, and being suspected by the same Holt, who was a dissembling wretch, to be one that favoured the Gospel, after a little talk had with him, he went into an honest house about Fleet-bridge, which was a bookseller's house. Then Holt, thinking he had found good occasion to show forth some fruit of his wickedness, sent for certain officers, who searched the house, and finding the same Andrew, apprehended him.

Andrew Hewet was brought before the Chancellor of the Bishop of London. When it was demanded of him what he thought as touching the sacrament of the last supper; he answered, 'Even as John Frith doth.' Then certain of the bishops smiled at him; and Stokesley, the Bishop of London, said, 'Why, Frith is a heretic, and already judged to be burned; and except thou revoke thine opinion, thou shalt be burned also with him.' 'Truly,' saith he, 'I am content therewithal.' Whereupon he was sent unto the prison to Frith, and afterwards they were carried together to the fire, 1533.

John Lambert

This Lambert, being born and brought up in Norfolk, studied in the University of Cambridge. After he had sufficiently profited both in Latin and Greek, and had translated out of both tongues sundry things into the English tongue, being forced at last by violence of the time, he departed beyond the seas, to Tyndale and Frith. There he remained the space of a year and more, being chaplain to the

English House at Antwerp, till he was disturbed by Sir Thomas More, and by the accusation of one Barlow carried from Antwerp to England; where he was brought to examination before Warham, the Archbishop of Canterbury.

Within short space after, the archbishop died; whereby it seemeth that Lambert for that time was delivered. He returned unto London, and there exercised himself about the Stocks, in teaching children both in the Greek and Latin tongue.

After that John Lambert had continued in this vocation, with great commendation, and no less commodity to the youth, it happened (1538) that he was present at a sermon in St Peter's Church at London. He that preached was named Dr Taylor.

When the sermon was done, Lambert went gently unto the preacher to talk with him. All the whole matter or controversy was concerning the sacrament of the body and blood of Christ. But Taylor desiring, as is supposed, of a good mind to satisfy Lambert, took counsel with Dr Barnes; which Barnes seemed not greatly to favour this cause.

Upon these originals Lambert's quarrel began of a private talk to be a public matter: for he was sent for by Archbishop Cranmer, and forced to defend his cause openly. For the archbishop had not yet favoured the doctrine of the sacrament, whereof afterwards he was an earnest professor. In that disputation, it is said that Lambert did appeal from the bishops to the King's majesty.

At last the King himself, all in white, did come as judge of that great controversy. On his right hand sat the bishops, and behind them the famous lawyers, clothed all in purple. On the left hand sat the peers of the realm, justices, and other nobles in their order; behind whom sat the gentlemen of the King's privy chamber. The manner and form of judgment was terrible enough of itself to abash any innocent; the King's look, his cruel countenance, and his brows bent into severity, did not a little augment this terror; plainly declaring a mind full of indignation. He beheld Lambert with a stern countenance; and then, turning himself unto his councillors, he called forth Dr Sampson, Bishop of Chichester, commanding him to declare unto the people the causes of this present assembly.

When he had made an end of his oration, the King, standing upon his feet, leaning upon a cushion of white cloth of tissue, turning himself toward Lambert with his brows bent, as it were threatening some grievous thing to him, said these words: 'Ho! good fellow; what is thy name?'

Then the humble lamb of Christ, humbly kneeling down upon his knee, said, 'My name is John Nicholson, although of many I be called Lambert.'

'What,' said the King, 'have you two names? I would not trust you, having two names, although you were my brother.'

'O most noble prince!' replied Lambert, 'your bishops forced me of necessity to change my name.'

And after much talk had in this manner, the King commanded him to declare what he thought as touching the sacrament of the altar.

Then Lambert, beginning to speak for himself, gave God thanks, Who had so inclined the heart of the King, that he himself would not disdain to hear and understand the controversies of religion.

Then the King with an angry voice, interrupting his oration: 'I came not hither,' said he, 'to hear mine own praises thus painted out in my presence; but briefly go to the matter, without any more circumstance. Answer as touching the sacrament of the altar, whether dost thou say, that it is the body of Christ, or wilt deny it?' And with that word the King lifted up his cap.

Lambert: 'I answer, with St Augustine, that it is the body of Christ, after a certain manner.'

The King: 'Answer me neither out of St Augustine, nor by the authority of any other; but tell me plainly, whether thou sayest it is the body of Christ, or no.'

Lambert: 'Then I deny it to be the body of Christ.'

The King: 'Mark well! for now thou shalt be condemned even by Christ's own words, "This is my body."'

Then the King commanded Thomas Cranmer, Archbishop of Canterbury, to refute his assertion.

It were too long to repeat the arguments of every bishop; and no less superfluous were it so to do, especially forasmuch as they were nothing forcible.

At last, when the day was passed, and torches began to be lighted, the King, minding to break up this disputation, said unto Lambert in this wise: 'What sayest thou now, after all these great labours which thou hast taken upon thee, and all the reasons and instructions of these learned men? art thou not yet satisfied? Wilt thou live or die? what sayest thou? thou hast yet free choice.'

Lambert answered, 'I yield and submit myself wholly unto the will of your majesty.'

Then said the King, 'Commit thyself unto the hands of God, and not unto mine.'

Lambert: 'I commend my soul unto the hands of God, but my body I wholly yield and submit unto your clemency.'

Then said the King, 'If you do commit yourself unto my judgment, you must die, for I will not be a patron unto heretics.' And, turning himself unto Cromwell, he said, 'Cromwell! read the sentence of condemnation against him.'

Of all other who have been burned at Smithfield, there was yet none so cruelly and piteously handled as this blessed martyr. For, after that his legs were burned up to the stumps, and that the wretched tormentors and enemies of God had withdrawn the fire from him, so that but a small fire were left under him, two that stood on each side of him with their halberts pitched him upon their pikes. Then he, lifting up such hands as he had, and his fingers' ends flaming with fire, cried unto the people in these words, 'None but Christ, none but Christ'; and so, being let down again from their halberts, fell into the fire, and there gave up his life, 1538.

STILE.

In the fellowship of these blessed saints and martyrs of Christ who innocently suffered within the time of King Henry's reign for the testimony of God's Word and truth, another good man cometh to my mind, not to be excluded out of this number, who was with like cruelty oppressed, and was burned in Smithfield about the latter end of the

322

time of Cuthbert Tonstall, Bishop of London. His name was called Stile, as is credibly reported unto us by a worthy and ancient knight, named Sir Robert Outred, who was the same time present himself at his burning. With him there was burned a book of the Apocalypse, which he was wont to read upon. This book when he saw fastened unto the stake, to be burned with him, lifting up his voice, 'O blessed Apocalypse,' said he 'how happy am I, that shall be burned with thee!' And so this good man, and the blessed Apocalypse, were both together in the fire consumed, 1539.

ROBERT BARNES, THOMAS GARRET, AND WILLIAM JEROME.

When the valiant standard-bearer and stay of the Church of England, Thomas Cromwell, was made away, pity it was to behold what miserable slaughter of good men and good women ensued. For Winchester, having now gotten free swing to exercise his cruelty, wonder it was to see what troubles he raised in the Lord's vineyard. He made his first assaults upon Robert Barnes, Thomas Garret, and William Jerome, whom within two days after Cromwell's death he caused to be put to execution.

Robert Barnes was prior and master of the house of the Augustines, Cambridge. He did read openly in the house Paul's Epistles; because he would have Christ there taught and His Holy Word, he, in short space, made divers good divines. Thus Barnes, what with his reading, disputation, and preaching, became famous and mighty in the Scriptures. Suddenly was sent down to Cambridge a serjeant-at-arms who arrested Dr Barnes openly in the convocation-house, to make all others afraid. In the morning he was carried to Cardinal Wolsey at Westminster. Then, by reason of Dr Gardiner, secretary to the Cardinal, and Master Foxe, Master of the Wards, he spake the same night to the cardinal in his chamber of estate, kneeling on his knees.

Then said the cardinal to them, 'Is this Dr Barnes your man that is accused of heresy?'

'Yea, and please your grace; we trust you shall find him reformable, for he is both well learned and wise.'

'What! master doctor,' said the cardinal; 'had you not a sufficient scope in the Scriptures to teach the people, but that my golden shoes, my pole-axes, my pillars, my golden cushions, my crosses did so sore offend you, that you must make us ridiculous amongst the people? We were jollily that day laughed to scorn. Verily it was a sermon more fit to be preached on a stage, than in a pulpit; for at the last you said, I wear a pair of red gloves (I should say bloody gloves, quoth you), that I should not be cold in the midst of my ceremonies.'

And Barnes answered, 'I spake nothing but the truth out of the Scriptures, according to my conscience, and according to the old doctors.' And then did Barnes deliver him six sheets of paper written, to confirm his sayings.

The cardinal received them smiling on him, and saying, 'We perceive then that you intend to stand to your articles, and to show your learning.'

'Yea,' said Barnes, 'that I do intend, by God's grace, with your lordship's favour.'

The cardinal answered, 'Such as you are do bear us and the catholic church little favour. I will ask you a question: "Whether do you think it more necessary that I should have all this royalty, because I represent the King's majesty's person in all the high courts of this realm, to the terror and keeping down of all the wicked and corrupt members of this commonwealth; or to be as simple as you would have us? to sell all these things, and give them to the poor, who shortly will cast it against the walls? and to pull away this majesty of a princely dignity, which is a terror to all the wicked, and to follow your counsel in this behalf?"'

Barnes answered, 'I think it necessary to be sold and given to the poor. For this is not comely for your calling.'

Then answered the cardinal, 'Lo, Master Doctors! here is the learned wise man, that you told me of.'

Then they kneeled down and said, 'We desire your grace to be good unto him, for he will be reformable.'

Then said the cardinal, 'Stand you up! for your sakes, and the University, we will be good unto him. How say you, Master Doctor; do you not know that I am able to dispense in all matters concerning religion within this realm, as much as the Pope may?'

He said, 'I know it to be so.'

'Will you then be ruled by us, and we will do all things for your honesty, and for the honesty of the University.'

Barnes answered, 'I thank your grace for your good will; I will stick to the holy Scripture, and to

God's Book, according to the simple talent that God hath lent me.'

'Well,' said the cardinal, 'thou shalt have thy learning tried to the uttermost, and thou shalt have the law.'

After Barnes had continued in the Fleet the space of half a year, at length being delivered, he was committed to be a free prisoner at the Austin Friars in London; whence he was removed to Northampton, there to be burned. One Master Horne, having intelligence of the writ which should shortly be sent down to burn him, gave him counsel to feign himself to be desperate; and that he should write a letter to the cardinal, and leave it on his table, to declare whither he was gone to drown himself; and to leave his clothes in the same place; and another letter to the mayor of the town, to search for him in the water, because he had a letter written in parchment about his neck, closed in wax, for the cardinal, which should teach all men to beware by him. Upon this, they were seven days in searching for him, but he was conveyed to London in poor man's apparel; took shipping to Antwerp, and so to Luther.

The said Dr Barnes returned in the beginning of the reign of Queen Anne, as others did, and continued a faithful preacher, being all her time well entertained and promoted. After that, he was sent ambassador by King Henry VIII. to the Duke of Cleves, for the marriage of the Lady Anne of Cleves between the King and her, and well accepted in the ambassade, and in all his doings until the time that Stephen Gardiner came out of France.

Not long after, Dr Barnes, with his brethren,

were apprehended and carried before the King's majesty to Hampton Court, and examined. The King with many high words rebuked his doings in his privy closet. Unto whom when Barnes had submitted himself, 'Nay,' said the King, 'yield thee not to me; I am a mortal man;' and therewith rising up and turning to the sacrament, and putting off his bonnet, said, 'Yonder is the Master of us all, Author of truth; yield in truth to Him and the truth will I defend; and otherwise yield not unto me.' The King, seeking the means of his safety, at Winchester's request granted him leave to go home with the bishop, to confer with him. But, as it happened, they not agreeing, Gardiner sought, by all subtle means, how to entrap Barnes and his brethren. They were enjoined to preach three sermons the next Easter following; at which sermons Stephen Gardiner was present, either to bear record of their recantation, or trip them in their talk. Shortly after they were sent for to Hampton Court; from thence they were carried to the Tower, and never came out till they came to their death.

Now let us consider the story of Thomas Garret.

In the year of our Lord 1526, or thereabout, Master Garret, curate of Honey-lane in London, came unto Oxford, and brought with him Tyndale's first translation of the New Testament in English, the which he sold to divers scholars. News came from London that he was searched for as an heretic, and so he was apprehended and committed to ward. Afterwards he was compelled to carry a faggot in open procession from St Mary's church to Friswide's, and then sent to Osney, there to be kept in prison till further order was taken.

The third companion who suffered with Barnes and Garret, was William Jerome, vicar of Stepney. He was charged before the King at Westminster for erroneous doctrine.

One Dr Wilson entered into disputation with him, and defended, that good works justified before God. To whom Jerome answered, that all works, whatsoever they were, were nothing worth, nor any part of salvation of themselves, but only referred to the mercy and love of God, which direct the workers thereof.

Thus then Barnes, Jerome, and Garret, being committed to the Tower after Easter, there remained till the thirtieth day of July, which was two days after the death of the Lord Cromwell. Then ensued process against them. Whereupon all those three good saints of God were brought together from the Tower to Smithfield, where they, preparing themselves to the fire, had there at the stake sundry exhortations.

'Take me not here,' said Dr Barnes, 'that I speak against good works, for they are to be done; and verily they that do them not shall never come into the Kingdom of God. We must do them, because they are commanded us of God, to show and set forth our profession, not to deserve or merit; for that is only the death of Christ.'

One asked him his opinion of praying to saints. Then said Dr Barnes: 'Throughout all Scripture we are not commanded to pray to any saints. Therefore I cannot preach to you that saints ought to be prayed unto; for then should I preach unto you a doctrine of mine own head. If saints do pray for us, then I trust to pray for you within this half hour, Master Sheriff.'

Then desired Dr Barnes all men to bear him witness that he abhorred all doctrines against the Word of God, and that he died in the faith of Jesu Christ. The like confession made also Jerome and Garret. They, taking themselves by the hands, and kissing one another, quietly and humbly offered themselves to the hands of the tormentors; and so took their death with such patience as might well testify the goodness of their cause, and quiet of their conscience.—1540.

Mistress Anne Askew, Daughter of Sir William Askew, Knight of Lincolnshire

Here follow the examinations of Anne Askew, according as she wrote them with her own hand, at the instant desire of certain faithful men and women.

The First Examinaton before the Inquisitors, A.D. 1545.

Christopher Dare examined me at Sadler's Hall, and asked me, wherefore I said, I had rather to read five lines in the Bible, than to hear five masses in the temple. I confessed that I said no less; not for the dispraise of either the epistle or the Gospel, but because the one did greatly edify me, and the other nothing at all. He laid unto my charge, that I should say, If an ill priest ministered, it was the devil and not God. My answer was, that I never spake any such thing. But this was my saying: that whosoever he were that ministered unto me, his ill conditions could not hurt my faith, but in spirit I received, nevertheless, the body and blood of Christ. He asked me what I said concerning confession. I answered him my meaning, which was, as St James saith, that every man ought to acknowledge his faults to other, and the one to pray for the other. Then he sent for a priest who asked me, if I did not think that private masses did help the souls departed. I said, it was great idolatry to believe more in them, than in the death which Christ died for us.

Then they had me unto my Lord Mayor, who laid one thing to my charge, which was never spoken of me, but by them; whether a mouse, eating the host, received God or no? I made them no answer, but smiled.

Then the bishop's chancellor rebuked me, and said that I was much to blame for uttering the Scriptures. For St Paul, he said, forbade women to speak or to talk of the Word of God. I answered him that I knew Paul's meaning as well as he, which is, in 1 Cor. xiv., that a woman ought not to speak in the congregation by the way of teaching: and then I asked him how many women he had seen go into the pulpit and preach? He said he never saw any. Then I said, he ought to find no fault in poor women, except they had offended the law.

Then was I had to the Compter, and there remained eleven days, no friend admitted to speak with me.

The sum of my Examination before the King's Council at Greenwich.

They said it was the King's pleasure that I should open the matter unto them. I answered them plainly, I would not so do; but if it were the King's pleasure to hear me, I would show him the truth.

They said, it was not meet for the King to be troubled with me. I answered, that Solomon was reckoned the wisest King that ever lived, yet misliked he not to hear two poor common women, much more his grace a simple woman and his faithful subject.

Then my Lord Chancellor asked my opinion in the sacrament. My answer was this, 'I believe that so oft as I, in a Christian congregation, do receive the bread in remembrance of Christ's death, and with thanksgiving, according to His holy institution, I receive therewith the fruits, also, of His most glorious passion. The Bishop of Winchester bade me make a direct answer: I said, I would not sing a new song of the Lord in a strange land. Then the bishop said, I spake in parables. I answered, it was best for him, 'for if I show the open truth,' quoth I, 'ye will not accept it.' I told him I was ready to suffer all things at his hands, not only his rebukes, but all that should follow besides, yea, and all that gladly.

My Lord Lisle, my Lord of Essex, and the Bishop of Winchester required me earnestly that I should confess the sacrament to be flesh, blood, and bone. Then, said I, that it was a great shame for them to counsel contrary to their knowledge.

Then the bishop said he would speak with me familiarly. I said, 'So did Judas, when he betrayed Christ.' Then desired the bishop to speak with me alone. But that I refused. He asked me, why. I said, that in the mouth of two or three witnesses every matter should stand.

Then the bishop said I should be burned. I answered, that I had searched all the Scriptures, yet could I never find that either Christ, or His apostles, put any creature to death. 'Well, well,' said I, 'God will laugh your threatenings to scorn.'

Then was I sent to Newgate.

My Handling since my Departure from Newgate.

I was sent from Newgate to the sign of the Crown, where Master Rich, and the Bishop of London, with all their power and flattering words went about to persuade me from God: but I did not esteem their glosing pretences.

Then came there to me Nicholas Shaxton, and counselled me to recant as he had done. I said to him, that it had been good for him never to have been born.

Then Master Rich sent me to the Tower, where I remained till three o'clock.

Then came Rich and one of the council, charging me upon my obedience, to show unto them, if I knew any manor woman of my sect. My answer was, that I knew none. Then said they unto me, that the King was informed that I could name, if I would, a great number of my sect. I answered, that the King was as well deceived in that behalf, as dissembled with in other matters.

Then commanded they me to show how I was maintained in the Compter, and who willed me to stick to my opinion. I said, that there was no creature that therein did strengthen me: and as for the help that I had in the Compter, it was by means of my maid. For as she went abroad in the streets, she made moan to the prentices, and they, by her, did send me money; but who they were I never knew.

They said that there were divers gentlewomen

that gave me money: but I knew not their names. Then they said that there were divers ladies that had sent me money. I answered, that there was a man in a blue coat who delivered me ten shillings, and said that my Lady of Hertford sent it me; and another in a violet coat gave me eight shillings, and said my Lady Denny sent it me: whether it were true or no, I cannot tell.

Then they did put me on the rack, because I confessed no ladies or gentlewomen to be of my opinion, and thereon they kept me a long time; and because I lay still, and did not cry, my Lord Chancellor and Master Rich took pains to rack me with their own hands, till I was nigh dead.

Then the Lieutenant caused me to be loosed from the rack. Incontinently I swooned, and then they recovered me again. After that I sat two long hours reasoning with my Lord Chancellor upon the bare floor; where he, with many flattering words, persuaded me to leave my opinion. But my Lord God (I thank His everlasting goodness) gave me grace to persevere, and will do, I hope, to the end.

Then was I brought to a house, and laid in a bed, with as weary and painful bones as ever had patient Job; I thank my Lord God therefor. Then my Lord Chancellor sent me word, if I would leave my opinion, I should want nothing; if I would not, I should forthwith to Newgate, and so be burned. I sent him again word, that I would rather die than break my faith.

The day of her execution being appointed, this good woman was brought into Smithfield in a chair, because she could not go on her feet, by means of her great torments. When she was brought unto the stake, she was tied with a chain, that held up her body. The multitude of the people was exceeding; the place where they stood being railed about to keep out the press. Upon the bench under St Bartholomew's Church sat Wriothesley, Chancellor of England; the old Duke of Norfolk, the old Earl of Bedford, the Lord Mayor, with divers others. Before the fire should be set unto them, one of the bench, hearing that they had gunpowder about them, and being alarmed lest the faggots, by strength of the gunpowder, would come flying about their ears, began to be afraid: but the Earl of Bedford declared unto him how the gunpowder was not laid under the faggots, but only about their bodies, to rid them out of their pains.

Then Wriothesley, Lord Chancellor, offered Anne Askew the King's pardon if she would recant; who made this answer, that she came not thither to deny her Lord and Master. And thus the good Anne Askew, being compassed in with flames of fire, as a blessed sacrifice unto God, slept in the Lord A.D. 1546, leaving behind her a singular example of Christian constancy for all men to follow.

John Lacels, John Adams, and Nicholas Belenian

There was, at the same time, burned with her, one Nicholas Belenian, priest of Shropshire; John Adams, a tailor; and John Lacels, gentleman of the court and household of King Henry. It happened well for them, that they died together with Anne

Askew: for, albeit that of themselves they were strong and stout men, yet, through the example and exhortation of her, they, being the more boldened, received occasion of greater comfort in that so painful and doleful kind of death: who, beholding her invincible constancy, and also stirred up through her persuasions, did set apart all kind of fear.

Master John Bradford

John Bradford was born at Manchester in Lancashire. His parents did bring him up in learning from his infancy, until he attained such knowledge in the Latin tongue, and skill in writing, that he was able to gain his own living in some honest condition. Then he became servant to Sir John Harrington, knight, who, in the great affairs of King Henry the Eighth, and King Edward the Sixth, when he was treasurer of the King's camps and buildings, had such experience of Bradford's activity, expertness, and faithful trustiness, that above all others he used his service.

But the Lord had elected him unto a better function, to preach the Gospel of Christ. Then did Bradford forsake his worldly affairs and forwardness in worldly wealth, and give himself wholly to the study of the Scriptures. To accomplish his purpose the better, he departed from the Temple at London, where the temporal law is studied, and went to the University of Cambridge, to learn by God's law how to further the building of the Lord's temple. Within one whole year the University did give him the degree of a Master of Arts, and immediately after, the Master and Fellows of

Pembroke Hall did give him a fellowship; yea that man of God, Martin Bucer, oftentimes exhorted him to bestow his talent in preaching. Unto which Bradford answered always, that he was unable to serve in that office through want of learning. To the which Bucer was wont to reply, saying, 'If thou have not fine manchet bread, yet give the poor people barley bread, or whatsoever else the Lord hath committed unto thee.' And while Bradford was thus persuaded to enter into the ministry, Dr Ridley, Bishop of London, called him to take the degree of a deacon, obtained for him a license to preach, and did give him a prebend in his cathedral church of St Paul's.

In this preaching office by the space of three years, how faithfully Bradford walked, how diligently he laboured, many parts of England can testify. Sharply he opened and reproved sin, sweetly he preached Christ crucified, pithily he impugned heresies and errors, earnestly he persuaded to godly life. When Queen Mary had gotten the crown, still continued Bradford diligent in preaching, until he was unjustly deprived both of his office and liberty by the Queen and her council.

The fact was this: the 13th of August, in the first year of the reign of Queen Mary, Master Bourn, then Bishop of Bath, made a sermon at Paul's Cross, to set popery abroad, in such sort that it moved the people to no small indignation, being almost ready to pull him out of the pulpit. Neither could the reverence of the place, nor the presence of Bishop Bonner, who then was his master, nor yet the commandment of the Lord Mayor of London, whom the people ought to have obeyed, stay their rage; but the more they spake, the more the people were incensed. At length Bourn, seeing the people in such a mood, and himself in such peril (whereof he was sufficiently warned by the hurling of a drawn dagger at him), desired Bradford, who stood in the pulpit behind him, to come forth, and to stand in his place and speak to the people. Good Bradford, at his request, was content, and spake to the people of godly and quiet obedience: whom as soon as the people saw, they cried with a great shout,—'Bradford, Bradford; God save thy life, Bradford!' Eftsoons all the raging ceased, and quietly departed each man to his house. Bourn desired Bradford not to go from him till he were in safety: which Bradford, according to his promise, performed. For while the Lord Mayor and Sheriffs did lead Bourn to the school-master's house, which is next to the pulpit, Bradford went at his back, shadowing him from the people with his gown.

The same Sunday in the afternoon, Bradford preached at the Bow Church in Cheapside, and reproved the people sharply for their seditious misdemeanour. Within three days, he was sent for to the Tower of London, where the Queen then was, to appear before the council. From the Tower he came to the King's Bench in Southwark: and after his condemnation, he was sent to the Compter in the Poultry in London: in which two places, for the time he did remain prisoner, he preached twice a day continually, unless sickness hindered him: such resort of good folks was daily to his lecture, that commonly his chamber was well nigh filled. Preaching, reading, and praying was his whole life. He did not eat above one meal a day; which was but very little when he took it; and his continual study was upon his knees. In the midst of dinner he used often to muse with himself, having his hat over his eyes, from whence came commonly plenty of tears dropping on his trencher. Very gentle he was to man and child.

Of personage he was somewhat tall and slender, spare of body, of a faint sanguine colour, with an auburn beard. He slept not commonly above four hours in the night; and in his bed, till sleep came, his book went not out of his hand. His chief recreation was in honest company, and comely talk, wherein he would spend a little time after dinner at the board; and so to prayer and his book again. He counted that hour not well spent, wherein he did not some good, either with his pen, study, or in exhorting of others. He was no niggard of his purse, but would liberally participate that he had, to his fellow-prisoners. And commonly once a week he visited the thieves, pick-purses, and such others that were with him in prison, unto whom he would give godly exhortation, and distribute among them some portion of money to their comfort. Neither was there ever any prisoner with him but by his company he greatly profited.

Walking in the keeper's chamber, suddenly the keeper's wife came up, as one half amazed, and seeming much troubled, being almost windless, said, 'O Master Bradford, I come to bring you heavy news.' 'What is that?' said he. 'Marry,' quoth she, 'to-morrow you must be burned; and your chain is now a buying, and soon you must go to Newgate.' With that Master Bradford put off his cap, and lifting up his eyes to heaven, said, 'I thank God for it; I have looked for the same a long time, and therefore it cometh not now to me suddenly, but as a thing waited for every day and hour; the Lord make me worthy thereof!'

They carried him to Newgate, about eleven or twelve o'clock in the night, when it was thought none would be stirring abroad: and yet, was there in Cheapside and other places (between the Compter and Newgate), a great multitude of people that came to see him, which most gently bade him farewell, praying for him with most lamentable and pitiful tears; and he again as gently bade them farewell, praying most heartily for them and their welfare. The next day at four a clock in the morning, there was in Smithfield a multitude of men and women; but it was nine a clock before Master Bradford was brought into Smithfield, with a great company of weaponed men, as the like was not seen at any man's burning. Bradford, being come to the place, fell flat to the ground, making his prayers to Almighty God. Then rising he went to the stake, and there suffered with a young man of twenty years of age, joyfully and constantly, whose name was John Leaf.

JOHN LEAF

John Leaf was an apprentice to Humfrey Gawdy, tallow-chandler, of the parish of Christ-Church in London, of the age of nineteen years and above. It is reported of him that two bills were sent unto him in the Compter in Bread Street, the one containing a recantation, the other his confessions, to know to which of them he would put his hand. The bill of recantation he refused. The other he well liked of, and instead of a pen he took a pin, and pricking his hand, sprinkled the blood upon the said bill, willing to show the bishop, that he had sealed it with his blood already.

When these two came to the stake Master Bradford took a faggot in his hand, and kissed it, and so likewise the stake. Holding up his hands, and casting his countenance up to heaven, he said, 'O England, England, repent thee of thy sins, repent thee of thy sins.' Turning his head unto the young man that suffered with him, he said, 'Be of good comfort, brother; for we shall have a merry supper with the Lord this night.' And thus they ended their mortal lives, without any alteration of their countenance, being void of all fear. 1535.

MASTER JOHN PHILPOT

Master John Philpot was a knight's son, born in Hampshire, brought up in the New College, Oxford. He was made Archdeacon of Winchester, and during the time of King Edward, continued to no small profit of those parts. When that King was taken away, and Mary his sister came in place, she caused a convocation of the prelates and learned men to be congregated to the accomplishment of her desire. In the which convocation Master Philpot sustained the cause of the Gospel manfully against the mass; for the which cause, he was called to account before Bishop Gardiner, and from thence was removed to Bonner and other commissioners, with whom he had sundry conflicts.

In the end the bishop, seeing his unmovable stedfastness in the truth, did pronounce the sentence of condemnation against him. 'I thank God', said Master Philpot, 'that I am a heretic out of your cursed church; I am no heretic before God. But God bless you, and give you grace to repent your wicked doings, and let all men beware of your bloody church.'

And so the officers delivered him to the keeper of Newgate. Then his man thrust to go in after his master, and one of the officers said unto him, 'Hence, fellow! what wouldst thou have?' And he said, 'I would go speak with my master.' Master Philpot turned him about, and said to him, 'To-morrow thou shalt speak with me.' Then the under-keeper said to Master Philpot, 'Is this your man?' and he said, 'Yea.' So he did license his man to go in with him; and Master Philpot and his man were turned into a little chamber on the right hand, and there remained a little time, until Alexander the chief keeper did come unto him; who, at his entering, greeted him with these words; 'Ah!' said he, 'hast not thou done well to bring thyself hither?'

'Well,' said Master Philpot, 'I must be content, for it is God's appointment: and I shall desire you to let me have your gentle favour; for you and I have been of old acquaintance.'

'Well,' said Alexander, 'I will show thee gentleness and favour, so thou wilt be ruled by me.'

Then said Master Philpot, 'I pray you show me what you would have me to do.'

He said, 'If you would recant, I will show you any pleasure I can.'

'Nay,' said Master Philpot, 'I will never recant, whilst I have my life, that which I have spoken, for it is most certain truth; and in witness hereof I will seal it with my blood.'

Then Alexander said, 'This is the saying of the whole pack of you heretics.' Whereupon he commanded him to be set upon the block, and as many irons upon his legs as he could bear.

'Good master Alexander, be so much my friend, that these irons may be taken off.'

'Well,' said Alexander, 'give me my fees, and I will take them off: if not, thou shalt wear them still.'

Then said Master Philpot, 'Sir, what is your fee?' He said four pound was his fees.

'Ah,' said Master Philpot, 'I have not so much; I am but a poor man, and I have been long in prison.'

'What wilt thou give me then?' said Alexander.

'Sir,' said he, 'I will give you twenty shillings, and that I will send my man for; or else I will my gown to gage.'

And with that Alexander departed from him, and commanded him to be had into limbo.

Then one Witterence, steward of the house, took Master Philpot on his back, and carried him down, his man knew not whither. Wherefore Master Philpot said to his man, 'Go to master sheriff, and show him how I am used, and desire master sheriff to be good unto me.' And so his servant went straightway, and took an honest man with him.

The sheriff took his ring off from his finger, and delivered it unto that honest man which came with Master Philpot's man, and bade him go unto Alexander, and command him to take off his irons, and to handle him more gently. And when they came to the said Alexander, and told their message from the sheriff, Alexander took the ring, and said,

'Ah! I perceive master sheriff is a bearer with him, and all such heretics as he is: therefore to-morrow I will show it to his betters.' Yet at ten of the clock he went in to Master Philpot, and took off his irons.

Upon Tuesday at supper, being the 17th day of December 1555, there came a messenger from the sheriffs, and bade Master Philpot make him ready, for the next day he should suffer. Master Philpot answered, "I am ready; God grant me strength, and a joyful resurrection.' And so he went into his chamber, and poured out his spirit unto the Lord God, giving Him most hearty thanks, that He of His mercy had made him worthy to suffer for His truth.

In the morning the sheriffs came, about eight of the clock, and he most joyfully came down unto them. And there his man did meet him, and said, 'Ah! dear master, farewell.' His master said unto him, 'Serve God, and He will help thee.' When he was entering into Smithfield, the way was foul, and two officers took him up to bear him to the stake. Then he said merrily, 'What! will ye make me a Pope? I am content to go to my journey's end on foot.'

When he was come to the place of suffering, he said, 'Shall I disdain to suffer at this stake, seeing my Redeemer did not refuse to suffer a most vile death upon the cross for me?' And when he had made an end of his prayers, he said to the officers, 'What have you done for me?' and every one of them declared what they had done; and he gave to every of them money. Then in the midst of the fiery flames he yielded his soul into the hands of Almighty God.

About the 27th day of January in anno 1556, were burned these seven persons: Thomas Whittle, priest; Bartlet Green, gentleman; John Tudson, artificer; John Went, artificer; Thomas Browne; Isabel Foster, wife; Joan Warne, alais Lashford, maid.

What an evil mess of handling Whittle had, and how he was by Bishop Bonner beaten and buffeted about the face, by this his own narration sent unto his friend, manifestly may appear:—

'The bishop sent for me, out of the porter's lodge, where I had been all night, lying upon the earth, upon a pallet, where I had as painful a night of sickness as ever I had. And when I came before him, he asked me if I would have come to mass that morning, if he had sent for me. Whereunto I answered, that I would have come to him at his commandment, "but to your mass," said I, "I have small affection." At which answer he was displeased sore, and said I should be fed with bread and water. And as I followed him through the great hall, he turned back and beat me with his fist, first on the one cheek, and then on the other. And then he led me into a little salt-house, where I had no straw nor bed, but lay two nights on a table, and slept soundly, I thank God.'

Whittle, strengthened with the grace of the Lord, stood strong and immovable. Wherefore he was brought to the fire with the other six.

Master Bartlet Green was of a good house, and was sent unto the University of Oxford. By his often repairing unto the lectures of Peter Martyr he saw the true light of Christ's Gospel.

As he was going to Newgate there met with him two gentlemen, being his special friends, minding to comfort their persecuted brother: but their loving and friendly hearts were manifested by the abundance of their pitiful tears. To whom Green said, 'Ah, my friends! is this your comfort you are come to give me, in this my occasion of heaviness? Must I, who needed to have comfort ministered to me, become now a comforter of you?'

When he was scourged with rods by Bishop Bonner he greatly rejoiced, yet his shamefaced modesty was such, that never would he express any mention therof, lest he should seem to glory in himself, save that only he opened the same to one Master Cotton of the Temple, a friend of his, a little before his death.

He was first apprehended, but last of them condemned, which was the 15th day of January, and afterward burned with the other six martyrs, the 27th of January, 1556.

Thomas Brown dwelled in the parish of St Bride's in Fleet Street, and because he came not to his parish church, was presented by the constable of the parish to Bonner. Being had to Fulham he was required to come into the chapel to hear mass, which, refusing to do, he went into the warren, and there kneeled among the trees. For this he was greatly charged of the bishop, 'Brown, ye have been before me many times and oft, and I have travailed with thee, to win thee from thine errors; yet thou, and such like, do report, that I go about to seek thy blood.' To whom the said Thomas Brown answered again; 'Yea, my lord,' saith he, 'indeed ye be a bloodsucker, and I would I had as much blood as is water in the sea, for you to suck.'

And so he was committed to be burned.

Joan Lashford, was the daughter of one Robert Lashford, cutler, who was persecuted for the Gospel of God to the burning fire; and after him his wife; and after her, this Joan Lashwood, her daughter; who, about the age of twenty years, ministering to her father and mother in prison, was known to be of the same doctrine. Her confession was that she came unto no popish mass service in the church, neither would be confessed.

Five other godly Martyrs burned at one Fire

In this story of persecuted martyrs, next in order follow five others burned in the year of the Lord 1557, April the 12th: Thomas Loseby, Henry Ramsey, Thomas Thirtel, Margaret Hide, and Agnes Stanley: who were apprehended for not coming to their parish churches.

Thomas Thirtel answered unto Bishop Bonner, 'My Lord, if you make me a heretic, you make Christ and all the twelve apostles heretics.'

Margaret Hide said, 'My lord, I would see you instruct me with some part of God's Word, and not to give me instructions of holy bread and holy water, for it is no part of the Scripture.'

Agnes Stanley made this answer: 'My Lord, as for these that ye say be burnt for heresy, I believe they are true martyrs before God: therefore I will not go from my opinion and faith as long as I live.'

Altogether in one fire most joyfully and constantly

these five martyrs ended their temporal lives, receiving there-for the life eternal.

John Hallingdale, William Sparrow, and Richard Gibson

These three faithful witnesses of the Lord's testament were tormented and put to death, 18th of November 1557.

John Hallingdale said that Cranmer, Latimer, Ridley, Hooper, and generally all that of late had been burnt for heretics, were no heretics at all, because they did preach truly the Gospel: upon whose preaching he grounded his faith and conscience. William Sparrow answered Bishop Bonner, 'that if every hair of my head were a man, I would burn them all, rather than go from the truth.'

The Martyrs of the Islington fields

Secretly, in a back close, in the field by the town of Islington, were assembled together a certain company of godly and innocent persons, to the number of forty, men and women, who there virtuously occupied in prayer and in the meditation of God's holy Word. Cometh a certain man to them unknown; who, saluted them, saying, that they looked like men that meant no hurt. One of the company asked the man, if he could tell whose close that was, and whether they might be so bold there to sit. 'Yea,' said he, 'for that ye seem unto me such persons as intend no harm,' and so departed.

Within a quarter of an hour cometh the constable of Islington with six or seven other, one with a bow, another with a bill, and others with weapons; the which six or seven persons the said constable left a little behind him in a close place, there to be ready if need should be, while he, came through them. Looking what they were doing, he bade them deliver their books. They, understanding that he was constable, refused not so to do. With that cometh forth the residue of his fellows who bade them stand, and not depart. They answered that they would be obedient and go whithersoever they would have them; and so were they first carried to a brewhouse but a little way off, while that some of the said soldiers ran to the justice next at hand. But the justice was not at home; whereupon they were had to Sir Roger Cholmley. In the mean time some of the women escaped. In fine, were sent to Newgate twenty-and-two. These were in prison seven weeks before they were examined. Of these foresaid two-and-twenty, were burnt thirteen; in Smithfield seven, at Brentford six.

The names of these seven were Henry Pond, Reinald Eastland, Robert Southam, Matthew Ricarby, John Floyd, John Holiday, Roger Holland; only the examination of Roger Holland came to our hand.

This Roger Holland, a merchant-tailor of London, was first an apprentice with one Master Kempton, at the Black Boy in Watling Street, giving himself to dancing, fencing, gaming, banqueting, and wanton company. He had received for his master certain money, to the sum of thirty pounds; and lost every groat at dice. Therefore he purposed to convey himself away beyond the seas, either into France or into Flanders.

He called betimes in the morning to a servant in

the house, a discreet maid, whose name was Elizabeth, which professed the Gospel, with a life agreeing unto the same. To whom he said, 'Elizabeth, I would I had followed thy gentle persuasions and friendly rebukes; which if I had done, I had never come to this shame and misery which I am now fallen into; for I have lost thirty pounds of my master's money, which to pay him, and to make up mine accounts, I am not able. But I pray you, desire my mistress, that she would entreat my master to take this bill of my hand, and if I be ever able, I will see him paid: desiring him that the matter may pass with silence, for if it should come unto my father's ears, it would bring his grey hairs oversoon unto his grave.' And so was he departing.

The maid considering that it might be his utter undoing, 'Stay,' said she; and having a piece of money lying by her, given unto her by the death of a kinsman, she brought unto him thirty pounds, saying, 'Roger, here is thus much money; I will let thee have it, and I will keep this bill. But thou shalt promise me to refuse all wild company, all swearing and ribaldry talk; and if ever I know thee to play one twelvepence at either dice or cards, then will I show this thy bill unto my master. And futhermore, thou shalt promise me to resort every day to the lecture at All-hallows, and the sermon at Paul's every Sunday, and to cast away all thy books of papistry and vain ballads, and get thee the Testament and Book of Service, and read the Scriptures with reverence and fear, calling unto God still, for His grace to direct thee in His truth. And pray unto God fervently, desiring Him to pardon thy former offences, and not to remember the sins of thy youth; and ever be afraid to break His laws, or offend His majesty. Then shall God keep thee, and send thee thy heart's desire.'

Within one half year God had wrought such a change in this man, that he was become an earnest professor of the truth. Then he repaired into Lancashire unto his father, and brought divers good books with him, and bestowed them upon his friends, so that his father and others began to taste of the Gospel, and to detest the mass, idolatry, and superstition; and in the end his father gave him a stock of money to begin the world withal, to the sum of fifty pounds.

Then Roger repaired to London again, and came to the maid that lent him the money to pay his master withal, and said unto her, 'Elizabeth, here is thy money I borrowed of thee; and for the friendship, good will, and the good connsel I have received at thy hands, to recompense thee I am not able, otherwise than to make thee my wife.' And soon after they were married, which was in the first year ot Queen Mary.

After this he remained in the congregations of the faithful, until, the last year of Queen Mary, he, with the six others aforesaid, were taken.

And after Roger Holland there was none suffered in Smithfield for the testimony of the Gospel, God be thanked.

Chapter Fifteen

THOMAS CRANMER,
ARCHBISHOP OF CANTERBURY

THOMAS CRANMER, coming of an ancient parentage, from the Conquest to be deducted, was born in a village called Aslacton in Nottinghamshire. He came in process of time unto the University of Cambridge ; and was chosen fellow of Jesus college. The tongues and other good learning began by little and little to spring up again, and the books of Faber and Erasmus to be much occupied and had in good estimation. In whom Cranmer taking no small pleasure, did daily rub away his old rustiness on them, as upon a whetstone, until at the length, when Martin Luther was risen up, the more bright and happy days of God's knowledge did waken men's minds to the clear light of the truth ; at which time, when he was about thirty years old, omitting all other studies, he gave his whole mind to discuss matters of religion. And, because he saw that he could not judge of these matters unless he beheld the very fountains thereof, before he would addict his mind to any opinion, he spent three whole years in reading over the books of holy Scriptures. After he had laid this foundation no less wisely than happily, when he thought himself sufficiently prepared, and being now instructed with more ripeness of judgment, like a merchant greedy of all good things, he gave his mind to read all kind of authors.

In the mean while, being addicted to no party or age, he weighed all men's opinions with secret judgment. He read the old writers, so as he despised not the new, and, all this while, in handling and conferring writers' judgments, he was a slow reader, but an earnest marker. He never came to any writer's book without pen and ink, but yet he exercised his memory no less than his pen. Whatsoever controversy came he gathered every author's sentence, briefly, and the diversity of their judgments, into common places, which he had prepared for that purpose; or else, if the matter were too long to write out, he noted the place of the author and the number of the leaf, whereby he might have the more help for his memory.

And so, being master of arts, and fellow of Jesus college, it chanced him to marry a gentleman's daughter: by means whereof he lost his fellowship there, and became the reader in Buckingham college. And for that he would with more diligence apply that his office of reading, he placed his said wife in an inn, called the 'Dolphin,' in Cambridge, the wife of the house being of affinity unto her. By reason whereof, and for his often resort unto his wife in that inn, he was much marked of some popish merchants: whereupon rose the report bruited abroad every where, after he was preferred to the Archbishopric of Canterbury, that he was but an hosteler, and therefore without all good learning.

Whilst this said Master Cranmer continued as

reader in Buckingham college, his wife died. The Master and fellows of Jesus college, desirous again of their old companion, chose him again fellow of the same college. In few years after he became the reader of divinity lecture in the same college, and in such reputation with the whole University, that, being doctor of divinity, he was commonly appointed one of the heads to examine such as yearly profess in commencement, either bachelors or doctors of divinity; by the approbation of these learned men the whole University licenseth them to proceed unto their degree; and by their disallowance the University rejecteth them, until they be better furnished with more knowledge.

Now Dr Cranmer, ever much favouring the knowledge of the Scripture, would never admit any to proceed in divinity, unless they were substantially seen in the story of the Bible: by means whereof certain friars, and other religious persons, who were principally brought up in the study of school authors without regard had to the authority of Scriptures, were commonly rejected by him; so that he was, for his severe examination, much hated, and had in great indignation. And yet it came to pass in the end, that divers of them, being thus compelled to study the Scriptures, became afterwards very well learned and well affected; insomuch, that when they proceeded doctors of divinity, they could not overmuch extol Master Doctor Cranmer's goodness towards them, who had for a time put them back, to aspire unto better knowledge and perfection.

While Dr Cranmer thus continued in Cambridge, the weighty cause of King Henry the Eighth, his divorce with the Lady Katherine dowager of Spain, came into question; which by the space of two or three years had been diversely disputed amongst the canonists and other learned men. It came to pass that Dr Cranmer, by reason that the plague was in Cambridge, resorted to Waltham Abbey, to one Master Cressy's house there, whose wife was of kin to the said Master Cranmer. He had two sons of the said Cressy with him at Cambridge as his pupils, wherefore he rested with the said two children, duringt hat summer-time, A.D. 1529. It chanced that the King had removed himself from London to Waltham for a night or twain, while Dr Stephen Gardiner, secretary, and Dr Foxe, almoner, were lodged in the house of the said Master Cressy.

When supper-time came, they all three doctors met together; and as they were of old acquaintance, the secretary and the almoner conferred with Dr Cranmer concerning the King's cause, what he thought therein.

Dr Cranmer answered, that in his opinion they made more ado in prosecuting the law ecclesiastical than needed. 'It were better, as I suppose,' quoth Dr Cranmer, 'that the question, whether a man may marry his brother's wife, or no? were decided by the Word of God, whereby the conscience of the prince might be quieted, than thus from year to year by frustratory delays to prolong the time. There is but one truth in it, which the Scripture will soon make manifest, being by learned men well handled, and that may be as well done in England in the Universities here, as at Rome. You might this way have made an end of this matter long since.'

The other two well liked of his device, and

conceived to instruct the King withal, who then was minded to send to Rome for a new commission. The next day, when the King removed to Greenwich, his mind being unquieted, and desirous of an end of his long and tedious suit, he called unto him Dr Stephen and Dr Foxe, saying unto them, 'What now, my masters,' quoth the King, 'shall we do in this infinite cause of mine? There must be a new commission procured from Rome; and when we shall have an end, God knoweth, and not I.' Dr Foxe answered, 'We trust that there shall be better ways devised for your majesty. It chanced us to be lodged at Waltham in Master Cressy's house this other night, where we met with an old acquaintance of ours, named Dr Cranmer. He thought that the next way were to instruct and quiet your majesty's conscience by trying your highness's question out by the authority of the Word of God, and thereupon to proceed to a final sentence.' The King said, 'Where is that Dr Cranmer? Is he still at Waltham?' They answered, that they left him there. 'Marry,' said the King, 'I will surely speak with him, and therefore let him be sent for out of hand. I perceive,' quoth the King, 'that that man hath the sow by the right ear: and if I had known this device but two years ago, it had been in my way a great piece of money, and had also rid me out of much disquietness.'

Whereupon Dr Cranmer was sent for. But when he came to London, he began to quarrel with these two his acquaintances, that he, by their means, was brought thither to be cumbered in a matter, wherein he had nothing at all travailed in study; and therefore most instantly entreated them,

that they would make his excuse that he might
be despatched away from coming into the King's
presence. But all was in vain; for the more they
began to excuse Dr Cranmer's absence, the more
the King chid with them; so that, no excuse
serving, he was fain to come to the court. 'Master
doctor,' said the King, 'I pray you, and nevertheless
because you are a subject, I charge and command
you (all your other business set apart), to take some
pains to see this my cause to be furthered according
to your device, as much as it may lie in you, so that
I may shortly understand whereunto I may trust.
For this I protest before God and the world, that I
seek not to be divorced from the Queen, if by any
means I might justly be persuaded that this our
matrimony were inviolable, and not against the laws
of God; for otherwise there was never cause to
move me to seek any such extremity: neither was
there ever prince had a more gentle, a more obedient
and loving companion and wife than the Queen is,
nor did I ever fancy woman in all respects better, if
this doubt had not risen; assuring you that for the
singular virtues wherewith she is endued, besides
the consideration of her noble stock, I could be right
well contented still to remain with her, if so it would
stand with the will and pleasure of Almighty God.'

Dr Cranmer besought the King's highness to
commit the examining of this matter by the Word
of God, unto the best learned men of both his
Universities, Cambridge and Oxford. 'You say
well,' said the King, 'and I am content therewith.
But yet nevertheless, I will have you specially to
write your mind therein.' After the King's departure, Dr Cranmer incontinent wrote his mind

concerning the King's question; adding to the same his opinion, that the Bishop of Rome had no such authority, as whereby he might dispense with the Word of God. When Dr Cranmer had committed this book to the King, the King said to him, 'Will you abide by this that you have here written before the Bishop of Rome?' 'That will I do by God's grace,' quoth Dr Cranmer, 'if your majesty do send me thither.' 'Marry,' quoth the King, 'I will send you even to him in a sure ambassage.'

And thus by means of Dr Cranmer's handling of this matter, in both the Universities of Cambridge and Oxford, it was concluded, that no such matrimony was by the Word of God lawful.

Whereupon a solemn ambassage was sent to the Bishop of Rome, then being at Bologna, wherein went Dr Cranmer and divers other learned men and gentlemen, A.D. 1530. And when the time came that they should declare the cause of their ambassage, the Bishop, sitting on high in his cloth of estate and in his rich apparel, offered his foot to be kissed of the ambassadors. The Earl of Wiltshire, disdaining thereat, stood still, and made no countenance thereunto, so that all the rest kept themselves from that idolatry. Howbeit, one thing is not here to be omitted, which then chanced by a spaniel of the Earl of Wiltshire. For he stood directly between the Earl and the Bishop of Rome, when the said Bishop had advanced forth his foot to be kissed. The spaniel straightway went directly to the Pope's feet, and not only kissed the same unmannerly, but took fast with his mouth the great toe of the Pope, so that in haste he pulled in his feet: our men smiling in their sleeves.

Without any further ceremony the Pope gave ear to the ambassadors, who declared that no man could or ought to marry his brother's wife, and that the Bishop of Rome by no means ought to dispense to the contrary. Divers promises were made, and sundry days appointed, wherein the question should have been disputed; and when our part was ready to answer, no man there appeared to dispute in that behalf. So in the end, the Pope, making to our ambassadors good countenance, and gratifying Dr Cranmer with the office of the penitentiaryship, dismissed them undisputed withal.

This matter thus prospering on Dr Cranmer's behalf, Warham, Archbishop of Canterbury, departed this life, whereby that dignity then being in the King's disposition, was immediately given to Dr Cranmer, as worthy for his travail of such a promotion.

Upon this question of the marriage riseth another question of the Pope's authority. The new archbishop was not a little helped by his old collections and notes, which he used in studying: for all the weight of the business was chiefly laid on his shoulders. He therefore-alone confuted all the objections of the papists. He showed that the Pope's lordship was brought in by no authority of the Scripture, but by ambitious tyranny of men; that the chiefest power in earth belonged to the Emperor, to Kings, and to other potentates, to whom the bishops, priests, popes, and cardinals, by God's commandment, were no less subject than other men of the commonwealth: that there was no cause why the Bishop of Rome should excel other bishops in authority, and therefore it were best that the ambitious lordship of this bishop, being driven out of England, should keep itself within his own Italy, as a river is kept within his banks.

Soon after the King and Queen, by the ecclesiastical law, were cited at Dunstable before the Archbishop of Canterbury and Stephen Gardiner, Bishop of Winchester, as judges, to hear the sentence of God's Word concerning the matter of their marriage. The King refused not to appear; but the Queen appealed to the Bishop of Rome. But forasmuch as the Pope's authority being banished out of the realm, and as by public authority it was enacted that no man should appeal out of the realm to Rome for any matter, the judges, making no delay, out of God's Word pronounced the marriage to be unlawful, and so made divorce. As the Pope's name and title were now abolished, the archbishop laboured also to banish out of the realm his errors, heresies, and corruptions. And not content therewith, he obtained of the King, partly by his own suit, and partly by other men's suit, that certain learned bishops should make a book of ecclesiastical institutions, which should be better purged from all popish superstitions. This book, by the title of the authors, they called *The Bishops' Book*. It appeareth that the Archbishop of Canterbury was not then well instructed in the doctrine of the sacrament, because there is granted a real presence. There was added also concerning worshipping of images, which article was none of the bishop's, but added and written by the King's hand.

The abolishing of monasteries now began to be talked of. The King's desire was, that all the abbey-lands should come to his coffers; the archbishop, and other men of the Church, thought it pertained more to Christian duty, that all the goods of monasteries (which were very great) should be put to the use of the poor, and erecting of schools. For which cause the King's will being somewhat bent against the archbishop and other maintainers of his doctrine, he set forth the Six Articles, containing the sum of popish religion, and by full consent of Parliament established them. What a slaughter by the space of eight years these Six Articles made, it were superfluous to repeat.

This Archbishop of Canterbury evermore gave himself to continual study; by five of the clock in the morning he was at his book, and so consuming the time in study and prayer until nine of the clock. He then applied himself (if the prince's affairs did not call him away) until dinner time to hear suitors, and to despatch such matters as appertained unto his special cure and charge, committing his temporal affairs unto his officers.

After dinner, if any suitors were attendant, he would very diligently hear them, and despatch them in such sort as every man commended his lenity and gentleness, although the case required that some while divers of them were committed by him to prison. And having no suitors after dinner, for an hour or thereabouts he would play at the chess, or behold such as could play. Then again to his ordinary study, at the which commonly he for the most part stood, and seldom sat; and there continuing until five of the clock, bestowed that hour in hearing the common prayer, and walking or using some honest pastime until supper time.

At supper, if he had no appetite (as many times he would not sup), yet would he sit down at the table, having his ordinary provision of his mess furnished with expedient company, he wearing on his hands his gloves, because he would (as it were) thereby wean himself from eating of meat, but yet keeping the company with such fruitful talk as did repast and much delight the hearers, so that by this means hospitality was well furnished, and the alms-chest well maintained for relief of the poor. After supper, he would consume one hour at the least in walking, or some other honest pastime, and then again until nine of the clock, at one kind of study or other; so that no hour of the day was spent in vain, but the same was so bestowed, as tended to the glory of God, the service of the prince, or the commodity of the Church; which his well-bestowing of his time procured to him most happily a good report of all men, to be in respect of other men's conversation faultless, as it became the minister of God.

It is required, 'that a bishop ought not to be stubborn:' with which kind of vice, without great wrong, this archbishop in no wise ought to be charged; whose nature was such as none more gentle, or sooner won to an honest suit or purpose; specially in such things, wherein by his word, writing, counsel, or deed, he might gratify either any gentle or noble man, or do good to any mean person, or else relieve the needy and poor. Only in causes pertaining to God or his prince, no man more stout, more constant, or more hard to be won. Such things as he granted, he did without any suspicion of rebraiding or meed therefore: so that he was rather culpable of overmuch facility and gentleness.

If overmuch patience may be a vice, this man may

seem peradventure to offend. For he had many cruel enemies, not for his own deserts, but only for his religion's sake: and yet whatsoever he was that sought his hindrance, either in goods, estimation, or life, and upon conference would seem never so slenderly to relent or excuse himself, the archbishop would forget the offence committed, and show such pleasure to him that it came into a proverb, 'Do unto my Lord of Canterbury displeasure, or a shrewd turn, and then you may be sure to have him your friend while he liveth.'

His quietness was such, that he never raged so far with any of his household servants, as once to call the meanest of them varlet or knave in anger, much less to reprove a stranger with any reproachful words.

How he was no niggard, all kind of people that knew him can well testify. And albeit such was his liberality to all sorts of men, that no man did lack whom he could do for, either in giving or lending; yet nevertheless such was again his circumspection, that when he was apprehended and committed by Queen Mary to the Tower, he owed no man living a penny: whereas no small sums of money were owing him of divers persons, which by breaking their bills and obligations he freely forgave and suppressed before his attainder. When he perceived the fatal end of King Edward should work to him no good success touching his body and goods, he incontinently called for his officers, commanding them in any wise to pay where any penny was owing, which was out of hand despatched. And then he said, 'Now I thank God, I am mine own man.'

Certain of the Council attempted the King against

the archbishop, declaring plainly, that the realm was so infected with heresies, that it was dangerous for his highness further to permit it unreformed, lest peradventure by long suffering, such contention should ensue in the realm, and thereby might spring horrible commotions and uproars, like as in some parts of Germany: the enormity whereof they could not impute to any so much, as to the Archbishop of Canterbury, who by his own preaching, and his chaplains, had filled the whole realm full of divers pernicious heresies. The King would needs know his accusers. They answered that forasmuch as he was a councillor, no man durst take upon him to accuse him; but, if it would please his highness to commit him to the Tower for a time, there would be accusations and proofs enow against him: for otherwise, just testimony and witness against him would not appear.

The King granted unto them that they should the next day commit him to the Tower for his trial. When midnight came, he sent Sir Anthony Denny to Lambeth to the archbishop, willing him forthwith to resort unto him at the court. The archbishop, coming into the gallery where the King walked, and tarried for him, his highness said, 'Ah, my Lord of Canterbury! I can tell you news. For divers weighty considerations it is determined by me, and the council, that you to-morrow, at nine of the clock, shall be committed to the Tower, for that you and your chaplains (as information is given us) have taught and preached, and sown within the realm, a number of execrable heresies: and therefore the council have requested me, for the trial of the matter, to suffer them to commit you to the Tower, or else no man dare come forth, as witness in these matters, you being a councillor.'

When the King had said his mind, the archbishop kneeled down and said, 'I am content, if it please your grace, with all my heart, to go thither at your highness's commandment. And I most humbly thank your majesty that I may come to my trial; for there be that have many ways slandered me: and now this way I hope to try myself not worthy of such report.'

The King, perceiving the man's uprightness, joined with such simplicity, said, 'O Lord, what manner a man be you! What simplicity is in you! Do you not know how many great enemies you have? Do you not consider what an easy thing it is to procure three or four false knaves to witness against you? Think you to have better luck that way than your Master Christ had? I see by it you will run headlong to your undoing, if I would suffer you. Your enemies shall not so prevail against you, for I have otherwise devised with myself to keep you out of their hands. Yet notwithstanding to-morrow, when the council shall send for you, resort unto them, and if they do commit you to the Tower, require of them, because you are one of them, a councillor, that you may have your accusers brought before them, and that you may answer their accusations before them, without any further endurance, and use for yourself as good persuasions that way as you may devise; and if no entreaty or reasonable request will serve, then deliver unto them this my ring (which then the King delivered unto the archbishop), and say unto them, "If there be no remedy, my lords, but that I must needs go to the

Tower, then I revoke my cause from you, and appeal to the King's own person by this his token unto you all," for' (said the King unto the archbishop) 'so soon as they shall see this my ring, they know it so well, that they shall understand that I have resumed the whole cause into mine own hands and determination, and that I have discharged them thereof.'

The archbishop, perceiving the King's benignity, had much ado to forbear tears.

On the morrow about nine of the clock before noon, the council sent a gentleman-usher for the archbishop, who when he came to the council-chamber door, could not be let in; but of purpose (as it seemed) was compelled there to wait among the pages, lackeys and serving-men all alone. Dr Buts, the King's physician, resorting that way, and espying how my Lord of Canterbury was handled, went to the King's highness, and said, 'My Lord of Canterbury, if it please your grace, is well promoted; for now he is become a lackey or a serving-man: for yonder he standeth this half hour without the council-chamber door amongst them.' 'It is not so,' quoth the King, 'I trow; the council hath not so little discretion as to use the metropolitan of the realm in that sort, specially being one of their own number. But let them alone,' said the King, 'and we shall hear more soon.'

Anon the archbishop was called into the council-chamber, to whom was alleged, as before is rehearsed. The archbishop answered in like sort as the King had advised him; and when he perceived that no manner of persuasion or entreaty could serve, he delivered them the King's ring, revoking his cause into the King's hands. The whole council being thereat somewhat amazed, the Earl of Bedford with a loud voice, confirming his words with a solemn oath, said, 'When you first began this matter, my lords, I told you what would come of it. Do you think that the King will suffer this man's finger to ache? Much more, I warrant you, will he defend his life against brabbling varlets! You do but cumber yourselves to hear tales and fables against him.' And so incontinently upon the receipt of the King's token, they all rose, and carried to the King his ring.

When they were come to the King's presence, his highness with a severe countenance said unto them, 'Ah, my lords! I thought I had wiser men of my council than now I find you. What discretion was this in you, thus to make the primate of the realm, and one of you in office, to wait at the council-chamber door amongst serving men? I protest, that if a prince may be beholden unto his subject, by the faith I owe to God, I take this man here, my Lord of Canterbury, to be of all other a most faithful subject unto us.' And with that one or two of the chiefest of the council, making their excuse, declared, that in requesting his endurance, it was rather meant for his trial, and his purgation against the common fame and slander of the world, than for any malice conceived against him. 'Well, well, my lords,' quoth the King, 'take him and well use him, as he is worthy to be, and make no more ado.' And with that every man caught him by the hand.

But yet look, where malice reigneth, there neither reason nor honesty can take place. And therefore it was procured by his ancient enemies, that not only the prebendaries of his cathedral church in Canterbury, but also the most famous justices of peace in the shire, should accuse him. The articles were delivered to the King's highness by some of the council's means. When the King had perused the book, he wrapt it up, and put it in his sleeve; and finding occasion to solace himself upon the Thames, came with his barge furnished with his musicians along by Lambeth bridge towards Chelsea. The noise of the musicians provoked the archbishop to resort to the bridge to salute his prince: whom when the King perceived, eftsoons he commanded the watermen to draw towards the shore, and so came straight to the bridge.

'Ah, my chaplain!' said the King to the archbishop, 'come into the barge to me.' The archbishop declared to his highness, that he would take his own barge and wait upon his majesty. 'No,' said the King, 'you must come into my barge, for I have to talk with you.' When the King and the archbishop, all alone in the barge, were set together, said the King to the archbishop, 'I have news out of Kent for you, my lord.' The archbishop answered, 'Good, I hope, if it please your highness.' 'Marry,' said the King, 'they be so good, that I now know the greatest heretic in Kent;' and with that pulled out of his sleeve the book of articles against both the said archbishop and his preachers, and gave the book to him, willing him to peruse the same.

When the archbishop had read the articles, and saw himself so uncourteously handled of the prebendaries of his cathedral church, and of such his neighbours as he had many ways gratified, the justices of the peace, it much grieved him; notwithstanding he kneeled down to the King, and besought his majesty to grant out a commission to whomsoever it pleased his highness, to try out the truth of this accusation. 'In very deed,' said the King, 'I do so mean; and you yourself shall be chief commissioner, to adjoin to you such two or three more as you shall think good yourself.' 'Then it will be thought,' quoth the archbishop to the King, 'that it is not indifferent, if it please your grace, that I should be mine own judge, and my chaplains also.' 'Well,' said the King, 'I will have none other but yourself, and such as you will appoint: for I am sure that you will not halt with me in any thing, although you be driven to accuse yourself. And if you handle the matter wisely, you shall find a pretty conspiracy devised against you. Whom will you have with you?' said the King. 'Whom it shall please your grace to name,' quoth the archbishop. 'I will appoint Dr Belhouse for one, name you the other,' said the King, 'meet for that purpose.' 'My chancellor, Dr Coxe, and Hussy my registrar,' said the archbishop, 'are men expert to examine such troublesome matters.' 'Well,' said the King, 'let there be a commission made forth, and out of hand get you into Kent, and advertise me of your doings.'

The commissioners came into Kent, and there they sat about three weeks to bolt out who was the first occasion of this accusation; for thereof the King would chiefly be advertised. Every man shrunk in his horns, and no man would confess any thing to the purpose: for Dr Coxe and Hussey, being friendly unto the papists, handled the matter so, that they would permit nothing material to come to light. This thing being well perceived by one of the archbishop's servants, his secretary, he wrote incontinently unto Dr Buts and Master Denny, declaring that if the King's majesty did not send some other to assist my lord, than those that then were there with him, it were not possible that any thing should come to light: and therefore wished that Dr Lee, or some other stout man that had been exercised in the King's ecclesiastical affairs, might be sent to the archbishop.

Dr Lee was sent for by the King, and appointed the archbishop to name a dozen or sixteen of his officers and gentlemen, such as had discretion, wit, and audacity, to whom he gave in commission from the King, to search the purses, chests, and chambers of all those that were suspected to be of this confederacy, both within the cathedral church and without. Such letters or writings as they could find they should bring to the archbishop and him. Within four hours the whole conspiracy was made manifest!

Amongst others came to my lord's hands two letters, one of the suffragan of Dover, and another of Dr Barber, whom continually the archbishop retained as a counsellor in the law. These two men being well promoted by the archbishop, he used ever in such familiarity, that when the suffragan, being a prebend of Canterbury, came to him, he always set him at his own mess, and the other never from his table, as men in whom he had much delight and comfort, when time of care and

369

pensiveness chanced. But that which they did, was altogether counterfeit, and the devil was turned into the angel of light, for they were both of this confederacy.

When my lord had gotten their letters into his hands, he called to him into his study the said suffragan of Dover and Dr Barber, saying, 'Come your ways with me, for I must have your advice in a matter.' When they were with him in his study altogether, he said to them, 'You twain be men in whom I have had much confidence and trust: you must now give me some good counsel, for I am shamefully abused with one or twain to whom I have showed all my secrets from time to time, and did trust them as myself. The matter is so now fallen out, that they not only have disclosed my secrets, but also have taken upon them to accuse me of heresy, and are become witnesses against me. I require you therefore, of your good advice, how I shall behave myself towards them. You are both my friends, and such as I always have used when I needed counsel. What say you to the matter?' quoth the Archbishop.

'Marry,' quoth Dr Barber, 'such villains and knaves (saving your honour) were worthy to be hanged out of hand without any other law.'

'Hanging were too good,' quoth the suffragan, 'and if there lacked one to do execution, I would be hangman myself.'

At these words, the archbishop cast up his hands to heaven, and said, 'O Lord, most merciful God, whom may a man trust now-a-days? Was never man handled as I am: but, O Lord, Thou hast evermore defended me, I praise Thy holy name there-for!' And with that he pulled out of his bosom the two letters, and said, 'Know ye these letters, my masters?'

With that they fell down upon their knees, and desired forgiveness, declaring how they a year before were tempted to do the same; and so, very lamentably bewailing their doings, besought his grace to pardon and forgive them. 'Well,' said the gentle archbishop, 'God make you both good men! I never deserved this at your hands: but ask God forgiveness, against Whom you have highly offended. If such men as you are not to be trusted, what should I do alive? I am brought to this point now, that I fear my left hand will accuse my right hand.' And so he dismissed them both with gentle and comfortable words.

This was the last push of the pike that was inferred against the said archbishop in King Henry the eighth's days: for never after durst any man move matter against him.

Until the entering of King Edward, it seemed that Cranmer was scarcely yet throughly persuaded in the right knowledge of the sacrament; shortly after, he, being confirmed by conference with Bishop Ridley, took upon him the defence of that whole doctrine, to refute the error of the papists, that men do eat the natural body of Christ.

King Edward, when he perceived that his death was at hand, and knowing that his sister Mary was wholly wedded to popish religion, bequeathed the succession to the Lady Jane (being niece to King Henry the eighth), by consent of all the council and lawyers of this realm. To this testament of the King's, when all the nobles and judges had subscribed, they sent for the archbishop, and required him that he also would subscribe. But he said, that it was otherwise in the testament of King Henry, and that he had sworn to the succession of Mary, as the next heir; by which oath he was bound. He was judge of no man's conscience but his own: and as concerning subscription, before he had spoken with the King himself, he utterly refused to do it. The King said, that the nobles and lawyers counselled him unto it, and with much ado the archbishop subscribed. Not long after King Edward died, A.D. 1553, being almost sixteen years old. It was commanded that the Lady Jane should be proclaimed Queen: which thing much misliked the common people. Mary, shifting for herself, eftsoons prevailed; came to London; and caused the two fathers, the Duke of Northumberland and the Duke of Suffolk, to be executed. After that the Lady Jane, in age tender, and innocent from this crime, could by no means be turned from the constancy of her faith, she together with her husband was beheaded.

The Archbishop of Canterbury, though he desired pardon, could obtain none, insomuch that the Queen would not once vouchsafe to see him: for the old grudge against the archbishop for the divorcement of her mother, remained hid in the bottom of her heart. Besides this divorce, she remembered the state of religion changed; all which was imputed to the archbishop, as the chief cause thereof.

While these things were in doing, a rumour was in all men's mouths, that the archbishop, to curry favour with the Queen, had promised to say a mass after the old custom in the funeral of King Edward her brother: neither wanted there some which reported that he had already said mass at Canterbury. This rumour thinking speedily to stay, Cranmer gave forth a writing of his purgation. This bill lying openly in a window in his chamber, cometh in by chance Master Scory, Bishop of Chichester, who, after he had read the same, required of the Archbishop to have a copy. By the occasion of Master Scory lending it to some friend of his, there were divers copies taken out, and the thing published abroad among the common people; insomuch that every scrivener's shop almost was occupied in copying out the same. Some of these copies coming to the commissioners, the matter was known, and the archbishop commanded to appear.

Whereupon Dr Cranmer appeared before the said commissioners. A bishop of the Queen's privy council, bringing in mention of the bill, 'My lord,' said he, 'there is a bill put forth in your name, wherein you seem to be aggrieved with setting up the mass again: we doubt not but you are sorry that it is gone abroad.' To whom the archbishop answered, saying, 'I do not deny myself to be the very author of that bill. I had minded to have set it on Paul's Church door, and on the doors of all the churches in London, with mine own seal joined thereto.' When they saw the constantness of the man, they dismissed him.

Not long after, he was sent to the Tower, and condemned of treason. The Queen, when she could not honestly deny him his pardon, seeing all the rest were discharged, released to him his action of treason, and accused him of heresy; which liked the archbishop right well, and came to pass as he wished, because the cause was not now his own, but Christ's; not the Queen's, but the Church's. It was determined, that he should be removed to Oxford, there to dispute with the doctors and divines. Although the Queen and the bishops had concluded before what should become of him, it pleased them that the matter should be debated with arguments, that under some honest show of disputation, the murder of the man might be covered.

We now proceed to his final judgment and order of condemnation, which was the 12th day of September, 1555, and eighteen days before the condemnation of Bishop Ridley and Master Latimer. This thing let us consider: how unjustly these three poor prisoned bishops were handled, which when they were compelled to dispute, yet were not suffered to speak, but at their adversary's appointment. And if they began to make any preface, or to speak somewhat largely for themselves, by and by they were commanded from the high chair of master prolocutor to go to the matter. If they prosecuted their arguments anything narrowly, straightway they heard, 'Short arguments, master doctor! short arguments, master doctor!'

And, so condemned, they carried the archbishop to prison with a great number of spearmen and billmen.

Cranmer was of stature mean; of complexion pure and somewhat sanguine, having no hair upon his head, at the time of his death; but a long beard, white and thick. He was of the age of sixty-six when he was burnt; and yet, being a man sore broken in studies, in all his time never used any spectacles.

After the disputations in Oxford between the doctors of both Universities, and the three worthy bishops, Cranmer, Ridley, and Latimer, they were judged to be heretics, and committed to the mayor and sheriffs of Oxford. But, forasmuch as the sentence given against them was void in law (for at that time the authority of the Pope was not yet received into the land), therefore was a new commission sent from Rome, and a new process framed for the conviction of these reverend and godly learned men.

At the coming down of the commissioners, which was upon Thursday, the 12th of September, 1555, in the church of St Mary, and in the east end of the said church at the high altar, was erected a solemn scaffold ten foot high, with cloth of state very richly and sumptuously adorned, for Bishop Brooks, the Pope's legate, apparelled in pontificals. The seat was made that he might sit under the sacrament of the altar. And on the right hand of the Pope's delegate beneath him sat Dr Martin, and on the left hand sat Dr Story, the King and Queen's commissioners, which were both doctors of the civil law, and underneath them other doctors, with the Pope's collector, and a rabblement of such other like.

The archbishop was sent for to come before them. He came forth of the prison to the church of St Mary, set forth with bills and glaves for fear he should start away, being clothed in a fair black gown, with his hood on both shoulders, such as doctors of divinity in the University use to wear, and in his hand a white staff. After he did see them sit in their pontificals, he did not put off his cap to any of them, but stood still till that he was called. And anon one of the proctors for the Pope called 'Thomas, Archbishop of Canterbury, appear here and make answer to that shall be laid to thy charge; that is to say, for blasphemy, incontinency, and heresy; and make answer here to the Bishop of Gloucester, representing the Pope's person.'

Being brought more near unto the scaffold, and spying where the King and Queen's majesty's proctors were, putting off his cap, he humbly bowing his knee to the ground, made reverence to the one, and after to the other.

That done, beholding the bishop in the face, he put on his bonnet again, making no manner of token of obedience towards him at all: whereat the bishop, being offended, said unto him, that it might beseem him right well, weighing the authority he did represent, to do his duty unto him. Whereunto Dr Cranmer answered, that he had taken a solemn oath, never to consent to the admitting of the Bishop of Rome's authority into this realm of England again; that he meant by God's grace to keep it; and therefore would commit nothing either by sign or token, which might argue his consent to the receiving of the same.

After they had received his answers to all their objections, they cited him to appear at Rome within fourscore days, to make there his personal answers: which he said, if the King and Queen would send him, he would be content to do. Thence he was carried to prison again, where he remained, notwithstanding that he was commanded to appear at Rome. But the Pope, contrary to all reason and justice, sent his letter unto the King and Queen to degrade and deprive him of his dignity: which thing he did not only before the eighty days were ended, but before there were twenty days spent!

Upon the receipt of this sentence definitive of the Pope, another session was appointed for the archbishop to appear the 14th day of February, before certain commissioners directed down by the Queen, the chief whereof was the Bishop of Ely, Dr Thirleby. With him was assigned Dr Bonner, Bishop of London, which two, coming to Oxford as the Pope's delegates, commanded the archbishop to come before them, in the choir of Christ's Church, before the high altar. They first began, as the fashion is, to read their commission, giving them full authority to proceed to deprivation and degradation of him, and so upon excommunication to deliver him up to the secular power.

Bonner, who, by the space of many years had borne, as it seemed, no great good will towards him, and now rejoiced to see this day wherein he might triumph over him, and take his pleasure at full, began to stretch out his eloquence, making his oration to the assembly after this manner:

'This is the man that hath ever despised the Pope's holiness, and now is to be judged by him: this is the man that hath pulled down so many churches, and now is come to be judged in a church: this is the man that contemned the blessed sacrament of the altar, and now is come to be condemned before that blessed sacrament hanging over the altar: this is the man that like Lucifer sat in the place of Christ upon an altar to judge others, and now is come before an altar to be judged himself.'

Bonner went on in his rhetorical repetition, beginning every sentence with, 'This is the man, this is the man,' till at length the Bishop of Ely divers times pulled him by the sleeve to make an end, and said to him afterward, when they went to dinner, that he had broken promise with him; for he had entreated him earnestly to use the archbishop with reverence.

This done, they began to bustle toward his degrading, and first to take from him his crosier-staff out of his hands, which he held fast and refused to deliver, and withal, imitating the example of Martin Luther, pulled an appeal out of his left sleeve under the wrist, which he there and then delivered unto them, saying, 'I appeal to the next General Council.' This appeal being put up to Thirleby the Bishop of Ely, he said, 'My lord, our commission is to proceed against you.'

When they came to take off his pall (which is a solemn vesture of an archbishop), he said, 'Which of you hath a pall, to take off my pall;' which imported as much as they, being his inferiors, could not disgrade him. Whereunto one of them said, in that they were but bishops, they were his inferiors, and not competent judges; but being the Pope's delegates, they might take his pall. And so proceeding took every thing in order from him, as it was put on. Then a barber clipped his hair round about, and the bishop scraped the tops of his fingers where he had been anointed, wherein Bishop Bonner behaved himself as roughly and unmannerly, as the other bishop was to him soft and gentle. Last of all they stripped him out of his gown into his jacket, and put upon him a poor yeoman-beadle's gown, full bare and nearly worn, and as evil favouredly made as one might lightly see, and a townsman's cap on his head; and so delivered him to the secular power.

After this pageant of degradation, then spake Lord Bonner, saying to him, 'Now are you no lord any more.' And thus, with great compassion of every man, was he carried to prison. There followed him a gentleman of Gloucestershire who asked him if he would drink. The archbishop answered, saying that if he had a piece of salt fish, he had better will to eat; for he had been that day somewhat troubled and had eaten little: 'but now that it is past, my heart,' said he, 'is well quieted.' Whereupon the gentleman gave money to the bailiffs that stood by, and said, that if they were good men, they would bestow it on him, 'for my Lord of Canterbury had not one penny in his purse to help him.'

While the archbishop was thus in durance (whom they had now kept in prison almost the space of three years), the doctors and divines of Oxford busied themselves all that ever they could to have him recant. And to the intent they might win him easily, they had him to the dean's house of Christ's Church, where he lacked no delicate fare, played at the bowls, had his pleasure for walking, and all other things that might bring him from Christ. They perceived what a great wound they should receive, if the archbishop stood steadfast; and again, how great profit they should get, if he, as the principal standard-bearer, should be overthrown. By reason whereof the wily papists flocked about him, with threatening, flattering, entreating, and promising. They put him in hope, that he should not only have his life, but also be restored to his ancient dignity, that there should be nothing in the realm that the Queen would not easily grant him, whether he would have riches or dignity. But if he refused, there was no hope of health and pardon; for the Queen was purposed, that she would have Cranmer a catholic, or else no Cranmer at all. At last the archbishop, being overcome, gave his hand.

The doctors and prelates without delay caused this recantation to be imprinted, and set abroad in all men's hands. All this while Cranmer was in uncertain assurance of his life, although the same was faithfully promised to him by the doctors. The Queen, having now gotten a time to revenge her old grief, received his recantation very gladly; but of her purpose to put him to death, she would nothing relent. Now was Cranmer's cause in a miserable taking, who neither inwardly had any quietness in his own conscience, nor yet outwardly any help in his adversaries. On the one side was praise, on the other side scorn, on both sides danger, so that neither he could die honestly, nor yet unhonestly live.

The Queen, taking secret counsel how to dispatch Cranmer out of the way (who looked for nothing less than death), appointed Dr Cole, and secretly gave him in commandment, that against the 21st of March, he should prepare a funeral sermon for Cranmer's burning.

Soon after, the Lord Williams of Thame, the Lord Chandos, Sir Thomas Bridges, and Sir John Brown, with other worshipful men and justices, were commanded in the Queen's name to be at Oxford at the same day, with their servants and retinue, lest Cranmer's death should raise any tumult.

Cole returned to Oxford, ready to play his part; who, the day before the execution, came into the prison to Cranmer, to try whether he abode in the catholic faith wherein he had left him. To whom Cranmer answered, that by God's grace he would daily be more confirmed in the catholic faith; Cole giving no signification as yet of his death that was prepared. In the morning appointed for Cranmer's execution, the said Cole, coming to him, asked if he had any money; to whom when he answered that he had none, he delivered fifteen crowns to give to the poor: and so exhorting him to constancy in faith departed.

The archbishop began to surmise what they went about.

Then because the day was not far past, and the lords and knights that were looked for were not yet come, there came to him the Spanish friar, witness of his recantation, bringing a paper with articles, which Cranmer should openly profess in his recantation before the people, earnestly desiring him that he would write the said instrument with his own hand, and sign it with his name: which when he had done, the said friar desired that he would write another copy thereof which should remain with him; and that he did also.

The archbishop being not ignorant whereunto their secret devices tended, and thinking that the time was at hand in which he could no longer dissemble the profession of his faith with Christ's people, put secretly in his bosom his prayer with his exhortation written in another paper, which he minded to recite to the people, before he should make the last profession of his faith, fearing lest, if they had heard the confession of his faith first, they would not afterward have suffered him to exhort the people.

Soon after, about nine of the clock, the Lord Williams, Sir Thomas Bridges, Sir John Brown, and the other justices, with certain other noblemen that were sent of the Queen's council, came to Oxford with a great train of waiting men. Also of the other multitude on every side was made a great concourse, and greater expectation. They that were of the Pope's side were in great hope that day to hear something of Cranmer that should stablish the vanity of their opinion: the other part could not yet doubt, that he, who by continual study and labour for so many years had set forth the doctrine of the Gospel, either would or could now in the last act of his life forsake his part.

Cranmer at length cometh from the prison of Bocardo unto St Mary's church in this order: the mayor went before ; next him the aldermen ; after them was Cranmer brought between two friars, who, mumbling certain psalms, answered one another until they came to the church door, and there they began the song of Simeon, *Nunc dimittis*. Entering into the church, the friars brought him to his standing, and there left him. There was a stage set over against the pulpit, of a mean height from the ground, where Cranmer had his standing, waiting until Cole made him ready to his sermon.

The lamentable case and sight of that man gave a sorrowful spectacle to all Christian eyes that beheld him. He that late was Archbishop, Metropolitan, and Primate of England, and the King's privy councillor, being now in a bare and ragged gown, and ill favouredly clothed, with an old square cap, exposed to the contempt of all men, did admonish men not only of his own calamity, but also of their state and fortune. For who would not pity his case, and bewail his fortune, and might not fear his own chance, to see such a prelate, so grave a councillor, and of so long continued honour, after so many dignities, in his old years to be deprived of his estate, from such fresh ornaments to descend to such vile and ragged apparel, adjudged to die, and in so painful a death to end his life?

When he had stood a good space upon the stage, turning to a pillar adjoining, he lifted up his hands to heaven, and prayed unto God, till at the length Dr Cole, coming into the pulpit, began his sermon.

The latter part he converted to the archbishop, whom he comforted and encouraged to take his death well, by the example of the three children, to whom God made the flame to seem like a pleasant dew; adding also the patience of St Lawrence on the fire; assuring him that God, to such as die in His faith, either would abate the fury of the flame, or give strength to abide it.

With what great grief of mind Cranmer stood hearing his sermon, the outward shows of his body and countenance did better express, than any man can declare; one while lifting up his hands and eyes unto heaven, and then again for shame letting them down to the earth. A man might have seen the living image of perfect sorrow in him expressed. More than twenty times the tears gushed out abundantly, dropping down from his fatherly face. Pity moved all men's hearts, that beheld so heavy a countenance.

Cole, after he had ended his sermon, called back the people that were ready to depart, to prayers. 'Brethren,' said he, 'lest any man should doubt of this man's earnest conversion, you shall hear him speak before you; therefore I pray you, Master Cranmer, openly express the true profession of your faith, that all men may understand that you are a catholic indeed.'

'I will do it,' said the Archbishop, 'and that with a good will;' who began to speak thus unto the people: 'Forasmuch as I am come to the end of my life, whereupon hangeth all my life to come, either to live with my Master Christ for ever in joy, or else to be in pain for ever with wicked devils in hell, and I see before mine eyes presently either heaven ready to receive me, or else hell ready to swallow me up: I shall therefore declare unto you my very faith, without any colour or dissimulation; for now is no time to dissemble, whatsoever I have said or written in time past.

'I believe in God the Father Almighty, maker of heaven and earth. And I believe every word and sentence taught by our Saviour Jesus Christ, His apostles and prophets, in the New and Old Testament.

'And now I come to the great thing, which so much troubleth my conscience, more than any thing that ever I did or said in my whole life, and that is the setting abroad of a writing contrary to the truth; which now here I renounce and refuse, as things written with my hand, contrary to the truth which I thought in my heart, and written for fear of

384

death, and to save my life if it might be; and that is, all such bills and papers which I have written or signed with my hand since my degradation; wherein I have written many things untrue. And forasmuch as my hand offended, writing contrary to my heart, my hand shall first be punished there-for; for, may I come to the fire, it shall be first burned.

'And as for the Pope, I refuse him, as Christ's enemy, and antichrist, with all his false doctrine.'

Here the standers-by, amazed, did look one upon another, whose expectation he had so notably deceived. Some began to admonish him of his recantation, and to accuse him of falsehood. It was a world to see the doctors beguiled of so great a hope. I think there was never cruelty more notably or better in time deluded; for they looked for a glorious victory and a perpetual triumph by this man's retractation. As soon as they heard these things, they began to let down their ears, to rage, fret, and fume; and so much the more, because they could not revenge their grief—for they could now no longer threaten or hurt him. For the most miserable man in the world can die but once.

And when he began to speak more of the sacrament and of the papacy, some of them began to cry out, yelp and bawl, and especially Cole cried out upon him, 'Stop the heretic's mouth and take him away.' And then being pulled down from the stage, Cranmer was led to the fire, accompanied with those friars, vexing, troubling and threatening him most cruelly. To whom he answered nothing, but directed all his talk to the people.

When he came to the place where the holy bishops and martyrs of God, Hugh Latimer and Nicholas

385

Ridley, were burnt before him, kneeling down, he prayed to God; and not long tarrying in his prayers, putting off his garments to his shirt, he prepared himself to death. His shirt was made long, down to his feet. His feet were bare; likewise his head. His beard was long and thick, covering his face with marvellous gravity.

Then the Spanish friars, John and Richard, began to exhort him and play their parts with him afresh, but with vain and lost labour. Cranmer, with steadfast purpose abiding in the profession of his doctrine, gave his hand to certain old men, and others that stood by, bidding them farewell.

And when he had thought to have done so likewise to Ely, the said Ely drew back his hand, and refused, saying, it was not lawful to salute heretics, and specially such a one as falsely returned unto the opinions that he had forsworn. And if he had known before that he would have done so, he would never have used his company so familiarly; and he chid those sergeants and citizens which had not refused to give Cranmer their hands. This Ely was a priest lately made, and student in divinity, being then one of the fellows of Brasenose.

Then was an iron chain tied about Cranmer. When they perceived him to be more steadfast than that he could be moved from his sentence, they commanded the fire to be set unto him.

And when the wood was kindled, and the fire began to burn near him, stretching out his arm, he put his right hand into the flame, which he held so steadfast and immovable (saving that once with the same hand he wiped his face), that all men might see his hand burned before his body was touched.

His body did abide the burning with such steadfastness, that he seemed to move no more than the stake to which he was bound; his eyes were lifted up into heaven, and he repeated 'his unworthy right hand,' so long as his voice would suffer him; and using often the words of Stephen, 'Lord Jesus, receive my spirit,' in the greatness of the flame, he gave up the ghost.

Chapter Sixteen

ANECDOTES AND SAYINGS
OF OTHER MARTYRS

—

When sentence was given against Jerome of Prague a great and long mitre of paper was brought unto him, painted about with red devils; which when he beheld, throwing away his hood upon the ground amongst the prelates, he took and put upon his head, saying: 'Our Lord Jesus Christ, when He should suffer death for me, most wretched sinner, did wear a crown of thorns upon His head; and I, for His sake, instead of that crown, will willingly wear this mitre and cap.'—Constance, 1416.

—There came unto George Carpenter a certain schoolmaster of St Peter saying, 'My friend George! dost thou not fear the death and punishment which thou must suffer? If thou wert let go, wouldst thou return to thy wife and children?'

Whereunto he answered, 'If I were set at liberty, whither should I rather go, than to my wife and well-beloved children?'

Then said the schoolmaster, 'Revoke your former sentence and opinion, and you shall be set at liberty.'

Whereunto George answered: 'My wife and my children are so dearly beloved unto me, that they cannot be bought from me for all the riches and possessions of the Duke of Bavaria; but, for the love of my Lord God, I will willingly forsake them.'—Munich, 1527.

—And so going forth they came to the place of execution, where Anthony Peerson, with a cheerful countenance, embraced the post in his arms, and kissing it, said, 'Now welcome mine own sweet wife! for this day shalt thou and I be married together in the love and peace of God.' And pulling the straw unto him, he laid a good deal thereof upon the top of his head, saying, 'This is God's hat; now am I dressed like a true soldier of Christ, by Whose merits only I trust this day to enter into His joy.'—Windsor, 1543.

—As Giles Tilleman was brought to the place of burning, where he saw a great heap of wood piled, he required the greater part thereof to be taken away, and to be given to the poor: a little (said he) would suffice him. Also seeing a poor man coming by, as he went, that lacked shoes, he gave his shoes unto him; better (said he) so to do, than to have his shoes burnt, and the poor to perish for cold. Standing at the stake, the hangman was ready to strangle him before; but he would not, saying that there was no such need that his pain should be mitigated; 'For I fear not,' said he, 'the fire; do thou therefore as thou art commanded.' And thus the blessed martyr, lifting up his eyes to heaven in the middle of the flame, died, to the great lamentation of all that stood by.—Brussels, 1544.

—Peter Miocius was let down into a deep dungeon, under the castle-ditch, full of toads and filthy vermin. Shortly after, the senate began to examine him of certain articles of religion. To whom, as he was about to answer boldly and expressly to every point, they, interrupting him, bade him say in two words, either yea or nay. 'Then,' said he, 'if ye will not suffer me to answer for myself in matters of such importance, send me to my prison again, among my toads and frogs, which will not interrupt me, while I talk with my Lord and my God.'—Dornick, 1545.

—Master Wingfield said to Kerby, 'Remember the fire is hot, take heed of thine enterprise, that thou take no more upon thee, than thou shalt be able to perform. The terror is great, the pain will be extreme, and life is sweet. Better it were betimes to stick to mercy, while there is hope of life, than rashly to begin, and then to shrink.'

To whom Kerby answered, 'Ah, Master Wingfield! be at my burning, and you shall say, there standeth a Christian soldier in the fire. For I know that fire and water, sword and all other things, are in the hands of God, and He will suffer no more to be laid upon us, than He will give us strength to bear.'—Ipswich, 1545.

—When the rope was put about Ann Audebert, she called it her wedding-girdle wherewith she should be married to Christ; and as she should be burned upon a Saturday, upon Michaelmas-even; 'Upon a Saturday,' said she, 'I was first married, and upon a Saturday I shall be married again.'—Orleans, 1549.

—About ten of the clock cometh riding the sheriff, with a great many other gentlemen and their retinue appointed to assist him, and with them Christopher Wade, riding pinioned, and by him one Margery Polley of Tunbridge; both singing of a psalm: which Margery, as soon as she espied afar off the multitude gathered about the place where he should suffer, waiting his coming, said unto him very loud and cheerfully, 'You may rejoice, Wade, to see such a company gathered to celebrate your marriage this day.'

Wade, coming straight to the stake, took it in his arms, embracing it, and kissed it, setting his back unto it, and standing in a pitchbarrel.

As soon as he was thus settled, he spake, with his hands and eyes lifted up to heaven, with a cheerful and loud voice, the last verse of Psalm lxxxvi.: 'Show some good token upon me, O Lord, that they which hate me, may see it, and be ashamed; because Thou, Lord, hast helped me, and comforted me.' The sheriff, often interrupted, saying, 'Be quiet, Wade! and die patiently.' 'I am,' said he, 'I thank God, quiet, master sheriff! and so trust to die.' Then the reeds being set about him, Wade pulled them, and embraced them in his arms, always with his hands making a hole against his face, that his voice might be heard, which they perceiving that were his tormentors, always cast faggots at the same hole, which not-withstanding, he still, as he could, put off, his face being hurt with the end of a faggot cast thereat. Then fire being put unto him, he cried unto God often, 'Lord Jesus! receive my soul;' without any token or sign of impatiency in the fire.—Dartford, 1555.

—When the time came that he should be brought out of Newgate to Smithfield, came to him Master Woodroofe, and asked him if he would revoke his evil opinion of the sacrament of the altar. Master Rogers answered and said, 'That which I have preached I will seal with my blood.

'Then,' quoth Master Woodroofe, 'Thou art a heretic.'

'That shall be known,' quoth Rogers, 'at the day of judgment.'

'Well,' quoth Master Woodroofe, 'I will never pray for thee.'

'But I will pray for *you*,' quoth Master Rogers.

His wife and children, being eleven in number, and ten able to go, and one sucking on her breast, met him by the way as he went towards Smithfield. This sorrowful sight of his own flesh and blood could nothing move him; but that he constantly and cheerfully took his death. When the fire had taken hold both upon his legs and shoulders, he, as one feeling no smart, washed his hands in the flame, as though it had been in cold water.— Smithfield, 1555.

—When the godly martyrs Master Cardmaker and John Warne were brought by the sheriffs to the place where they should suffer, the sheriffs called Cardmaker aside, and talked with him secretly so long, that in the mean time Warne had made his prayers, was chained to the stake, and had wood and reed set about him, so that nothing wanted but the firing; but still abode Cardmaker talking with the sheriffs.

The people which before had heard that Cardmaker would recant, on beholding this manner of doing, were in a marvellous dump and sadness, thinking indeed that Cardmaker should now recant at the burning of Warne. At length Cardmaker departed from the sheriffs, and came towards the stake, and, in his garments as he was, kneeled down and made a long prayer in silence to himself: yet the people confirmed themselves in their fantasy of his recanting, seeing him in his garments, praying secretly, and no semblance of any burning.

His prayers being ended, he rose up, put off his clothes unto his shirt, went with bold courage to the stake, and kissed it sweetly: he took Warne by the hand, and comforted him heartily; and so gave himself to be also bound to the stake most gladly. The people seeing this so suddenly done, contrary to their fearful expectation, as men delivered out of a great doubt, cried out for joy, saying, 'God be praised; the Lord strengthen thee, Cardmaker; the Lord Jesus receive thy spirit!'—Smithfield, 1555.

—When this good man, Rawlins White, while he was on his way to the stake, came to a place where his poor wife and children stood weeping and making great lamentation, the sudden sight of them so pierced his heart that the tears trickled down his face. But he soon after, as though he had misliked this infirmity of his flesh, began to be as it were altogether angry with himself; insomuch that in striking his breast with his hand he used these words: 'Ah flesh! stayest thou me so? wouldest thou fain prevail? Well, I tell thee, do what thou canst, thou shalt not, by God's grace, have the victory.' Then went he cheerfully and very joyfully, and set his back close unto the stake.—Cardiff, 1555.

—Thomas Hauker being bound to the stake, the fire was set unto him. In the which when he continued long, and when his speech was taken away by violence of the flame, his skin also drawn together, and his fingers consumed with the fire, so that now all men thought certainly he had been gone, suddenly, and contrary to all expectation, the blessed servant of God reached up his hands burning on a light fire, which was marvellous to behold, over his head to the living God, and with great rejoicing, as it seemed, struck or clapped them three times together. Which thing he had promised certain of his friends to do; and so, secretly between them, it was agreed, that if the rage of the pain were tolerable and might be suffered, then he should lift up his hands above his head towards heaven, before he gave up the ghost.—Coggeshall, 1555.

—A godly letter of John Bradford—'To my dear Fathers, Dr Cranmer, Dr Ridley, and Dr Latimer.

Our dear brother Rogers hath broken the ice valiantly, as this day, I think, or to-morrow at the uttermost, hearty Hooper, sincere Saunders, and trusty Taylor, end their course, and receive their crown. The next am I, who hourly look for the porter to open me the gates after them, to enter into the desired rest. God forgive me mine unthankfulness for this exceeding great mercy, that, amongst so many thousands, it pleaseth His mercy to choose me to be one, in whom He will suffer. Oh! what am I, Lord, that Thou shouldest thus magnify me, so vile a man and wretched, as always I have been? Is this Thy wont, to send for such a wretch and hypocrite, as I have been, in a fiery chariot, as Thou didst for Elias? Oh! dear fathers, be thankful for me, and pray for me, that I still might be found worthy, in whom the Lord would sanctify His holy name. And for your part, make you ready: for we are but your gentlemen-ushers: "The marriage of the Lamb is prepared, come unto the marriage." '—Smithfield, 1555.

—When Robert Samuel was brought forth to be burned, certain there were that heard him declare what strange things had happened unto him during the time of his imprisonment; to wit, that after he had been famished or pined with hunger two or three days together, he then fell into a sleep, as it were one half in a slumber, at which time one clad all in white seemed to stand before him, who ministered comfort unto him by these words: 'Samuel, Samuel, be of good cheer, and take a good heart unto thee: for after this day shalt thou never be either hungry or thirsty.'

No less memorable it is, and worthy to be noted, concerning the three ladders which he told to divers he saw in his sleep, set up toward heaven; of the which there was one somewhat longer than the rest, but yet at length they became one, joining (as it were) all three together.

As this godly martyr was going to the fire, there came a certain maid to him, which took him about the neck, and kissed him, who, being marked by them that were present, was sought for the next day after, to be had to prison and burned, as the very party herself informed me: howbeit, as God of His goodness would have it, she escaped their fiery hands, keeping herself secret in the town a good while after.

But as this maid, called Rose Nottingham, was marvellously preserved by the providence of God, so there were other two honest women who did fall into the rage and fury of that time. The one was a brewer's wife, the other was a shoemaker's wife, but both together now espoused to a new husband, Christ.

With these two was this maid aforesaid very familiar and well acquainted, who, on a time giving counsel to the one of them, that she should convey herself away while she had time and space, had this answer at her hands again : 'I know well,' saith she, 'that it is lawful enough to fly away; which remedy you may use, if you list. But my case standeth otherwise. I am tied to a husband, and have besides young children at home ; therefore I am minded, for the love of Christ and His truth, to stand to the extremity of the matter.'

And so the next day after Samuel suffered, these two godly wives, the one called Anne Potten, the other called Joan Trunchfield, the wife of Michael Trunchfield, shoemaker, of Ipswich, were apprehended, and had both into one prison together. As they were both by sex and nature somewhat tender, so were they at first less able to endure the straitness of the prison ; and especially the brewer's wife was cast into marvellous great agonies and troubles of mind thereby. But Christ, beholding the weak infirmity of His servant, did not fail to help her when she was in this necessity; so at the length they both suffered after Samuel, in 1556, February 19. And these, no doubt, were those two ladders, which, being joined with the third, Samuel saw stretched up into heaven. This blessed Samuel, the servant of Christ, suffered the 31st of August 1555.

The report goeth among some that were there present, and saw him burn, that his body in burning did shine in the eyes of them that stood by, as bright and white as new-tried silver.—Norwich, 1555 and 1556.

—Suffered at the town of Derby a certain poor honest godly woman, being blind from her birth, and unmarried, about the age of twenty-two, named Joan Waste. This Joan was the daughter of one William Waste, an honest poor man, and by his science a barber, who sometime also used to make ropes. She was born blind, and when about twelve or fourteen years old, she learned to knit hosen and sleeves, and other things, which in time she could do very well. Furthermore, as time served, she would help her father to turn ropes, and do such other things as she was able, and in no case would be idle.

In the time of King Edward the Sixth, of blessed memory, she gave herself daily to go to the church to hear divine service read in the vulgar tongue. And thus, by hearing homilies and sermons, she became marvellously well affected to the religion then taught. So at length, having by her labour gotten and saved so much money as would buy her a New Testament, she caused one to be provided for her. And though she was of herself unlearned, and by reason of her blindness unable to read, yet, for the great desire she had to understand and have printed in her memory the sayings of the holy Scriptures contained in the New Testament, she acquainted herself chiefly with one John Hurt, then prisoner in the common hall of Derby for debts. The same John Hurt being a sober grave man, of the age of threescore and ten years, by her earnest entreaty, and being a prisoner, and many times idle and without company, did for his exercise daily read unto her some one chapter of the New Testament.

And if at any time the said John Hurt were otherwise occupied or letted through sickness, she would repair unto some other person which could read, and sometimes she would give a penny or two (as she might spare) to such persons as would not freely read unto her; appointing unto them aforehand how many chapters of the New Testament they should read, or how often they should repeat one chapter, upon a price.

Moreover, in the said Joan Waste this was notorious, that she, being utterly blind, could notwithstanding, without a guide, go to any church within the said town of Derby, or at any other place or person, with whom she had any such exercise. By the which exercise she so profited, that she was able not only to recite many chapters of the New Testament without book, but also could aptly impugn, by divers places of Scriptures, as well sin, as such abuses in religion, as then were too much in use in divers and sundry persons.

Nothwithstanding the general backsliding of the greatest part of the whole realm into the old papism again, this poor blind woman, continuing in a constant conscience, proceeded still in her former exercise.—Derby, 1556.

—Then both the bishops waxed weary of the said William Tyms, for he had troubled them about six or seven hours. Then the bishop began to pity Tyms' case, and to flatter him, saying, 'Ah! good fellow,' said they, 'thou art bold, and thou hast a good fresh spirit; we would thou hadst learning to thy spirit.'

'I thank you, my lords,' said Tyms, 'and both you be learned, and I would you had a good spirit to your learning.'—London, 1556.

—Hugh Laverock, a lame old man and John Apprice, a blind man, were carried from Newgate in a cart to Stratford-le-Bow, and most quietly in the fire, praising God, yielded up their souls into His hands. Hugh Laverock, after he was chained, cast away his crutch; and comforting John Apprice, his fellow-martyr, said unto him, 'Be of good comfort, my brother; for my lord of London is our physician. He will heal us both shortly; thee of thy blindness, and me of my lameness.'—Stratford-le-Bow, 1556.

—There followed in this happy and blessed order of martyrs, burnt in one fire eleven men and two women, whose dwellings were in sundry places in Essex, and whose names hereafter follow:—Henry Adlington, Laurence Parnam, Henry Wye, William Hallywel, Thomas Bowyer, George Searles, Edmund Hurst, Lyon Cawch, Ralph Jackson, John Derifall, John Routh, Elizabeth Pepper, and Agnes George.

When these thirteen were condemned, and the day appointed they should suffer, they were divided into two parts, in two several chambers.

The sheriff came to the one part, and told them that the other had recanted, and their lives therefore should be saved, willing and exhorting them to do the like, and not to cast away themselves: unto whom they answered, that their faith was not builded on man, but on Christ crucified.

Then the sheriff, perceiving no good to be done with them, went to the other part, and said the like to them, that they whom he had been with before had recanted, and should therefore not suffer death, counselling them to do the like, and not wilfully to kill themselves, but to play the wise men; unto

399

whom they answered as their brethren had done before, that their faith was not builded on man, but on Christ and His sure word.

Now when he saw it booted not to persuade (for they were, God be praised, surely grounded on the Rock, Jesus Christ), he led them to the place where they should suffer: and being all there together, most earnestly they prayed unto God, and joyfully went to the stake, and kissed it, and embraced it very heartily.

The eleven men were tied to three stakes, and the two women loose in the midst without any stake; and so they were all burnt in one fire, with such love to each other, and constancy in our Saviour Christ, that it made all the lookers-on to marvel.—Stratford-le-Bow, 1556.

—A blind boy, named Thomas Drowry, suffered martyrdom at Gloucester. Dr Williams, then Chancellor of Gloucester, ministered unto the boy such articles as are accustomed in such cases:

Chancellor: 'Dost thou not believe that after the words of consecration spoken by the priest, there remaineth the very real body of Christ in the sacrament of the altar?'

To whom the blind boy answered, 'No, that I do not.'

Chancellor: 'Then thou art a heretic, and shalt be burned. But who hath taught thee this heresy?'

Thomas: 'You, master chancellor.'

Chancellor: 'Where, I pray thee?'

Thomas: 'Even in yonder place;' pointing towards the pulpit.

Chancellor: 'When did I teach thee so?'

Thomas: 'When you preached a sermon to all men as well as to me upon the sacrament. You said, the sacrament was to be received spiritually by faith and not carnally and really, as the papists have heretofore taught.'

Chancellor: 'Then do as I have done, and thou shalt live as I do, and escape burning.'

Thomas: 'Though you can so easily dispense with yourself, and mock with God, the world, and your conscience, yet will I not so do.'

Chancellor: 'Then God have mercy upon thee; for I will read the condemnation sentence against thee.

Thomas: 'God's will be fulfilled.'

The registrar being herewith somewhat moved, stood up, and said to the chancellor:

Registrar: 'Fie for shame, man! will you read the sentence against him, and condemn yourself? Away, away, and substitute some other to give sentence and judgment.'

Chancellor: 'No, registrar, I will obey the law, and give sentence myself, according to mine office.' —Gloucester, 1556.

—Sir Richard Abridges sent for Julius Palmer to his lodging; and there friendly exhorted him to revoke his opinion, to spare his young years, wit, and learning. 'If thou wilt be conformable, and show thyself corrigible and repentant, in good faith,' said he, 'I promise thee, I will give thee meat and drink, and books, and ten pound yearly, so long as thou wilt dwell with me. And if thou wilt set thy mind to marriage, I will procure thee a wife and a farm, and help to stuff and frit thy farm for thee. How sayst thou?'

Palmer thanked him very courteously, but very modestly and reverently concluded that as he had already in two places renounced his living for Christ's sake, so he would with God's grace be ready to surrender and yield up his life also for the same, when God should send time.

When Sir Richard perceived that he would by no means relent: 'Well, Palmer,' saith he, 'then I perceive one of us twain shall be damned: for we be of two faiths, and certain I am there is but one faith that leadeth to life and salvation.'

Palmer: 'O sir, I hope that we both shall be saved.'

Sir Richard: 'How may that be?'

Palmer: 'Right well, sir. For as it hath pleased our merciful Saviour, according to the Gospel's parable, to call me at the third hour of the day, even in my flowers, at the age of four and twenty years, even so I trust He hath called, and will call you, at the eleventh hour of this your old age, and give you everlasting life for your portion.'

Sir Richard: 'Sayest thou so? Well, Palmer, well, I would I might have thee but one month in my house: I doubt not but I would convert thee, or thou shouldst convert me.'

Then said Master Winchcomb, 'Take pity on thy golden years, and pleasant flowers of lusty youth, before it be too late.'

Palmer: 'Sir, I long for those springing flowers that shall never fade away.'—Newbury, 1556.

—— Agnes Bongeor, who should have suffered with the six that went out of Mote-hall was kept back at the time, because her name was wrong written within the writ. When the said six were called

out to go to their martyrdom and when the said Agnes
Bongeor saw herself so separated from her prison-
fellows, what piteous moan that good woman
made, how bitterly she wept, what strange thoughts
came into her mind, how naked and desolate she
esteemed herself, and into what plunge of despair
and care her poor soul was brought, it was piteous
and wonderful to see; which all came because she
went not with them to give her life in the defence
of her Christ; for of all things in the world, life
was least looked for at her hands.

For that morning in which she was kept back
from burning, had she put on a smock, that she
had prepared only for that purpose. And also
having a child, a little young infant sucking on her,
whom she kept with her tenderly all the time that
she was in prison, against that day likewise did she
send away to another nurse, and prepared herself
presently to give herself for the testimony of the
glorious Gospel of Jesus Christ. So little did she
look for life, and so greatly did God's gifts work in
her above nature, that death seemed a great deal
better welcome than life.

Being in this great perplexity of mind, a friend
of hers came to her, and required to know whether
Abraham's obedience was accepted before God, for
that he did sacrifice his son Isaac, or in that he
would have offered him? Unto which she answered
thus: 'I know,' quod she, 'that Abraham's will
before God was allowed for the deed, in that he
would have done it, if the angel of the Lord had
not stayed him: but I,' said she, 'am unhappy, the
Lord thinketh me not worthy of this dignity: and
therefore Abraham's case and mine are not alike.'

'Why,' quod her friend, 'would ye not willingly have gone with your company, if God should so have suffered it?'

'Yes,' said she, 'with all my heart; and because I did not, it is now my chief and greatest grief.'

Then said her friend, 'My dear sister, I pray thee consider Abraham and thyself well, and thou shalt see thou dost nothing differ with him in will at all.'

'Alas, nay,' quod she, 'there is a far greater matter in Abraham than in me; for Abraham was tried with the offering of his own child, but so am not I: and therefore our cases are not alike.'

'Good sister,' quod her friend, 'weigh the matter but indifferently. Abraham, I grant,' said he, 'would have offered his son: and have not you done the like, in your little sucking babe? But consider further than this, my good sister,' said he, 'whereas Abraham was commanded but to offer his son, you are heavy and grieved because you offer not yourself, which goeth somewhat more near you, than Abraham's obedience did; and therefore before God, assuredly, is no less accepted and allowed in His holy presence.' After which talk between them, she began a little to stay herself, and gave her whole exercise to reading and prayer, wherein she found no little comfort.

In a short time came a writ from London for the burning, which, according to the effect thereof, was executed.—Colchester, 1557.

—Elizabeth Cooper being condemned, and at the stake with Simon Miller, to be burnt, when the fire came unto her, she a little shrank thereat, with a voice crying, 'Hah!' When the said Simon Miller heard the same, he put his hand behind him toward her, and willed her to be strong and of good cheer: 'for, good sister,' said he, 'we shall have a joyful and a sweet supper:' whereat she, being as it seemed thereby strengthened, stood as still and as quiet as one most glad to finish that good work which before most happily she had begun.— Norwich, 1557.

Master Tyrrel with a certain of his company went into the chamber where the said father Mount and his wife lay, willing them to rise: 'for,' said he, 'you must go with us to Colchester castle.' Mother Mount, hearing that, being very sick, desired that her daughter might first fetch her some drink; for she was (she said) very ill at ease.

Then he gave her leave and bade her go. So her daughter Rose Allin, maid, took a stone pot in one hand, and a candle in the other, and went to draw drink for her mother: and as she came back again toward the house, Tyrrel met her, and willed her to give her father and mother good counsel, and advertise them to be better catholic people.

Rose : 'Sir, they have a better instructor than I; for the Holy Ghost doth teach them, I hope, which I trust will not suffer them to err.'

'Why,' said Master Tyrrel, 'art thou still in that mind, thou naughty housewife? Marry it is time to look upon such heretics indeed.'

Rose : 'Sir, with that which you call heresy, do I worship my Lord God; I tell you troth.'

Tyrrel : 'Then I perceive you will burn, gossip, with the rest, for company's sake.'

Rose : 'No, sir, not for company's sake, but for my Christ's sake, if so I be compelled; and I hope in His mercies if He call me to it, He will enable me to bear it.'

So he, turning to his company, said, 'Sirs, this gossip will burn: do you not think it?' 'Marry, sir,' quoth one, 'prove her, and you shall see what she will do by and by.'

Then that cruel Tyrrel, taking the candle from her, held her wrist, and the burning candle under her hand, burning cross-wise over the back thereof so long, till the very sinews cracked asunder. In which time of his tyranny, he said often to her, 'Why, wilt thou not cry? wilt thou not cry?' Unto which always she answered, that she had no cause, she thanked God, but rather to rejoice. He had (she said) more cause to weep, than she, if he considered the matter well. In the end, he thrust her from him violently.

But she, quietly suffering his rage for the time, at the last said, 'Sir, have ye done what ye will do?'

And he said, 'Yea, and if thou think it be not well, then mend it.'

'Mend it!' said Rose; 'nay, the Lord mend you, and give you repentance, if it be His will. And now, if you think it good, begin at the feet, and burn to the head also. For he that set you a work, shall pay you your wages one day, I warrant you.'

And so she went and carried her mother drink, as she was commanded.—Colchester, 1557.

—When these six constant martyrs had made their prayers, they rose, and made them ready to the fire. And Elizabeth Folkes, when she had plucked off her petticoat, would have given it to her mother (which came and kissed her at the stake, and exhorted her to be strong in the Lord): but the wicked there attending, would not suffer her to give it. Therefore, taking the said petticoat in her hand, she threw it away from her, saying, 'Farewell, all the world! farewell Faith! farewell Hope!' and so taking the stake in her arms, said, 'Welcome love!'

Now she being at the stake, and one of the officers nailing the chain about her, in the striking in of the staple he missed the place, and struck her with a great stroke of the hammer on the shoulder-bone; whereat she suddenly turned her head, lifting up her eyes to the Lord, and prayed smilingly, and gave herself to exhorting the people again.

When all the six were also nailed likewise at their stakes, and the fire about them, they clapped their hands for joy in the fire, that the standers-by, which were, by estimation, thousands, cried 'The Lord strengthen them; the Lord comfort them; the Lord pour His mercies upon them; with such like words, as was wonderful to hear.—Colchester, 1557.

—Master Rough, being at the burning of Austoo in Smithfield, and returning homeward again, met with one Master Farrar, a merchant of Halifax, who asked him, where he had been. Unto whom he answered, 'I have been,' saith he, 'where I would not for one of mine eyes but I had been.' 'Where have you been?' said Master Farrar. 'Forsooth,' said he, 'to learn the way.' And so he told him he had been at the burning of Austoo, where shortly after he was burnt himself.—Smithfield, 1557.

—After John Fetty had lain in the prison by the space of fifteen days, hanging in the stocks, sometimes by the one leg, and the one arm, sometimes by the other, and otherwhiles by both, it happened that one of his children (a boy of the age of eight or nine years) came unto the bishop's house, to see if he could get leave to speak with his father. At his coming thither, one of the bishop's chaplains met with him, and asked him what he lacked and whom he would have. The child answered, that he came to see his father. The chaplain asked again, who was his father. The boy then told him, and pointing towards Lollards' Tower, showed him that his father was there in prison.

'Why,' quoth the priest, 'thy father is a heretic.'

The child, being of a bold and quick spirit, and also godly brought up, and instructed by his father in the knowledge of God, answered and said, 'My father is no heretic; but you are an heretic, for you have Balaam's mark.'

With that the priest took the child by the hand, and carried him into the bishop's house, and there, amongst them, they did most shamefully and without all pity so whip and scourge, being naked, this tender child, that he was all in a gore-blood; and then they carried the child in his shirt unto his father, the blood running down by his heels.

At his coming unto his father the child fell down upon his knees, and asked him blessing. The poor man then, beholding his child, and seeing him so cruelly arrayed, cried out for sorrow, and said, 'Alas, Will! who hath done this to thee?'

The boy answered that as he was seeking how to come to see his father, a priest with Balaam's mark took him into the bishop's house, and there was he so handled. Cluney therewith violently plucked the child away out of his father's hands, and carried him back again into the bishop's house, where they kept him three days after.

Bonner, bethinking in himself of the danger which the child was in by their whipping, and what peril might ensue thereupon, thought better to discharge the said Fetty, willing him to go home and carry his child with him; which he so did, and that with a heavy heart, to see his poor boy in such extreme pain and grief. But within fourteen days after the child died.—London, 1558.

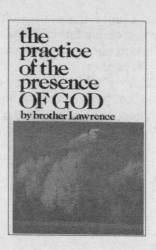

The Practice of the Presence of God
Brother Lawrence

Brother Lawrence was a man of humble beginnings who discovered the secret of living moment by moment with a sense of God's presence. It is the art of "practicing the presence of God in one single act that does not end." For centuries, this unparalleled classic has given both blessing and guidance to millions who can be content with nothing less than knowing God in all His majesty and experiencing His loving presence throughout each day.

ISBN: 978-0-88368-105-3 • Mass Market • 96 pages

WHITAKER
HOUSE